SPEECHWRITING:
THE EXPERT GUIDE

SIMON LANCASTER

ROBERT HALE · LONDON

© Simon Lancaster 2010
First published in Great Britain 2010

ISBN 978-0-7090-8917-9

Robert Hale Limited
Clerkenwell House
Clerkenwell Green
London EC1R 0HT

www.halebooks.com

All illustrations by Paul Rainey

A catalogue record for this book is available from the British Library

10 9 8 7

Typeset by Derek Doyle and Associates, Shaw Heath
Printed in Great Britain by Berforts Information Press Ltd

SPEECHWRITING:
THE EXPERT GUIDE

Simon Lancaster runs Bespoke, a specialist speechwriting agency. Over the last ten years, Simon has written hundreds of speeches for top politicians and business leaders. He runs courses in Creative Speechwriting and hosts regular Speechwriters' Networking Evenings.

Six years ago I got married. Since then, my life has just got better and better. This book is dedicated to my lovely wife, Lucy.

Contents

Acknowledgements   9

Introduction   15

Chapter One   The Art of Speechwriting   21
Chapter Two   The Craft of Speechwriting   46
Chapter Three   The Art of Persuasion   75
Chapter Four   The Art of Argument   106
Chapter Five   The Art of Story-telling   137
Chapter Six   The Art of Metaphor   160
Chapter Seven   The Craft of Editing   177
Chapter Eight   The Craft of Soundbites   188
Chapter Nine   The Craft of Media Manipulation   209
Chapter Ten   The Craft of Performance   226
Chapter Eleven   The Craft of Strategy   242

Epilogue   250
Glossary   252
Bibliography   263
Notes and References   272
Index   280

Acknowledgements

Eleven years ago, I was on a train to Harrogate with the newly appointed industry minister, Alan Johnson. Alan was on his way to deliver a speech on employment rights in Harrogate. I was his private secretary, there to do his bidding. I had wanted to be a minister's private secretary ever since watching *Yes Minister* at school. I'd loved watching the tension between the loquacious, verbose Sir Humphrey and pithy, plain-speaking Hacker and here I was observing one of those classic *Yes Minister* moments up close. 'This is f***ing diabolical,' said Alan, as he tore through the draft speech prepared by the civil service. 'I'm starting again,' he said, taking out his pen. The civil service isn't keen on ministers winging it, particularly not on contentious issues like employment rights, particularly not before hardened audiences of trade unionists and hacks. But, as soon as he started speaking, the whole room was captivated. During the two hours it took to get from London to Harrogate, Alan had assembled all the essential components of a successful speech.

There was a throat-grabbing opening which expertly exposed the central thesis: 'Stalin. Mussolini. Hitler. The first thing every despot did on their march to power was destroy the trade union movement. That's because they knew that free independent trade unions are a fundamental part of a functioning democracy.' A stat: 'The Conservative Party have held power for longer in Britain in the twentieth century than the Communists did in Russia.' A good joke (at my expense): 'This is the first time my private secretary's been north of Watford. He thought Harrogate was a scandal at a top public school.' A metaphor: 'Employment rights are a safety net, not a trampoline.' Imagery: 'I was there at the TUC conferences of the 1970s in my tank top and flares and we voted against a national minimum wage. With 13 million members, this was the glam rock era of the trade union movement.' A story: 'When I became General Secretary of the Communication Workers Union, there was a special white phone on my desk. My predecessor, Alan Tuffin, was told by Tom Jackson – his predecessor and a famous public figure in the 1970s – that when the white phone rang it would be a top civil servant or a Government Minister contacting him on important issues concerning BT or the Post Office. Alan spent his ten years as General Secretary under a Tory Government. When he handed over to me he said plaintively that the phone had only rung once. It was a woman asking if that was Sainsburys.'

The speech was not reported in any of the papers and has probably been long-since forgotten by everyone else who attended but it scorched deep on my memory. In that fifteen-minute speech, Alan Johnson irreversibly changed the way I thought about two things: one political and one personal. First, politically: I was brought up in the 1980s with media images of fighting miners and combative party conferences; I'd generally agreed with Margaret Thatcher's view that trade unions were 'the enemy within'. But Alan's speech gave me a completely new perspective on the history of trade unions and their role in modern society; I didn't go rushing straight out to sign up but he had definitely nudged my thinking along.

On a personal level, I was struck far more profoundly though by the way that Alan's persuasive skill had helped him shake off the shackles of a poor upbringing and climb up the social ladder, first becoming leader of a trade union, then an MP and then a minister. I found his story amazingly inspiring. A number of people approached me during the coffee break and said what a smashing speech by a smashing person it had been. I agreed wholeheartedly.

I decided there and then that I wanted to be a speechwriter. Two years later, I got my first full-time speechwriting gig writing Patricia Hewitt's speeches as Secretary of State for Trade and Industry and Minister for Women and Equality. When Alan Johnson joined the Cabinet a few years later, he asked me to write his speeches and I then worked with him across a string of departments, eventually becoming Whitehall's longest serving speechwriter. I left government in 2007 and set up Britain's first speechwriting agency: Bespoke. Since then, I have written for all sorts of incredible people, including the CEOs of HSBC and Cadbury, top politicians from left and right, Britpop rock stars, Olympic gold medallists, famous celebrities and rabble rousers. I've never looked back, so my deepest thanks to Alan for setting me off on this amazing journey and for remaining such a profound inspiration to me and many others.

This book contains the fruits of ten years writing and studying speeches. As well as working with many great speakers, I've worked with many of Britain's best speechwriters, including Julie Braithwaite, Charlotte Carr, Sam Coates, Phil Collins, Sarah Gibbons, Nicola Gilbert, Tom Greeves, Sara Halliday, Andrew Kaye, Tim Kiddell, Michael Lea, Mark Morris, Fiona Murray, Jo Nadin, Jenny Poole and Matt Shinn. I've also worked with some great communication gurus including Professor Marion Banks, Aileen Boughen, David Cracknell, Sheree Dodd, Mario Dunn, Jim Godfrey, Iain Hepplewhite, Sian Jarvis, Deb Lincoln, Bron Madson, Jo Moore, Clare Montagu, Chris Norton, Roger Sharp, Vickie Sheriff, John Shield, Mike Snowdon, Matt Tee, Kitty Ussher, Ben Wilson and Caroline Wright. I also owe a huge debt to Andrew Adonis, Bryan Holden, Tracy Vegro and Mela Watts for giving me a leg up the career ladder at crucial points.

Writing this book has been an unusually isolating experience. I'm incredibly grateful to all those who interrupted my solitude to review early drafts. Particular thanks go to Mike Edwards, Lyndsey Jenkins, Peter Steggle, David Tinline and Tom 'four brains' Clark, for providing comments that were far crisper and clearer than my early drafts. I am also inordinately grateful to Paul Rainey (www.pbrainey.com) for taking my childlike doodles and turning them into the fantastic illustrations that now feature throughout this book. I'm grateful to Scott Mason for the number crunching. I'm also grateful to all those at Robert Hale, particularly Alexander Stilwell, Nikki Edwards and Victoria Lyle, for being so kind, considerate and supportive throughout the whole writing process.

But most thanks must go to my family: my mum for instilling in me a love of reading and writing from the earliest age, my brother for his unstinting friendship and support and my lovely wife and wonderful daughter for being the big, big loves of my life. Lucy has not only supported me all the way, she has also lent her own communications expertise to shaping the ideas in this book. She has read the manuscript several times as well as allowing our dinner conversations to drift on to the subject of 'how to win an argument' far more times than can be healthy in a marriage. My hilariously funny daughter, Lottie, also made a number of perceptive comments during the drafting process. She aimed carefully targeted splats of baby porridge at the manuscript in the early days and has intervened latterly with long lines of green felt-tip pen. Nothing makes me prouder than seeing Lottie on the floor doodling on the manuscript because she has seen me do the same.

Those are the thanks. Now for the apologies. There are well over 70,000 words in this book and some offence is inevitable. Indeed, if this book didn't cause offence, I'd be sure I'd have failed. So here goes.

Apology one: I use the male third person pronoun throughout the book. This is simple short-hand and is not designed to offend the fairer sex, of whom I am inordinately fond.

Apology two: I use some pretty abominable reference points in the book, quoting Adolf Hitler, Robert Mugabe and Nick Griffin amongst others. I'm not endorsing them in any way: for the record, I find them all repugnant. But oratory does have a murky side as well as a bright side and a rounded view is necessary.

Apology three: this book contains some pretty nasty and

Machiavellian techniques: in sharing them, I do not want to add to the sum of global evil. On the contrary, I rather hope that sharing some of these techniques might help people to spot when they are being spun against, and restore some of the democratic deficit that has built up in the decades since rhetoric was removed from the school curriculum.

Apology four: although I have taken great care to ensure this book's accuracy, if you do find something that makes you raise your eyebrows, please write to me at simon@bespokespeeches.com so that I can correct future editions.

Otherwise, jump on board, put on your seat belt and enjoy the ride. I hope you enjoy your journey through the dark arts of rhetoric as much as I, and if you're interested in finding out more about speechwriting, do get in touch. I love nothing more than chatting about this extraordinary art which continues to shape so many aspects of the world we live in.

Simon Lancaster
Westminster
Summer 2010

Introduction

Speeches don't put food on the table. Speeches don't fill up your tank or fill your prescription or do anything about that stack of bills that keeps you up at night. There's a big difference between Obama and I – speeches versus solutions, talk versus action.

Hillary Clinton, seeking the Democratic Party's nomination
for the Presidency in 2008

Everybody here sort of lives with the reality that the President is the best speechwriter in the group.

David Axelrod, Senior Adviser to President Obama

Even before the starting gun was fired in the 2010 General Election, the commentators declared it the first-ever 'social media election'. They said the battle would not be fought on soap-boxes or doorsteps but on PCs and palm-tops, with blogs, emails and tweets as weapons, instead of speeches. This tired old refrain that speeches no longer matter has become common in recent years, usually repeated by those who want to puff up their own achievements by harking back to some mythical golden age that never existed, but it is not new. Tacitus moaned that Ancient Rome was 'bereft of eloquence'. But Tacitus was wrong in AD 97 and so were the election commentators in 2010.

In fact, speeches provided the current which powered the election: the Prime Minister's dissolution speech sparked the campaign into life; the manifesto launches provided further surges; and the biggest shock came from Britain's first televised leaders' debates. The debates got the nation talking in a manner barely seen since Den and Angie's heyday. Their impact on the polls was instant and immense, transforming Nick Clegg into Britain's most popular leader since Winston Churchill, albeit fleetingly.

During the five-week campaign, the three candidates made 1,500 speeches totalling a million words (the televised debates alone comprised 18,000 words). 30 million people responded by going out to vote: 3 million more than in 2005 and twelve times the average viewing audience for *Big Brother*, for those who consider the comparison valid. But the speeches didn't stop when the ballot boxes closed. After polling day, the three leaders used speeches to navigate through the ensuing constitutional crisis, using speeches to issue offers (Cameron), to barter (Clegg) and, occasionally, to throw a spanner in the works (Brown). It's no surprise speeches were such a force, no fewer than six of the principal negotiators were ex-speechwriters: Ed Balls, Andrew Adonis, Oliver Letwin, George Osborne, David Miliband and Ed Miliband were former speechwriters for Gordon Brown, Tony Blair, Margaret Thatcher, William Hague, Neil Kinnock and Harriet Harman respectively. Of course, social media did play a role; people were tweeting, blogging and emailing like crazy – 600,000 tweets were sent in the first leaders' debates alone – but they were tweeting about speeches! The medium is important, but it will never be more important than the message or the man.

So it is patently nonsense to say that speeches are now irrelevant. The two standard-bearers of next-generation Western leadership both used speeches to rise to power. It was David Cameron's spectacular 'look no notes' performance before Conservative Party conference in 2005 which lifted him from 25/1 outsider to favourite almost overnight. David Davis, meanwhile, the former bookies' favourite, was forced to fetch his coat after serving up a limp, lacklustre performance at the same conference. Speeches also hoisted Barack Obama up from 150/1 rank outsider to become president of the United States. Hillary Clinton dismissed him as 'just an orator' but it was good enough for the American people and rightly so: oratorical skill is a reliable indicator of leadership ability. Obama won the largest share of the House of Representatives in eighty years and became the first black president in history to walk into the White House.

Speeches are evidently crucial in politics, but they also mark the dividing line between success and failure in many other walks of life, like business. Richard Branson, Steve Jobs and Anita Roddick all deliberately used speeches to project their personalities on to their companies, turning Virgin, Apple and the Body Shop into three of the most powerful brands in the world in the process. Their personalization of their companies gave them a magical 'X Factor' which set them apart from their competitors. It allowed them to create richer, more emotive connections with their customers and employees, so their shoppers shopped longer and their workers worked harder.

CEO speeches have a huge impact on corporate performance: as a strong speech is a sign of a strong company, so a weak speech is a sign of a weak company. A 2003 study of CEO capital showed that half of a company's reputation flows from the reputation of the chief executive,[i] so it is extraordinary that companies will merrily spend millions designing new websites whilst their chief executive is frequently left to scribble his own speeches on the back of an envelope. The consequences would be comic were they not so catastrophic. In 1991, Gerald Ratner wiped half a billion pounds from his company's value after joking to an Institute of Directors conference that his products were 'total crap', adding that some were 'cheaper than a prawn sandwich but probably wouldn't last as long'. The public were outraged. Eventually Ratner was forced out of his own family firm and the company had to change its name.

Great orators wield a mighty power. It is the power over the hearts and minds of men; the power to inspire and shame; the power to build a bridge from the past to the future. It was ever so: the history of the world can be told through the history of speeches. As power has shifted, so has rhetorical skill: from the citizens of Ancient Greece to the Emperors of Ancient Rome, to the Popes, to the monarchs, to the politicians, to the business leaders. Oratory has also been a powerful weapon for the oppressed and marginalized. In some ways, it was the original rock 'n' roll. In the past, people travelled hundreds of miles to see speeches, just as eager fans travel hundreds of miles to attend top gigs today. Speeches were edgy, dangerous, subversive events where ideas were challenged and egos paraded. Vivid pictures of history's angry rebels remain imprinted on the cultural conscience: John Ball on Blackheath Common during the Peasant's Revolt calling for the fellow common man to 'Cast off the yoke of bondage'; Cromwell's cries outside Parliament to another generation of corrupt MPs: 'In the name of God! Go!' or Malcolm X's rat-a-tat-tat 'ballot or bullet' speech. As Cicero said, '[Rhetoric can] raise up those who are cast down, bestow security, set free from peril and maintain men in their civil rights.'

But if rhetoric is an ancient art, it is also something of a lost art. In Ancient Greece, every citizen was entitled to free tuition in rhetoric. Even in Renaissance Britain, a London child could receive a free education in rhetoric but not in maths. Rhetorical skill was rightly seen as an essential part of a successfully functioning society. How could citizens possibly exercise their civil, legal and democratic rights if they were inarticulate? Curiously, rhetoric was removed from the curriculum at about the same time as education provision was extended to the masses. This should be a cause for concern, for the fewer of us who understand rhetoric, the harder it is to guard against its abuses.

We all know that oratory can be a powerful force for good – every speech anthology pompously proclaims oratory's mighty contribution in the struggle for global peace, freedom and equality – but oratory also has a darker side, about which we hear rather less. Oratory did help to grow formidable movements against apartheid, colonialism and totalitarianism, but it also played an equally crucial role in the execution of the Holocaust, the Iraq War and the Rwandan genocide. Wherever there has been some appalling abomination in history, oratory's fingerprints have invariably been found all over the crime scene. At its most innocent, oratory is only a form of mass communication; in the wrong hands, it can be a weapon of mass destruction. That is why it remains an essential part of the arsenal of every despotic dictator on the planet from Zimbabwe to North Korea to Turkmenistan.

Oratory isn't to blame for their crimes any more than the pen is responsible for the writing of *Mein Kampf*. The speech itself is morally neutral, only as good or as wicked as its perpetrator, but the important question for society is who should possess this skill? Should it be concentrated amongst a small élite or should it be spread across the masses? Ultimately, this is a question for our democracy. I agree with the historian Hayden White that rhetoric should be restored to the curriculum. This would represent a genuine commitment to people power. There could have been no prouder nor more apposite legacy for the last New Labour government than to have had rows of school children sitting in lines rehearsing soundbites (I say this only slightly tongue-in-cheek: a nation better versed in rhetoric might have been better equipped to avert the Iraq War).

This book sets out everything you need to know to be a great rhetorician, whether you work in politics, business, entertainment or PR. Rhetoric is a skill, but it can be learnt. This book reveals how to win an argument, how to structure a soundbite and how to tell a story, exposing the secrets behind a great metaphor, a brilliant performance and a successful persuasive act. The book is based on extensive academic research and practical experience, mixing techniques from Ancient Greece and modern advertising. It is intended to fill the gap between the numerous excruciating guides on 'How to write a best man speech' and the eminently worthy but ultimately inaccessible academic texts on rhetoric. This book draws back the curtain and reveals all the trade secrets. You'll never be able to watch a speech or hear an interview quite the same again.

Rhetoric is an essential skill whether or not you want to be a speechwriter. It provides the key to personal, political and professional power. Rhetoric shapes the way we think, feel and behave; it determines how we're governed, by whom and in what style; it will be pivotal in the resolution of issues such as climate change, poverty and terrorism. Rhetoric can turn preachers into presidents, paupers into prime ministers, the parochial into the profound. We may not all achieve herculean heights but perhaps, in some modest way, we might be able to use these techniques to make a small difference. Be good.

Chapter One

The Art of Speechwriting

Of all the talents bestowed upon men, none is so precious as the gift of oratory, [anyone] who enjoys it wields a power more durable than that of the great king.

Winston Churchill

[Rhetoric is one of the] greatest dangers of modern civilisation.

Stan Baldwin

Rhetoric is . . . older than the church, older than Roman law, older than all Latin literature, it descends from the age of the Greek Sophists. Like the Church and the law it survived the fall of the empire, rides into the renascentia and the Reformation like waves, and penetrates far into the eighteenth century; through all these ages, not the tyrant, but the darling of humanity; soavissima, as Dante says, 'the sweetest of all the other sciences'.

C.S. Lewis, *English Literature in the Sixteenth Century*[1]

Aristotle's Golden Triangle of Speechwriting

In 350 BC, Aristotle produced *The Art of Rhetoric*. It was the first definitive account of the art of speechwriting. Over the centuries, it has been subjected to intense scrutiny from some of the greatest minds in history but emerged unscathed, surviving profound technological, political and social change. As Thomas Babington Macaulay wrote in a nineteenth-century essay about rhetoric, 'both in analysis and in combination, that great man was without a rival'[ii]. *The Art of Rhetoric* comprises three lectures spread out across three books. It was not a work of invention or deduction but observation, meaning that Aristotle did not make up the techniques himself but sat around the tavernas and temples of Ancient Greece studying the techniques of the 'naturally eloquent'[iii] and noticing what worked and what didn't. Judging by the depravity of techniques he suggests, he must have come across a right motley crew of Del Boys: some of the techniques in *The Art of Rhetoric* would make Alastair Campbell's eyes water. It remains the ultimate guide to the art of spin.

Aristotle boiled persuasive speaking down to three essential ingredients: *ethos* (meaning the character and credibility of the speaker, not in its more widely understood modern meaning of 'the spirit of an organization'), *pathos* (meaning the emotions of the audience and the emotions of the argument – not, again, in its more widely understood modern meaning of 'suffering') and *logos* (meaning the proof, or *apparent* proof – Aristotle himself was careful to draw this distinction). Aristotle argued that each of these three elements were not only equally crucial components in any act of persuasive speaking, they were all also mutually supportive. For instance, a speaker would be more likely to sweep his audience along with an emotional appeal if he had previously established his credibility and constructed a robust argument.

We will keep coming back to Aristotle's golden triangle throughout this book. It remains the cornerstone for any speechwriter. But this chapter also sets out three further golden

triangles of speechwriting: the three golden principles, the three golden rhetorical techniques and also the three blackest lies about speechwriting.

The Three Golden Principles of Speechwriting

The first golden principle of speechwriting is that *the audience is more important than the speaker.* By this, I mean that the true measure of the success of a speech is not how smug and self-satisfied the speaker feels as he leans back into the lush, leather seats of his chauffer-driven car roaring away from the venue, but what the audience is saying as they gather around for that awkward coffee and soggy biscuit back in the conference hall. Most of us will, at some time or other, have experienced that excruciating moment when a fellow delegate asks what we thought of someone's speech and we realize we can't remember a damn thing about it – even though we watched it just minutes before.

Audience focus is crucial for a great speech and always has been. Aristotle opens *The Art of Rhetoric* arguing that: 'of the three elements in speech-making – speaker, subject and person addressed – it is the last one, the hearer, that determines the speech's end and object.' Today, top US communications adviser, Frank Luntz, opens his book, *Words that Work*, with remarkably similar advice: 'It's not what you say – it's what people hear. You can have the best message in the world, but the person on the receiving end will always understand it through the prism of his or her own emotions, preconceptions, prejudices and pre-existing beliefs.'[iv] In the past, there was a belief that you could plant an opinion into someone's mind in the same way as a syringe pumps a drug into someone's veins: the 'hypodermic needle model'. Now, it is understood that any communication activity must begin with an understanding of why the audience is there and what they want: the 'uses and gratifications model'.

Audience focus underpins modern communications theory, as well as the arts of hypnosis, propaganda and advertising. Hypnosis is based on the audience-led approach of 'pacing and leading'.[v] Pacing is when the hypnotist aligns himself with his subject through empathy and mimicry, e.g. 'You are sitting in your chair. You can hear the soft hum of traffic outside.' The leading comes when the hypnotist starts implanting messages, e.g. 'You know you can give up smoking.' Advertising is also fundamentally audience led, driven by customer insights: for instance, the Ronseal 'it does exactly what it says on the tin' campaign was based on the insight that DIY customers wanted plain, simple instructions.

The audience must come first. A lack of audience focus has lain behind all of the cause célèbre speech disasters of recent years, perhaps the most famous of which was Tony Blair's speech to the Women's Institute in 2000. Blair's fatal error was to try to lecture 5,000 fundamentally conservative people about the evils of conservatism.[vi] He said the word 'new' thirty-two times in his speech, always in a positive light, whilst the word 'old' appeared twenty-nine times, always in a pejorative sense. No wonder he was slow-handclapped and forced to finish his speech early. He had profoundly upset their values. It was like walking into someone's house and putting your feet on the sofa. The blowback may have been fierce and furious but it was also utterly predictable.

A successful speech is one in which the speaker and audience are aligned: in appearance, if not in fact. A good speaker will not storm into a conference and aggressively impose and assert his views. This would be bound to fail. No one wants to feel hectored or harassed when they listen to a speech. Nor do we go to speeches to be told that what we know is wrong. Rather depressingly, the truth is that we go to speeches looking for information that reinforces our own views, confirming that we have been right along. The academic, Stuart Hall, says that people hail messages in the same way that they hail taxis. So audiences look out for particular messages which they like, take those and leave the rest behind. That's why racist political parties trawl through speeches by the equality lobby; not because they wish to be converted, but because they are looking for evidence that proves ethnic minorities receive preferential treatment. So the successful speaker will not challenge the audience overtly but instead weaves their proposition in amongst the audience's pre-existing ideas, almost leaving them with the impression that they came up with the idea themselves. This is not as hard as it sounds. It is actually just a matter of framing. We flash the audience's views above the front door in blazing neon lights whilst surreptitiously smuggling in our speaker's opinions through the back door. This is all an illusion but it is a necessary one. We do not seduce someone by telling them how wonderful we are. We seduce someone by telling them how wonderful *they* are. As John F. Kennedy might have said, ask not what your audience can do for the speaker, ask what the speaker can do for your audience.

The deeper we analyse our audience, the higher our ambitions can be for the speech. Some people may balk at these tactics – they do look sinister in black and white – but they are part and parcel of everyday human interactions. Just observe yourself the next time you are in conversation. We all constantly adapt the style and content of our speech to match the people we are addressing. We speak louder to older people; we use baby talk to toddlers. We refer back to things people have said to us before to encourage them to agree with us. Speechwriting is about translating those same processes to the podium. Anyone who considers themselves too righteous for such techniques might remember Michael Corleone's immortal line from *The Godfather*: 'We're all part of the same hypocrisy, Senator.'

The second golden principle of speechwriting is that *emotions are far more powerful than logic*. This seems counter intuitive because it is so seriously counter cultural. From childhood, we are taught that reason must trump emotion ('Stop crying!' 'Pull yourself together!') When we start working, that conditioning becomes even stronger – we are encouraged to leave our emotions at the door along with our hat and coat. In speechwriting, however, we must flip this back completely. Emotion is the nuclear button of communication: guaranteed to cause an explosive response. The brain's limbic system, which governs our emotions, is five times more powerful than the neo-cortex that controls our logical minds.[vii] And the emotional part of our brain is wired right through to the decision-making side. Every great speech in history has involved some form of emotional appeal.

There are many emotions we can appeal to: hopes or fears, anger or affection, pride or shame. The emotion we appeal to must be rooted in knowledge of our audience. Different audiences are predisposed to different emotions. You're not going to garner pity from an audience that is predominately angry, nor will you find much optimism amongst a crowd that is feeling fearful. Emotional appeals cannot be made randomly. We should find out what the dominant emotion in the room is and play to that. We will usually know what it is either by instinct, intuition or insight. For instance, trade union audiences often seem to be angry, which is why they respond so well to speakers such as Nye Bevan, Arthur Scargill and John Prescott. Charitable audiences, on the other hand, tend to prefer appeals to pity. We must judge the emotional appeal carefully: if the speaker appeals to one emotion when another emotion is more prevalent, we could set our speaker on course for a catastrophic collision. This is what happened to Cherie Booth: she tried to play for pity when many people felt angry about her involvement with a convicted Australian fraudster. Likewise, George Galloway's appeals to shame over Iraq alienated many people who disliked the war but were proud of 'our boys'. Both suffered severe backlashes. So we should proceed with care when it comes to emotional appeals. Emotions are like a can of worms: once released, they are impossible to contain again.

Logic is actually an optional extra when it comes to speeches. Speeches move too fast. Logic doesn't matter. As Macaulay said, we should not imagine that audiences, 'pause at every line, reconsidering every argument ... [when in fact they are] hurried from point to point too rapidly to detect the fallacies through which

they were conducted; [with] no time to disentangle sophisms, or to notice slight inaccuracies of expression.' The truth is that most speeches are stuffed to the brim with logical fallacies and no one even notices. By way of example, one of the most oft-repeated lines in ministerial speeches during the first ten years of New Labour was the (now forgotten) mantra that: 'In 1997, we gave independence to the Bank of England. Since then, we have experienced the longest, uninterrupted period of growth in the nation's history.' This line sought to credit the government for the sustained economic growth using the ancient rhetorical device *post hoc ergo propter hoc*, meaning 'after this, therefore because of this.' This device misleads the listener into assuming a causal connection between two actually unconnected factors because they are placed next to one another. Interestingly, film directors use the same technique to suggest a narrative flow between scenes. It is, however, illusory and therefore useful for deceit.

Most logical fallacies sound deceptively reassuring. When Virgin Galactic's president, Will Whitehorn, tried to extinguish safety concerns about Richard Branson's first foray into commercial space flights, he said, 'Virgin operates three airlines. Our name is a byword for safety.' Whitehorn was making a general assertion (Virgin is safe) on the basis of a specific truth (that Virgin's airlines are safe) in order to make an unproven suggestion (that Virgin Galactic will be safe). No connection can be drawn between the safety record of Virgin's airlines and their future safety in the uncharted territory of space, but the fallacy provided a soothing sense of comfort and that was all that the audience required. Job done!

Again, those who feel a bit uncomfortable about these techniques should bear in mind that even that great and most noble of philosophers, Aristotle, only insisted that a speaker need to create the *illusion* of logic, they didn't need to bother whether it was supported or not.

The third principle is that *less is more*. Gordon Brown's speeches are packed full with facts, stats and clever lines but the end result is speeches that seem so brutally assertive that the audience is left feeling almost battered and bruised by the end, as if they have been on the receiving end of 'a boot stamping on a human face,' to quote George Orwell's memorable line. Audiences like to be mentally involved in speeches and will turn off if they are not. We should leave the audience space to think about what we're saying, to find their own connections and paint their own pictures, if they want, rather than imposing our own ideas upon them. Our speeches should contain what graphic designers call 'white space'.

It's worth being modest in our ambitions for a speech. A speaker who presents ten pieces of information on a PowerPoint slide is unlikely to get his audience to remember them. More realistically, the audience will simply think, 'That speaker had ten bits of information (but I can't remember what any of them were).' Likewise, a speaker who reels off a long list of statistics is likely only to leave his audience with the impression that he likes statistics. Speeches should always be judged in terms of net achievement, not

gross activity – i.e. not what we say, but what they hear. This is something of a paradigm shift, meaning that instead of looking to cram a speech with piles of information, speechwriters should instead focus upon a single brilliant idea or image they want to impress.

Less is also more in terms of the number of speeches a speaker makes – people shouldn't make speeches unless they have something to say. Every day, all across Whitehall you can see politicians and businesspeople scurrying between business breakfasts, lunches, conferences, seminars and dinners to give speeches they don't care about to audiences who will barely listen. What's the point? Save the speeches for when it really matters. And that is why it is so important to prepare speech strategies, covered in the final chapter of this book.

Less is also more when it comes to the length of speeches. Twenty minutes seems to be as much as most people can stomach these days. Reducing the speech down focuses the writing more clearly on a particular message. It reminds me of Mark Twain's apology for 'writing a long letter because [he] didn't have time to write a short one.' The same could easily be said in respect of a speech. The best speeches are strikingly simple: the Gettysburg Address, which included the immortal line, 'Government of the people, by the people, for the people,' comprised just 269 words. Of these, 205 were just one syllable.

Less is also more in terms of the length of words. Winston Churchill once said, 'Broadly speaking, the short words are best, and the old ones are the best of all.'[viii] Or, as Richard Nixon's speechwriter William Safire subsequently joshed, 'Never pick a long word where a diminutive one will do.'

The Three Golden Rhetorical Devices

Next, comes the three golden rhetorical devices. These devices are formulae for constructing sentences to give your words more impact. They are the easiest tricks for any speechwriter to learn to make their writing sound instantly more like a speech and less like an essay. These devices also form the essence of what we today label pejoratively as 'soundbites'. We all know these devices instinctively and use them unconsciously in everyday conversation whenever we are saying something we care about. They are not, as some have claimed, 'claptraps': the only sure-fire way to make an audience applaud is to hand out ten pound notes. Rhetorical devices are, however, a way of signifying importance to our audience. They tell them, 'this bit matters'. There are literally dozens of rhetorical devices. Some are particularly good at advancing ethos, some pathos and some logos. They are all covered more extensively in the chapter The Craft of Soundbites (see page 188).

The top three rhetorical devices are helpfully set out by that master rhetorician Shakespeare in the first three lines of Mark Antony's speech in Act 3, Scene 2 of *Julius Caesar*.

'Friends, Romans, Countrymen	Rule of Three
Lend me your ears	Imagery
I come to bury Caesar, not to praise him.'	Contrast

Shakespeare knew what he was doing with these three lines. He was showing us the three easiest ways to grab an audience's attention.

The rule of three comes up again and again in speechwriting. When we make our points in lists of three it creates a sense of completeness and an illusion of finality. This is because we are so used to hearing arguments in twos (left or right, black or white, up or down), that when a third is added it feels like a final nail has been hammered in: our case proved beyond doubt. We use the rule of three habitually in everyday conversation (e.g. 'this, that and the other', 'ready, steady, go', 'three, two, one'). We often grapple around for a third even when none comes instantly to mind. The rule of three also has relevance, in a different way, to the way that we receive and process visual images, which is why photographers and artists are often encouraged to think of their pictures as three by three grids.

Many of the best-known lines from speeches have been based on three-part lists, from Abraham Lincoln's 'Government of the people, by the people, for the people' to O.J. Simpson's 'I could not, would not, did not commit this crime.' Many speeches open with three-part lists, as Mark Antony did, and as Earl Spencer also did in his eulogy for Princess Diana: 'I stand before you today, the representative of a *family* in grief, in a *country* in mourning, before a *world* in shock.' When the rule of three is used to repeat a single word, it gives it a shocking force, as with Margaret Thatcher's 'No! No! No!'

The second line of Mark Antony's speech, 'Lend me your ears,' is an impeccable example of *imagery*. Imagery allows the speechwriter to bypass rational scrutiny and strike the message deep into their audience's hearts. We can use imagery to predispose our audience to particular emotions or opinions without giving them any clue what we are doing. Mark Antony's 'Lend me your ears' plea laid the ground for his speech. It was rather pleading, demonstrating that he was putting the fraught and raucous mob's needs before his own. It contrasted sharply with Brutus's far more aggrandising 'Hear me for my cause, and be silent that you may hear.' The metaphors characterized the two different approaches to rhetoric and the mob. Antony's imploring metaphor cast him in a much more favourable light than Brutus's crushing fist approach.

Many of the most famous speeches are centred around a single, fresh image, including Charles De Gaulle's 'Flame of French resistance,' Nelson Mandela's 'Road to freedom,' Winston Churchill's 'Iron curtain,' Harold Macmillan's 'Wind of change,' Margaret Thatcher's 'Lady's not for turning' and Tony Blair's 'Hand of history.' Aristotle said the gift of metaphor was the most important skill for any orator.

The third line of Mark Antony's speech, 'I come to bury Caesar, not to praise him' is a classic example of a *contrast*. Contrast is the bread and butter of speechwriting. It works on a number of levels, many of which are primeval. It heightens the senses, makes our speeches more interesting and forces our audience to pick sides.

Different contrasts achieve different effects. George W. Bush's short, sharp contrasts presented a short, sharp view of the world: 'You're either with us or you're against us', 'We want Osama dead or alive'. John F. Kennedy's more long-winded contrasts projected grandeur and intellect: 'Ask not what your country can do for you, ask what you can do for your country', 'Liberty without learning is always in peril. Learning without liberty is always in vain.'

Contrast is often used at the beginning of speeches when typically a number of contrasts are issued in rapid succession. This was the case with J.F.K.'s inaugural ('We observe today not a victory of party, but a celebration of freedom; symbolising an end, as well a beginning; signifying renewal, as well as change'), Obama's inaugural ('We have chosen hope over fear, unity of purpose over discord') and Jonny Cochran's closing speech in the O.J. Simpson trial ('There should be no rich, no poor, no high, no low, no white, no black, but common country, common citizenship, equal rights and a common destiny'). The effect is presidential, but it is also slightly disorientating, almost bewildering. It feels like a conjuror performing rapid hand moves in front of your eyes before suddenly pulling a rabbit from a hat. It enhances the speaker's authority and makes the audience more malleable. In an episode of the *West Wing*, Toby Ziegler – speechwriter extraordinaire – explains how it works:

> Food is cheaper, clothes are cheaper, steel is cheaper, cars are cheaper, phone service is cheaper. You feel me building a rhythm here? That's 'cause I'm a speechwriter and I know how to make a point. . . It lowers prices, it raises income. You see what I did with 'lowers' and 'raises' there? It's called the science of listener attention. We did repetition, we did floating opposites and now you end with the one that's not like the others. Ready? Free trade stops wars. And that's it. Free trade stops wars!

The Top Three Myths of Speechwriting

Now we move from the three best tricks of successful speechwriting to the three big myths. When I first became a speechwriter, I was given a number of pieces of advice which seemed to have been passed from speechwriter to speechwriter for generations: keep your sentences short, write in the active and know your grammar. Since then, the more I've researched rhetoric, the more I've discovered that these pieces of advice were complete nonsense.

First, this *myth that speechwriters must write in short sentences.* When Tony Blair was prime minister, an unspoken rule circulated around Whitehall that no sentence should ever contain more than seven words. This rule arose presumably because everyone knew that Blair loved short, verbless, ungrammatical sentences. But this wasn't everyone's style and it didn't suit every occasion. It was just Blair's style when he deliberately wanted to whip up a sense of fear or drama. It is based upon the old Ancient Roman rhetorical technique of asyndeton, where connective words are deliberately removed to create a breathless effect, so it sounds as if the speaker is almost hyperventilating. Blair used this style to get people going. It created a sense of urgency about what he was proposing, whether he was talking about promoting science, reforming health or invading Iraq.

But short sentences are not always appropriate. Obama's speech to the Democratic National Convention in 2004 – the one which first thrust him into the public eye – ended with a single sentence peroration that was 108 words long. It is hard, even now, to look at this sentence and find a single word that could be struck out without changing the feeling or meaning:

> Tonight, if you feel the same energy that I do, if you feel the same urgency that I do, if you feel the same passion that I do, if you feel the same hopefulness that I do – if we do what we must do, then I have no doubt that all across the country, from Florida to Oregon, from Washington to Maine, the people will

rise up in November, and John Kerry will be sworn in as president, and John Edwards will be sworn in as vice president, and this country will reclaim its promise, and out of this long political darkness a brighter day will come.

Obama needed a long sentence like that. Why? Because it created the sense that he was leading his audience upon a long and winding journey: a journey that would not finish in one day or one week or even one year; a journey that would require a multitude of effort from a multitude of people; a journey that would take them from each side of the country to the other, from north to south, east to west and around again. Could he have achieved that effect with a short sentence? No chance. Not. A. Hope. In. Hell.

The *second myth is that speechwriters must always write in the active, not the passive voice*, i.e. subject – verb – object. Yes, this is normally true, because we normally want to clearly let our audience know who the main actor is, what the main act is and whom that act is affecting. The active voice achieves all this. But clarity is not always our aim, particularly in politics and business, and particularly if our speaker has been up to no good. In these cases, we might actively want to draw a veil over some parts of the action, and the passive voice can achieve this.

'Mistakes were made' is probably one of the best examples of the passive voice in all its cruel, deceptive glory. Richard Nixon used it during the Watergate scandal, George Bush Senior during the Iran-Contra affair and Bill Clinton during the Monica Lewinsky scandal. Its genius is that it creates the impression that the speaker accepts some responsibility whilst he is actually doing nothing of the sort. The passive voice can also be helpful in other situations. It means the speaker can grab credit for things he had little to do with, because there is no requirement to reveal the protagonist, as in this two-part construction: 'In 1997, we introduced the minimum wage and the New Deal. Since then, 2 million jobs have been created.'[ix]

The *third myth is that you need an incredible mastery of English grammar to be a great speechwriter*. Speeches are written for the ear, not the eye. No one will notice or even care about grammar. They should be tailor-made for the speaker in all their authentic glory.

Many of the greatest speakers in history were technically illiterate. And, in many of these cases, it was their inarticulacy which gave their oratory its potency, for example, Sojourner Truth's 'Ain't I a woman' speech: 'I tink dat 'twixt de niggers of de Souf and de womin at de Norf, all talkin' bout rights, de white men will be in a fix pretty soon. . . .' Her dialect was part of the message. Had she sounded like some pompous, pretentious nineteenth-century lawyer abounding with rhetorical flourishes, i.e. speaking in the familiar style of the day, it would have totally undermined what she was saying.

John Prescott has also often been lampooned for his use of English, but his mangled style was a guaranteed roof-raiser at Labour Party conference:

Look I've got my old pledge card a bit battered and crumpled . . . We said we'd provide more turches churches teachers . . . And we have . . . I can remember when people used to say the Japanese are better than us, the Germans are better than us, the French are better than us, well it's great to be able to say we're better than them. I think Mr Kennedy, well we all congratulate on his baby, and the Tories. Are you remembering what I'm remembering? Boom and bust? Negative equity? Remember! Mr Howard! I mean, are you thinking what I'm thinking. I'm remembering it's all a bit wonky isn't it?

Minus ten for grammar. Minus ten for coherency. But full marks for authenticity, passion and impact.

Summary

We all have a latent talent for speechwriting. We all know these principles and rhetorical devices instinctively. We use them in ordinary conversation. Many of today's greatest speeches are probably not being delivered in Parliament or at posh banquets but in two-up two-downs across the country about such profound topics as, 'Why I wish you'd pick your socks up from the floor' and 'Why I wish you wouldn't hide my car keys when I'm already late for a meeting.' The trick is transferring those techniques from our personal lives into a professional setting. This book shows you how to do that. It's not about emulating Barack Obama, David Cameron or Tony Blair. On the contrary, the constant challenge for Obama, Cameron and Blair's speechwriters is to emulate the authentic voice of the ordinary man on the street.

Aristotle's big three of speechwriting
- Ethos (the character of the speaker)
- Pathos (the emotions of the audience)
- Logos (the reasoning of the argument)

The top three principles of speechwriting
- The audience is more important than the speaker
- Emotions are more powerful than logic
- Less is more

The top three rhetorical devices
- The rule of three
- Imagery
- Contrast

The top three myths about speechwriting
- Always write short sentences
- Always write in the active
- Always check your grammar

Case Study

I have selected Barack Obama's inaugural address to illustrate the techniques in this chapter. The speech was penned by Jon Favreau. With his glamorous girlfriends, Police sunglasses, Armani suit and $170k salary, 'Favs' epitomised the rebirth of speechwriter cool. Obama called him his 'mind reader'. Legend had it that Favreau wrote the inaugural in a Washington Starbucks, fuelled by espressos. The story had great mythical qualities but the truth was rather different. He went out and spoke to world-renowned historians. He studied speeches from other past crises.[x] He sought advice from other notable presidential speechwriters including Peggy Noonan, Reagan's speechwriter, and Ted Sorensen, Kennedy's speechwriter. He wrote the speech with tremendous care, elegantly moving Obama along from the poetry of his campaign rhetoric to the more serious, statesmanlike tones required by a leader. He used a number of different techniques.

Edited version of Obama's Inaugural Address, Washington DC, 20 January 2009

I stand here today humbled by the task before us, grateful for the trust you've bestowed, mindful of the sacrifices borne by our ancestors.

Forty-four Americans have now taken the presidential oath. Their words have been spoken during rising tides of prosperity and the still waters of peace. Yet, every so often, the oath is taken amidst gathering clouds and raging storms.

Our nation is at war. Our economy is badly weakened. Homes have been lost, jobs shed, businesses shuttered.

The challenges we face are real. They are serious and they are many. They will not be met easily or in a short span of time. But know this America: they will be met.

We gather because we have chosen hope over fear, unity of purpose over conflict and discord. In the words of scripture, the time has come to set aside childish things; to reaffirm our enduring spirit; to choose our better history; to carry forward that precious gift, that noble idea passed on from generation to generation: the God-given promise that all are equal, all are free, and all deserve a chance to pursue their full measure of happiness.

In reaffirming the greatness of our nation we understand that greatness is never a given.

Our journey has never been one of short-cuts or settling for less. It has not been the path for the faint-hearted, for those that prefer leisure over work, or seek only the pleasures of riches and fame. Rather, it has been the risk-takers, the doers, the makers of things who have carried us up the long rugged path towards prosperity and freedom.

For us, they packed up their few worldly possessions and travelled across oceans in search of a new life. For us, they toiled in sweatshops, and settled the West, endured the lash of the whip, and plowed the hard earth. For us, they fought and died in places like Concord and Gettysburg, Normandy and Khe Sahn.

Time and again these men and women struggled and sacrificed and worked till their hands were raw so that we might live a better life.

This is the journey we continue today. We remain the most prosperous, powerful nation on Earth. But our time of standing pat has surely passed. Starting today, we must pick ourselves up, dust ourselves off, and begin again the work of remaking America.

Everywhere we look, there is work to be done. The state of our economy calls for action. We will build the roads and bridges. We'll restore science to its rightful place. We will harness the sun and the winds and the soil to fuel our cars and run our factories. And we will transform our schools and colleges and universities.

There are some who question the scale of our ambitions. Their memories are short. They have forgotten what this country has already done, what free men and women can achieve when imagination is joined to common purpose, and necessity to courage.

We reject as false the choice between our safety and our ideals. Our Founding Fathers, faced with perils that we can scarcely imagine, drafted a charter to assure the rule of law and the rights of man. Those ideals still light the world.

And so, to all the other peoples and governments, from the grandest capitals to the small village where my father was born, know that America is a friend of each nation, and every man, woman and child who seeks a future of peace and dignity.

We will not apologize for our way of life, nor will we waver in its defence. And for those who seek to advance their aims by inducing terror and slaughtering innocents, we say to you that our spirit is stronger and cannot be broken.

Our patchwork heritage is a strength, not a weakness. We are a nation of Christians and Muslims, Jews and Hindus, and non-believers. We are shaped by every language and culture; and because we have tasted the bitter swill of civil war and segregation, and emerged from that dark chapter stronger and more united, we cannot help but believe that the old hatreds shall someday pass.

To those leaders around the globe who sow conflict, know that your people will judge you on what you can build, not what you destroy.

To those who cling to power through the silencing of dissent, know that you are on the wrong side of history, but that we will extend a hand if you are willing to unclench your fist.

To the people of poor nations, we pledge to work alongside you to make your farms flourish and let clean waters flow.

We remember with humble gratitude those brave Americans who patrol far-off deserts and distant mountains. They have something to tell us, just as the fallen heroes who lie in Arlington whisper through the ages.

They embody the spirit of service. For as much as government can do, it is ultimately the faith and determination of the American people upon which this nation relies. It is the kindness to take in a stranger when the levees break, the selflessness of workers who would rather cut their hours than see a friend lose their job which sees us through our darkest hours. It is the firefighter's courage to storm a stairway filled with smoke, but also a parent's willingness to nurture a child that finally decides our fate.

Our challenges may be new. But those values upon which our success depends are old. They have been the quiet force of progress throughout our history.

What is demanded now is a new era of responsibility – a recognition on the part of every American that we have duties to ourselves, our nation and the world.

This is the price and the promise of citizenship. This is the source of our confidence. This is the meaning of our liberty and our creed. This is why a man whose father less than sixty years ago might not have been served in a local restaurant can now stand before you to take a most sacred oath.

So let us mark this day with remembrance of who we are and how far we have traveled. In the year of America's birth, in the coldest of months, a small band of patriots huddled by dying campfires on the shores of an icy river. The capital was abandoned. The enemy was advancing. The snow was stained with blood. At the moment when the outcome of our revolution was most in doubt, the father of our nation ordered these words to be read to the people:

'Let it be told to the future world ... that in the depth of winter, when nothing but hope and virtue could survive . . . that the city and the country, alarmed at one common danger, came forth to meet [it].'

America: In the face of our common dangers, in this winter of our hardship, let us remember these timeless words. With hope and virtue, let us brave once more the icy currents, and endure what storms may come. Let it be said by our children's children that when we were tested we refused to let this journey end, that we did not turn back nor did we falter; and with eyes fixed on the horizon and God's grace upon us, we carried forth that great gift of freedom and delivered it safely to future generations.

Thank you. God bless you. And God bless the United States of America.

Aristotle's big three

The speech balances ethos, pathos and logos.

The ethos is evident. Many commentators remarked that Obama instantly took on the appearance of a ready made president. This was surely no accident. He associated himself with great American leaders through mimicking their style. Sometimes, he sounded like Martin Luther King: 'We remain a young nation, but in the words of scripture, the time has come to set aside these childish things. The time has come to reaffirm our enduring spirit; to choose our better history; to carry forward that precious gift, that noble idea, passed on from generation to generation: the God-given promise that all are equal, all are free, and all deserve a chance to pursue their full measure of happiness.' On other occasions, he sounded like John F. Kennedy: 'In reaffirming the greatness of our nation, we understand that greatness is never a given.' He sometimes drifted into Abraham Lincoln's trademark monosyllabic simplicity: 'Our Founding Fathers, faced with perils we can scarcely imagine, drafted a charter to assure the rule of law and the rights of man, a charter expanded by the blood of generations. Those ideals still light the world, and we will not give them up for expedience's sake.' He also echoed Ronald Reagan: 'We must pick ourselves up, dust ourselves off, and begin again the work of remaking America.' He was also very happy to talk about his ethnicity, reminding the audience that 'less than sixty years ago [he] might not have been served at a local restaurant'.

The pathos comes through exquisite use of metaphor. The journey metaphor was used throughout his candidacy: this is a strong metaphor for political campaigns as it appeals to people's hopes and ambitions. 'Our journey has never been one of shortcuts . . . It has not been a path for the fainthearted . . . up the long rugged path toward prosperity and freedom.' It was often ambiguous whether he was talking about his own journey or that of America. This blurring intertwined Obama's interests with America's, effectively making the American people an offer they could not refuse: if you believe in America, you must vote for me. He also appealed to pathos by evoking powerful images from the national consciousness: 'The kindness to take in a stranger ... the selflessness of workers who would rather cut their hours than see a friend lose their job.... The firefighter's courage to storm a stairway filled with smoke, but also a parent's willingness to nurture a child.'

The logos comes from one very simple argument that runs throughout the speech like a backbone: America has always been a fundamentally great country because it comprises fundamentally great people; by mobilizing those fundamentally great people once again, America can be great once again.

The principles of speechwriting
This speech clearly placed the audience (the American people) in the position of protagonist, with Obama a distant second. This speech was not about self-aggrandizement but audience appeal.

The speech was filled with emotion and the rhetorical device of repetition e.g. *'For us*, they fought and died in places like Concord and Gettysburg, Normandy and Khe Sahn', *'This* is the price and the promise of citizenship. *This* is the source of our confidence. . . . *This* is the meaning of our liberty and our creed.'

The less-is-more principle was clearly applied. This speech does not delve into the detail. It is built around a simple linear argument. There are no statistics or incomprehensible sentences.

Three rhetorical devices
There are plenty of instances of the rule of three, e.g.: 'I stand here today *humbled* by the task before us, *grateful* for the trust you have bestowed, *mindful* of the sacrifices borne by our ancestors.' '*Homes* have been lost, *jobs* shed, *businesses* shuttered.'

The speech is loaded with powerful imagery, particularly when he talked about the 'small band of patriots huddled by dying campfires on the shores of an icy river. The capital was abandoned. The enemy was advancing. The snow was stained with blood.'

And the speech is also stuffed with contrasts: 'We have chosen hope over fear, unity of purpose over conflict and discord', 'Our patchwork heritage is a strength, not a weakness.'

Favreau had previously compared being Obama's speechwriter with being 'Ted Williams' batting coach'. With this speech, he scored a home run. This was speechwriting at its best, as it had been throughout the campaign, hoisting a 'skinny kid with a funny name' into the most powerful position in the world.

Chapter Two

The Craft of Speechwriting

I can see him now, pacing slowly up and down the room, his hands clasped behind his back, his shoulders hunched, his head sunk forward in deep thought, slowly and haltingly dictating the beginning of a speech or an article. I wait, my pencil poised in mid-air, as he whispers phrases to himself, carefully weighing each word and striving to make his thoughts balance. Nothing may be put down until it has been tested aloud and found satisfactory. A happy choice brings a glint of triumph to his eye; a poor one is instantly discarded. He will continue the search until every detail – of sound, rhythm and harmony – is to his liking. Sometimes there are long halts, during which he patiently sounds out a phrase a dozen times, this way and that, making the cigar in his hand serve as a baton to punctuate the rhythm of his words.

Phyllis Moir, from *I was Winston Churchill's Private Secretary*

He would be standing at or bent over his desk, working on the punch lines for a speech. Before the dictation, I would not exist for him, and I doubt whether he saw me as a person when I was at my typist's desk. A while would pass in silence. Then he would close in on the typewriter and begin to dictate calmly and with expansive gestures. Gradually, getting into his stride, he would speak faster. Without pause, one sentence would then follow another while he strolled around the room. Occasionally, he would halt, lost in thought, in front of Lenbach's portrait of Bismarck, gathering himself before resuming his wandering. His face would become florid and the anger would shine in his eyes. He would stand rooted to the spot as though confronting the particular enemy he was imagining.

Christa Schroder, from *The Memoirs of Adolf Hitler's Secretary*

Sam Rosenman, Ted Roosevelt's former speechwriter, once described speechwriting as a mix of 'the glamour and the grind.' As jobs go, overall, it must be said that most speechwriters don't get a bad deal. At a relatively young age (most speechwriters start in their twenties), we gain an influence that extends far beyond our pay grade, getting to mix with the great and the good, walking down the corridors of power, occasionally even witnessing a little piece of history being made. It can be the greatest job in the world, but it can be the worst too. In private, speechwriters can be subjected to the most ferocious, vicious abuse. The trouble is that speeches have a cruel capacity to reduce even the most powerful people into nervous wrecks. As a result, speechwriters can often find themselves on the receiving end of the most furious rants and rages. I know of one speechwriter who once walked in to her boss's office to see he had smashed his own computer on the floor because he was so angry at the draft speech she had submitted. He looked at her furiously and said, 'You broke my computer.' She found it difficult to believe she had such a profoundly infuriating effect on the prime minister of Great Britain.

The truth is, easy as it is to theorize and pontificate about speechwriting, it is never ever an easy job. Still, to this day, whenever I get a writing commission, a tight knot develops in my stomach that does not loosen until the moment the draft has been submitted. Until then, I am battling with a demon, swinging between

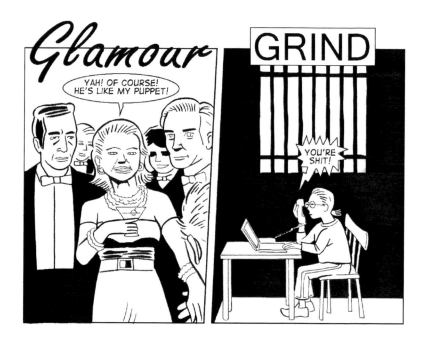

polar extremes, from wild cockiness to utter depression, from manic typing to desperate avoidance strategies – ringing friends I've not spoken to in years and even offering to help around the house. If I'm lucky, I finally find my groove as the deadline looms; then I write like a man possessed, fuelled by caffeine, crisps and adrenalin until the early hours when the job is done.

There is no single way of approaching speechwriting. Everyone has their own method; for them, that will usually be the best. This chapter doesn't seek to impose a single simple way to write a speech. Instead, it is intended to provide a clear process for anyone who is struggling to beat the blank sheet of paper blues. This chapter is based on a few starting principles.

First, don't start writing too soon. A builder would not start building a house without seeing the finalized plans, and nor should a speechwriter try writing a speech without knowing what shape the final speech will take.

Second, the speaker is always right. The speechwriting process should be based ninety-nine per cent around what the speaker wants and one per cent around what everyone else wants. This is true whether we agree with the speaker or not. It is their speech, their job and their judgement on the line. The speechwriter's role is more an essential efficiency saving than anything else: to write the same speech the speaker would write, if only they had the time. This approach should be heeded as a matter of self-preservation if nothing else: by looking after our speaker, we're looking after ourselves. The speechwriter who writes for self-gratification will have a very short career span indeed. Plus, they'll regularly face the miserable task of consigning 3,000 words of carefully honed text to the dustbin because they've missed the spot.

Third, take charge of the speechwriting process. You wouldn't let a car drive itself, nor can a speech be allowed to write itself. If we do not take charge, the risk is that no one will or everyone will – either of which spells disaster for the speech. This is not to say that we must work in isolation: far from it, we should absorb influences and welcome feedback, but equally we must know when to slam the door shut – when we are actually doing the writing. No good speech was ever written by committee. As J.F.K.'s speechwriter, Theodore Sorensen, has said, 'The boldness and strength of a statement is in inverse proportion to the number of people who have to clear it.'[i]

Fourth, we should separate the creative and rational parts of the process. They use different parts of the brain. By mixing the two, we reduce our effectiveness. How many times have you had a great idea, run to the keyboard, typed it up and then you start fiddling with it, shifting the order, changing the words and, before you know it, the sentence has lost all its freshness and your original burst of inspiration has vanished. John Lennon and Paul McCartney wrote 'Hard Days Night' in half an hour flat. If they had stopped five minutes through to have a big debate about whether it sounded better in G or A, they would never have made it to the end. Keep your creative and critical faculties separate.

Fifth, we should keep our role and influence private. Many

speakers are embarrassed to admit using speechwriters for the very good reason that the revelation could lead to them being lampooned. Nero was the first politician to get into trouble for using a speechwriter.[ii] Kennedy too was characterized as Sorenson's 'puppet'.[iii] I have attended conferences where my biography was doctored to delete my speechwriting activities. I have been variously introduced as a 'political adviser', 'secretary' and even 'friend' to conceal my true role. I even watched one of my clients conclude a speech by telling the audience a story about a speechwriter that I had given him, and then brazenly declare that this could never happen to him as he wrote all of his own speeches! If you're wondering, the (undoubtedly apocryphal) story went like this: one of Alan Clark's speechwriters wanted to get his own back, after a series of bruising encounters. Clark was due to deliver a speech at a major conference on employment law. The speechwriter presented Clark with the draft. The first page said, 'Good morning. I'm delighted to be here. Today, I will today run through seventeen complex issues in employment law which are in desperate need of reform.' The second page said, 'You're on your own now, you bastard.'

There are three questions I'm often asked.

The first is how long it takes to write a speech. My answer is Parkinson's Law: if you have three weeks, it takes three weeks; if you have three hours, it takes three hours. My rule of thumb is that it takes one hour to produce a minute of carefully crafted text.

The second question is what attributes a good speechwriter must possess. My answer is seemingly contradictory skills. You need a certain level of emotional immaturity, but combined with wisdom and experience. You need a sharp intellect and clear ideas, but alongside a willingness to subject those ideas to the harshest scrutiny. You need a certain sensitivity and vulnerability, but along with one hell of a thick skin.

The third question is how I go about writing a speech. This chapter sets out my answer to that question.

Step One: Researching the Speaker, Issue and Audience

Aristotle's golden triangle of ethos, logos and pathos (the character of the speaker, the logic of the argument and the emotions of the audience, see page 22) militates against any kind of speech-by-numbers approach. It means every speech must be an original composition, based on an analysis of the unique congregation of speaker, issue and audience. Our starting point must be to research each one of these.

We must be able to sink into our *speaker's* skin. Speechwriting is like an act of psychological transference. We must think, feel and write like our speaker, becoming their eyes and ears, heart and hands. This can leave the speechwriter facing a bit of an identity crisis. In recent years, I have been a forty-something, high-heel wearing, powerful CEO one moment and then quickly had to convert myself into a seventy-something senior member of the

House of Lords. I've argued on one side of the issue then leapt across to argue from the other. This kind of intellectual and emotional cross-dressing is an inescapable and intrinsic part of the speechwriting process. When we're writing a speech, we must cast our own peccadilloes and prejudices to one side and replace them with our speakers. It was said of J.F.K.'s speechwriter, Theodore Sorensen, 'When Jack is wounded, Ted bleeds.' This kind of transferral is not unusual. I have noticed that in Whitehall many speechwriters come to mimic their speakers after a while. In some cases, they even began, quite comically, to resemble them. If speaker and speechwriter are unable to achieve this rapport or empathy, the relationship is much more fraught. Bob Shrum walked out on Jimmy Carter after just a week.[iv] President Roosevelt and his speechwriter Raymond Moley often had heated arguments at dinner parties, embarrassing the guests.[v]

If we write for the same person for a long time, we will eventually absorb their thoughts and ideas almost by osmosis, making us far more likely to anticipate not just the position they will take but also their preferred soundbites, metaphors, speech structures and even jokes. I have now written speeches for Alan Johnson on-and-off for over ten years. The longer I've done it, the easier it's become. I often judged my success by the ratio of words in the final draft that were mine against the ratio that were his: over ninety-five per cent left me very chuffed. After a while though, I could hear Alan's voice in my head very clearly whilst I was writing.

If you don't have this kind of history with the speaker, you should try and secure some access. If you do get a meeting, make sure you go with focused and specific recommendations. Don't put them too on the spot or they'll be defensive. The response you'll probably provoke will in fact be, 'What bloody speech?' rapidly followed with a, 'How the hell do I get out of it?'

If you can't get a meeting, try to tap members of their entourage for advice, e.g. PAs, deputies, private secretaries, press secretaries and special advisers. If you are writing for someone in the public eye, you may be able to discover some past interviews or even speeches on YouTube. If that fails, you can always resort to guerrilla tactics. One minister I worked for was so difficult to pin down I used to lurk by the lift lobby so I could spend the twenty-two seconds it took to get to the ground floor bombarding him with questions about my speech. This was not ideal, but it was better than nothing. Without meaningful access, speechwriting becomes almost impossible. As one of Jimmy Carter's speechwriters once complained, 'I can't get into the head of Jimmy Carter because I've never met Jimmy Carter . . . [It] is like writing in a vacuum.'[vi]

One of the first things to get to grips with is a speaker's style. Everyone has a unique style of speech. To take two of the most recent prime ministers, Tony Blair was imperious and spoke instinctively in soundbites whilst John Major was more demure and fiercely anti-rhetoric.[vii] They were almost complete opposites. Major couldn't deliver a Blair speech, nor could Blair deliver a Major speech. You must write in the authentic style of the speaker. Matthew Parris once wrote a speech for John Major and, because he knew John Major liked to drone, he 'put in a section that could be droned.'[viii] If we write Obama-like speeches for an insipid middle-manager he will crash down like a lead balloon. The trick to learning someone's style is to listen not just to *what* they say but *how* they say it. A few basic pointers act as a good guide: do they prefer long or short sentences? Do they like humble or pompous words? Is their style florid or plain? We might also add to this, what are their favourite metaphors? What are their preferred frames of reference? How do they tend to structure an argument? What rhetorical devices do they prefer?

Most people have a style that can be boiled down to just two or three things. Gordon Brown's style is based around a) amassing huge piles of sub-clauses; b) constructing extensive alliterative pairings (e.g. boom and bust, listen and learn, challenge and change); and c) unleashing wave after wave of statistic. George Osborne's style is based on very short and pithy sentences, no unnecessary information and points of reference that would appeal to a housewife. Prince Charles, on the other hand, has a tremendously ornate and grandiose style, based on using as many intensifiers as possible (e.g. 'I am *extremely* grateful to you all for sparing your *hugely* important time from your *hideously* busy schedules.') Russell Brand's style is based around a) exchanging every 'was' for a 'were'; b) inserting plenty of oiky fillers such as 'like' and 'right', and c) making dramatic swoops, from highly ornate Victorian-like flourishes to gutter-like cries of 'an' it were me ball bag!'

We must also really research the *issue*. Writing a speech without knowledge is like trying to climb Kilimanjaro without legs. That is why some writers resort to jargon, as a veil for their ignorance (amazingly, this often works, as a fear of looking foolish means jargon frequently goes unchallenged). The best cure for ignorance is reading. Peggy Noonan, Ronald Reagan's speechwriter, said, 'Reading is collecting wisdom, writing is spending it.' A speech is only as good as the material it contains. And also, by going over the issue as thoroughly as you can, you reduce the chance of your speaker slipping over any banana skins.

Invariably, the best information comes from reaching beyond the usual sources, so cast your net far and wide. Pore over encyclopedias, hunt through Hansard, scour through libraries. Read academic journals and think-tank pamphlets (both are usually packed with facts and figures). Check out media sources: LexisNexis, *The Economist* and broadsheet websites. Trawl Internet search engines, Wikipedia and blogs. Check what people in other parties, countries and companies are saying. Try thinking laterally to expose serendipitous routes. So, if you are writing about corruption in Africa, try looking at corruption in Italy in the twelfth century. If you are writing about what intellectuals in Washington think about climate change, try seeing the issue from the perspective of African maize farmers. If you are writing about the IT revolution, why not read about the industrial revolution. Don't be afraid to bounce between different perspectives, from populist to intellectual, economic to social, local to global, emotional to logical, practical to ideological, scientific to instinctive, conservative to progressive. It's these leaps that make a speech exciting.

Finally, we must really understand and research our *audience*. We should analyse them with the same care as a doctor would a patient. Delving into their backgrounds serves many purposes but in particular it helps us to discover a) a reasonable persuasive aim for our speech and b) what triggers, images and ideas will work best.

We should work out why they are listening to the speech. What gratification are they seeking? Are they just there because their boss has told them to go? Or are they so desperately concerned that they are there of their own volition? Are they an audience which is likely to hector and harangue? Or are they there to listen and learn? Are they there to get away from home for a few days? Or are they there to build up their contacts?

Who are they? How old? What gender? What social class? What

profession? In today's politically correct age, it's not always easy to admit that different demographic groups demand different persuasive strategies, but that is clearly the case. Female audiences tend to be more receptive to new information than male audiences. Audiences who perceive themselves to be minorities are more prone to anger and shame but also to pride. Young audiences tend to be more fixed in their opinions than older audiences (the older we get the less certain we are in our opinions, probably because we know more, so we become more confused).

How does our audience feel? Are they likely to be relaxed or tense, business-like or fun, intellectual or accessible? What will the predominant emotions be? Anger or sadness? Hope or fear? Pride or shame? What will the strength of feeling be? Maybe they don't feel strongly about the issue we are talking about but do feel strongly about something else. Can we connect the two?

What motivates them? Who are their role models? What has motivated them in the past? This information will prove crucial: we could inspire an audience of teenagers to do something by telling them that Lily Allen has just done it, but saying the same thing to an audience of pensioners might elicit a reaction of, 'Huh?'

And how much do they know? Do they have any advance knowledge of the issue? We don't want to risk talking over their heads or talking down to them. And do we agree or not? It is best to be clear about any disagreements up front.

There are all sorts of places we can go to find out about our audience: some we may know intuitively, the rest can usually be tracked down easily enough from the web. If we're lucky, there might even be some formal pre-prepared audience research we can look at. I will often spend a lot of time talking to the organizers in advance, even exchanging drafts, off the record, with the Head of Public Affairs or PR. They are normally happy to help – it's in everyone's interest for the speech to go well.

At the end, we should have a really clear picture of our audience in our mind. We should know their age, gender, race, what car they drive, what paper they read, what programmes they watch on TV.

That person will become our imaginary friend, our omnipresent sounding board for ideas during the writing process.

Step Two: Setting a Clear Aim for the Speech

The reason most speeches ramble around aimlessly is because they are literally that – aimless. Geoffrey Howe, in all probability, did not start writing his famous November 1990 resignation speech by staring at a blank page, thinking, 'Well, I'll just start writing and see what happens.' He knew, with every bone in his body, that he wanted to use his speech to destabilize and preferably even destroy Margaret Thatcher: both aims which were achieved with devastating success. As Ronald Millar, Thatcher's speechwriter, acknowledged: 'Every word in the speech was sharpened to inflict the deepest possible cut.' The clarity in the writing came from the clarity of the purpose. Such conviction is equally evident in many other persuasive speeches, from Steve Jobs' frenzied product launches to Michael Moore's dense polemics. Our own speeches may not be as grand in intent, but it is no less important to be clear about why we're there.

It is easy to think of a speech as an end in itself – but it is not. It is not about simply getting the speaker through but winning the audience over. There are two points at stake: a) who our speech is aiming to influence; and b) what is the change in behaviour, emotion or thinking we are seeking. So, instead of just saying, 'The CEO is giving a speech to staff,' when we are asked about our speech, we might say, 'The CEO will use this speech to staff to reassure high-performers that they have nothing to fear from the impending redundancy programme.'

Our aim must be realistic. Speech-making is rarely about achieving dramatic results; more often, it is about making minor contributions to a steady process of gradual change.[ix] It's 'salami tactics': one slice at a time. Even supposedly landmark speeches, such as the speech which set out the Truman Doctrine, had little discernible impact at the time.[x] So, instead of thinking that our speech might transport someone from John O'Groats to Lands End we might instead think about nudging them from Islington North to Islington South. Even Barack Obama could not convince an audience of evangelists that abortion was morally legitimate, but he might realistically persuade them that he was not a relative of Satan. One way to identify a realistic aim is to imagine a thirty-minute conversation with a member of our audience and predict what sort of outcome that might produce.

Generally, the aim of our speech will be based upon one of three things: changing the way our audience thinks, feels or behaves. The nature of our objective will, to some extent, dictate the content of the speech. For instance, if we are looking to change the way our audience thinks, we should pile our speech high with facts, statistics and endorsements. If we want to change the way our audience feels, we should go heavy on stories, images and metaphors. If we want to change the way our audience behaves, we should serve up lots of real-life examples, role models and rewards. This is why it is so important that we clearly pinpoint the intended change we are seeking. Once we have established this, everything else can be wrapped around it.

Many major speeches have multiple audiences, including an audience inside and outside the room. We may want to prioritize between these different audiences and consider whether there should be separate aims for each. A party conference speech can involve a very complex design. There might be one aim for business, one for the media and one for the voters. A CEO's AGM speech might comprise different aims for customers, investors and employers. When Nelson Mandela made his statement from the dock in the 1964 Rivonia Trial, he might have had as many as three different audiences and aims in mind:

a) To convince the court to stop short of imposing the death penalty (which he achieved by convincing them he would become a martyr, if executed);

b) To persuade his colleagues in the African National Congress they should stand by him (which he achieved by expressly articulating his loyalty to Chief Luthili); and,

c) To attract support from the wider global community (which he achieved by explicitly denouncing communism and expressing his support for the British Parliament and American Congress).

Often, the true aims for our speech will remain covert because to articulate them would make our speaker appear mercenary. If we are honest, the true purpose of many political speeches is to win votes and the aim of many business speeches is to make money, but to admit this would make the whole fragile edifice of credibility collapse.

Step Three: Discovering the 'Big Idea' for the Speech

All of the best speeches are based around a single big idea which can be articulated in a few simple words. The speech may drift off occasionally, disappear down back alleys, but it will always return to this single, brilliant idea. It might be a compelling claim (Earl Spencer's 'Diana was hunted'), a moving metaphor (the 'wind of change'), a war of words (Neil Kinnock's gutsy attack on the Militant Tendency), an unusual connection (NHS managers can copy techniques from football managers), a provocative question (is the American dream alive?) or an incredible vision (J.F.K.'s pledge to put a man on the moon). Finding that big idea is the most important step of the process. Once you've discovered that, the title, quote and structure for the speech are usually obvious.

The big idea might emerge organically whilst you're researching. That's why it's good to always keep a little notebook or some sort of recording device handy: you never know when inspiration will strike. Wolfgang Mozart's ideas came to him when he was travelling,[xi] Paul McCartney woke up one morning with the melody to 'Yesterday' in his head – it felt so perfect to him he was sure he couldn't have composed it himself, and was convinced it was an old jazz tune – and William Blake described how 'Jerusalem' came to him almost at once.

If no idea comes, there are plenty of ways to kick-start creativity. Often, it is not so much about finding new ideas as finding new connections between old ideas. As James Webb Young said, new ideas are 'nothing more ... than a new combination of old elements.'[xii] The iPhone was not based on any new technologies but simply combined existing technologies into one exquisitely beautiful product. George Lucas described *Star Wars* as little more than Cowboys and Indians set in space. Oasis's music combined Johnny Rotten's voice with the Beatles' sound. The very origin of the word 'intelligent' lies in the Latin for 'reading between'.

Random connections provide the key to creative speechwriting. Who would have expected Martin Luther King to use religious imagery to make the case for civil rights ('I have seen the Promised Land. I may not get there with you. But I want you to know that we as a people will reach the Promised Land.') Who would have thought Ronald Reagan would use an old poem by a Canadian air pilot to eulogize the astronauts who perished in the Challenger disaster ('Oh, I have slipped the surly bonds of earth . . . put out my hand and touched the face of God.') Who would have imagined that Barack Obama would devote almost a quarter of his election victory speech to talking about a 106-year-old lady ('Tonight, I think about all that she's seen throughout her century in America – the heartache and hope; the struggle and the progress; the times we were told that we can't, and the people who pressed on with that American creed – yes we can.') These were random connections. The delight came from the unexpected.

Such connections come from thinking outside of our traditional thought patterns. Sometimes we can achieve that leap naturally; other times we have to force it. Our mind works a bit like the tube map: when you're on an eastern point on the District line, you can't just jump onto a Central line train. But advertising agencies use a number of techniques to give them the energy to achieve such massive mental leaps.

The first technique is to pick something completely random and then riff from it, picking every possible word that is triggered by that topic until something interesting emerges. The random something can be whatever you want: something you see in the room or anything else that pops into your mind. So, if the speech we're writing is about Islamic fundamentalism, and we start riffing from an angle-poise lamp, we might come up with, 'The dark shadow of Islamic fundamentalism.' If we start riffing from a fountain pen, we might be, 'Writing the next page of history.'

The second is *related words*. We simply play a word association game, as you do as a child, until an intriguing idea emerges. So, as an example, if we start with 'child', we might think child > toy > play > game. . . 'We can't play games with Middle East politics.'

The third technique is *reversal*. With this, we simply take the opposite of our usual perspective. So, instead of thinking about the *best* way to speak about the Middle East, think about the worst way. Then flip it back and see if any interesting ideas have emerged.

The fourth technique is *revolution*: break all the rules. Rip it up and start again. Start the argument from somewhere completely new.

The fifth technique is *steal and twist*, where we take an existing idea and adapt it. This has led to some great innovations, in business and in rhetoric. The easyJet airline was originally conceived as McDonald's in the sky. The roll-on deodorant took the design principle of the ballpoint pen and applied it to personal hygiene. Blair's 'I have no reverse gear' was a twist on Margaret Thatcher's, 'The lady is not for turning.' (Ironically, Thatcher's 'The lady is not for turning' was itself a twist on a then popular West End play called *The Lady is Not for Burning*.)

Another good brainstorming technique is *De Bono's Hats*, a technique used by many large companies to break people out of traditional patterns of thinking. De Bono came up with the hats idea in frustration at the way that people's behaviour in meetings was pre-determined by their characteristics, i.e. whether they were naturally emotional or negative or creative etc. This is a barrier to effective thinking. To shake off these mental shackles, De Bono assigned a hat to different viewpoints: a red hat represented an emotional thinker, a yellow hat was a positive thinker, a black hat was a critical thinker, a white hat was a rational thinker, a green hat was a creative thinker and a blue hat was a big-picture thinker. A chairperson then guides the discussion through each of the hats systematically, getting everyone in the room to think in the way that the hat demands. Once you get over the silliness of literally wearing hats, it is immensely productive. It brings immediate advantages over a more conventional meeting. Because it depersonalizes the act of thinking, people feel liberated to think more creatively. Plus, because the format is so collaborative, you experience the rare treat of having everyone in the room pushing in the same direction. A single session with the hats can generate a mass of ideas very quickly. I have run one-hour sessions for communications teams that have generated enough ideas for a whole year's worth of speeches.

These techniques can take some time to work. Be patient if they do not work immediately or if the ideas they produce are not very good. For every brilliant idea that emerges, there will be a dozen or so appalling ones. But your final speeches are bound to be more original and intriguing. If all else fails, you can go for the F.D.R. approach. Franklin Roosevelt used to get his team brainstorming by getting them altogether in the Oval Office and refilling their glasses with bourbon until an idea came!

Step Four: Organizing the Argument

The next step is to organize our argument into a logical structure. There are all sorts of ways of doing this. You can scribble out the most salient ideas on Post-it notes and jumble them around until you find a sequence you like (David Bowie uses a similar technique for writing songs). You can cut and paste blocks on a computer. For me though, the best way to start writing a speech is to talk about it. There is no better bullshit detector than a real human conversation, with all the to-and-fro that entails. As I talk someone through my ideas for the speech, soundbites, structure and stories tend to emerge organically, because it is a genuine conversation and I am genuinely trying to persuade them. If I am afraid to test this method, it is usually because subconsciously I know my ideas are rubbish – but it's better to work that out now than when the speaker is at the podium!

If no structure emerges, there are a number of off-the-shelf speech structures that can be used.

For political or argumentative speeches, *Cicero's structure*, outlined in *Ad Herennium*, is without rival. It creates the impression of balance: giving equal space to both sides of the argument, placing the audience as arbiter, therefore appealing to their desire for control. It also has a very clear beginning, middle and end. This structure remains common in political speeches: around eighty per cent of all major party conference speeches follow this structure, and not because of any conscious effort on the part of the writer, but because it naturally flows so well.

a) Exposition (*exordium*) – outline the central issue that the speech will address.

b) History (*narratio*) – provide a summary of the agreed facts.

c) Areas of contention (*partitio*) – summarize areas of agreement and set out the main areas of contention.

d) Evidence in support of your argument (*confirmatio*) – provide the strongest evidence in support of your own case.

e) Refutation of your opponent's argument (*refutatio*) – dismantle your opponent's argument.

f) Conclusion – wrap up your speech with an inspiring peroration.

For annual reviews or celebratory events, a *timeline structure* works well:

a) Past – what we have done.

b) Present – where we are now.

c) Future – where we must go in the future.

For motivational or inspirational speeches, a *story-teller's structure* creates an intrinsic sense of drama:

a) Exposition – make people care about the character or issues you are talking about.

b) Conflict – show why the character or issues you are talking about are under threat.

c) Resolution – explain how they can be protected.

For persuasive speeches, there is the *propagandist's structure*:

a) Create fear.

b) Provide solution.

For speeches that are responding to a serious emergency, there is a *crisis structure:*

a) Authoritative statement of facts.

b) Narrative of the situation to date, highlighting the enemy's duplicity.

c) Actions to be taken.

d) A call to shared values.[xiii]

For social or celebratory speeches, we want to make people feel good. The following components work well:

a) Icebreaker.

b) Story about how everyone else is brilliant.

c) Story to illustrate the brilliance of the speaker.

d) Argument to show how the brilliant speaker and the brilliant room reinforce one another's brilliance.

e) Inspiring vision.

For policy statements, or any speech where we have to get through a lot of disparate information, a list can help the audience navigate through. The *countdown structure* can be based around any kind of list. It could be three questions, three points or three issues. Simply announce at the beginning of the speech that the speaker will run through a certain number of points and then do so. The countdown structure might also be based on an acronym so, for instance, a speech based around the acronym COAST could lead the audience through the steps Concentration, Observation, Awareness, Space and Time. If the acronym spells a word that suits the message (e.g. MAMA for Mothers Against Male Aggression) it is known as an apronym. Motivational speakers often use acronyms or apronyms because they are so easy to remember.

One warning about using the countdown structure, if it's not too obvious: take care that you count correctly. I once wrote a parliamentary statement for a cabinet minister, using a countdown structure. The early drafts had her addressing seven points. By the time the speech was delivered, this had been whittled down to three. I almost had a heart attack when I watched her stand up and say, 'There are seven things I wish to announce today …' Fortunately, the kindly Hansard writers changed the record.

Step Five: Writing the First Draft

Now is the time to write. Find a quiet room, shut the doors, turn off the phones, log out of email and order a pizza. Nothing less than complete isolation will do. Interruptions ruin your flow and coherency, leaving you with a muddled mish-mash. Usually, speechwriters are placed in the very least conducive environment possible for good writing. I used to sit with Alan Johnson's special advisers, who were the noisiest, if loveliest, people in the world. Margaret Thatcher's private secretary described how, 'Speechwriting for Mrs Thatcher was chaos. She wanted everyone to chip in but no-one knew what was going on.'[xiv] Alastair Campbell's diary records: 'Usual last-minute pre-speech nightmares . . . The worst attack of lastminutitis . . . Telly on in the background . . . A Sky reporter saying T.B. appearing any second . . . Tony losing it . . . shouting "Where's the fucking speech?" 'xv I find the best way to produce a complete first draft is simply to hide away, lock the door and not leave until it's done. This prevents the process becoming too pained and protracted. Funnily enough, this was how the Rolling Stones' manager, Andrew Loog Oldham, forced Mick Jagger and Keith Richards to write their first song (they emerged with 'Satisfaction').

Some people prefer writing by hand, others by computer. I am increasingly using voice-recognition software and dictating my first drafts. There are some excellent software packages available. MacSpeech or Dragon Naturally Speaking have an accuracy rating of more than ninety-five per cent. The other advantage of using voice recognition software is that it ensures your final product will be spoken rather than written English.

Whilst you're writing, try to keep moving forward, relentlessly moving your argument on to the next natural or logical point. Keep your speaker, audience and aim at the front of your mind all the time. If you hit a mental block, try asking the question you suspect will be at the forefront of the audience's mind at that point in the speech. The question will usually be a variation on 'So what?', 'Why's that?', 'Who says?', 'How come?' or 'What next?' If that doesn't work, shift direction, using a connecting word like 'now', 'but' or an address to the chair (Mr President, Mr Chairman, Mr Speaker) to signify the shift. Never drift so far away from your central idea that you can't get back. Simplicity is key. Remember Churchill's advice: 'Tell 'em what you're going to say; then tell 'em it; and finally tell 'em what you just told 'em.' The King of Hearts in Lewis Carol's *Alice in Wonderland* had similarly sage advice: 'Begin at the beginning and go on till you come to the end: then stop.'

Some key don'ts at this stage. Don't read emails. Don't check something on the Internet. Don't start editing what you write. Don't update your Facebook status to say, 'Simon is writing a speech' (because Simon is clearly not writing a speech if he is updating his Facebook status). The main thing is just to keep going until it is done. It doesn't matter if it is messy and muddled at first – this is a sign of a successful creative process and, anyway, it can all be sorted out later in the editing. The most important thing is that you wind up with something that looks ever so slightly and ever so vaguely like a speech and maybe – just maybe – that knot in your stomach will have untightened a little.

Summary

- Starting principles: don't start writing too soon; stay close to the speaker; take charge of the speech; keep the research and creative process separate.
- Step one: research the speaker, the issue and the audience.
- Step two: establish a clear aim.
- Step three: discover a 'big idea'.
- Step four: organize the argument.
- Step five: produce a first draft.

Case Study

Speechwriters must quickly learn a speaker's unique style of speech. This is particularly hard for freelancers who write for a number of clients. Whenever I meet a new client, I carefully observe not just what they say but how they say it. I ask some simple questions. Do they speak in long sentences or short sentences? Do they use long words or short words? Do they prefer statistics or stories? What kind of metaphors do they prefer? What kind of rhetorical devices do they deploy most often?

In the run up to the 2010 general election, I analysed the speaking styles of the leading players in all of the main political parties, based on their 2009 party conference speeches, to help cabinet speechwriters prepare for the imminent change in administration. My analysis revealed an enormous variance both between individual speakers and the different political parties. The findings reinforce the need for speechwriters to prepare personalized style guides. They might also provide a blueprint for anyone else who wants to develop their own style guide.

Length of Words and Sentences
The average Labour sentence is nineteen words long; the average Conservative and Liberal Democrat sentence is fourteen words.

The gap is even wider between individuals. The average Alan Johnson sentence (twenty-four words) is twice as long as the average David Cameron sentence (twelve words). The average William Hague sentence (forty words) is more than three times as long as the average Nick Clegg sentence (twelve words). Curiously, almost all of the wordiest politicians were educated at state schools (Hague, Johnson, Brown) whereas the most clipped were educated at top private schools (Cameron, Osborne, Darling, Clegg, Huhne).

Here is a grand William Hague sentence:

We will be clear that our forces will not be there forever and that whenever the British Army is sent to war, it must be whenever possible on the basis of agreed objectives, proper co-ordination with development assistance, every effort to provide the right equipment and an explanation of their mission from the highest levels of government at the very outset.

Here is a clipped sequence of David Miliband sentences:

The Tories are not a government in waiting. They are a national embarrassment. David Cameron has shown not leadership but pandering. Not judgement but dogma. Not patriotic defence of national interest but the white flag of surrender to euro-extremists in his own party.

	Sentences	Words	Words per Sentence	Syllables per Word	Characters per Word
Brown	293	6469	22	1.2	4.3
Darling	156	2493	16	1.2	4.5
Miliband	150	2241	15	1.2	4.4
Johnson	43	1022	24	1.4	4.8
Labour	642	12225	19	1.2	4.4
Cameron	493	6407	13	1.2	4.3
Osborne	252	3555	14	1.3	4.5
Hague	41	1648	40	1.4	4.7
Grayling	167	1853	11	1.3	4.5
Conservative	953	13463	14	1.3	4.4
Clegg	430	5145	12	1.3	4.4
Cable	131	2187	17	1.5	4.8
Davey	107	2548	24	1.4	4.7
Huhne	164	1940	12	1.3	4.4

Longer sentences are typically associated with a grander style whereas shorter sentences are indicative of a plain style. Professor James W. Pennebaker, one of the world's leading linguists, argues that longer sentences and longer words tend to suggest honesty (issues are complex; why pretend they're not).

It is also interesting to note that the three people who would probably be instantly described as the best communicators in the three parties, namely Alan Johnson, William Hague and Vince Cable consistently produced the words with the most syllables and characters.

Statistics Versus Stories

Labour and the Liberal Democrats use statistics two and a half times as often as the Conservatives. Chris Huhne and Alan Johnson use a statistic once every hundred words. Gordon Brown uses a statistic once every 359 words. The Conservatives tell two and a half times as many stories as Labour. Statistics and stories have a very different effect. To illustrate the difference, Alan Johnson says, 'Crime is down by thirty-six per cent, violent crime by forty-one per cent, domestic burglary by fifty-four per cent and vehicle related theft by fifty-seven per cent.' David Cameron says, 'I got an email from a lady. She says, 'During the cold spell this winter, we sat watching TV with blankets wrapped around us. The drug dealer and the druggies who live nearby had their windows wide open and the heating full on. We don't bother watching police dramas. We just look out of the window.'

	Stats	Words	Words per Stat	Stories
Brown	18	6469	359	1
Darling	8	2493	312	
Miliband	4	2241	560	
Johnson	9	1022	114	1
Labour	39	12225	313	2
Cameron	8	6407	801	3
Osborne	8	3555	444	
Hague	2	1648	824	
Grayling	0	1853	N/A	2
Conservative	18	13463	748	5
Clegg	9	5145	572	
Cable	5	2187	437	
Davey	1	2548	2548	
Huhne	19	1940	102	
Lib Dems	34	11820	348	

Metaphors

Labour uses war or conflict metaphors twice as often as the Conservatives and three times as often as the Liberal Democrats. Gordon Brown in particular seemed particularly drawn to the metaphors of 'politics as war' and 'political challenge as physical threat.' These metaphors appear on average once every 180 words in his speech, making up one in five of his total metaphors.

The Liberal Democrats' metaphors have changed with time. When Nick Clegg first became leader, he habitually used Labour's war rhetoric. This now seems to have been deliberately expunged from the lexicon and replaced with journey metaphors. This brought a number of advantages: it bolstered Nick Clegg's leadership credentials (because he was telling us about our journey, we assumed he was our leader), it reinforced the impression that the Liberal Democrats were a progressive party but, perhaps most significantly, it also triggered associations with Obama, Clinton and Blair – the journey metaphor was also their metaphor of choice.

The Conservatives use nature metaphors twice as often as Labour. Cameron uses nature metaphors four times as often as Brown. They feature an average of once every 149 words. Cameron uses the metaphor of natural forces eleven times as often as Brown. He uses the metaphor of personalization twice as often as Brown.

The different metaphors activate different thoughts, ideas and associations, giving us fleeting insights into the different leaders' takes on the world: Nick Clegg says, 'Britain needs a change of direction,' David Cameron says, 'We can put Britain back on its feet,' and Gordon Brown says, 'We need to fight; not bow out, not walk away, not give in, not give up, but fight.'

Rhetorical devices

The one area where there is clear common ground across the parties is in the use of rhetorical devices. Gordon Brown and William Hague both have a penchant for alliterative pairs: Brown's speech was called 'the change we choose' and Hague's speech was called 'renew and reinforce'. Miliband and Cameron both use asyndeton:

	Brown	Darling	Miliband	Johnson	Cameron	Osborne
Words in speech	6469	2493	2241	1022	6407	3555
Total Metaphors	180	162	110	61	233	168
Words per Metaphor	35.94	15.39	20.37	16.75	27.50	21.16
Construction	17	18	10	6	17	13
%	9.44%	11.11%	9.09%	9.84%	7.30%	7.74%
Machinery/Tools	10	5	5	6	28	7
%	5.56%	3.09%	4.55%	9.84%	12.02%	4.17%
Super-strength alcohol = fuel						
%						
Nature	10	16	9	8	43	21
%	5.56%	9.88%	8.18%	13.11%	18.45%	12.50%
Plant	1	5	1		4	2
%	10.00%	31.25%	11.11%		9.30%	9.52%
The elements/natural forces	2	6	1	5	22	15
%	20.00%	37.50%	11.11%	62.50%	51.16%	71.43%
Animal	1	1	2			
%	10.00%	6.25%	22.22%			
Earth/materials	6	4	5	3	15	4
%	60.00%	25.00%	55.56%	37.50%	34.88%	19.05%
Disease					2	
%					4.65%	
War/Conflict	36	3	12	3	16	11
%	20.00%	1.85%	10.91%	4.92%	6.87%	6.55%
Political challenge = physical threat	14	1	4		9	7
%	38.89%	33.33%	33.33%		56.25%	63.64%
Personalization	25	37	27	10	40	30
%	13.89%	22.84%	24.55%	16.39%	17.17%	17.86%
Human action	16	18	14	4	14	18
%	64.00%	48.65%	51.85%	40.00%	35.00%	60.00%
Human anatomy	5	7	2		5	4
%	20.00%	18.92%	7.41%		12.50%	13.33%
Human qualities/emotions	4	12	10	5	21	8
%	16.00%	32.43%	37.04%	50.00%	52.50%	26.67%
People			1	1		
%			3.70%	10.00%		
Education	2	2	1		2	
%	1.11%	1.23%	0.91%		0.86%	
Economic/Financial	5	1	1		2	5
%	2.78%	0.62%	0.91%		0.86%	2.98%
National Economy = Household Budget						2
%						40.00%
Journey	11	7	2		7	8
%	6.11%	4.32%	1.82%		3.00%	4.76%
Sports/Games	8	6	7	3	7	5
%	4.44%	3.70%	6.36%	4.92%	3.00%	2.98%
Transformation	30	29	10	10	42	34
%	16.67%	17.90%	9.09%	16.39%	18.03%	20.24%
Conceptual	12	25	18	13	4	20
%	6.67%	15.43%	16.36%	21.31%	1.72%	11.90%
Master/Servant	5			1	6	1
%	2.78%			1.64%	2.58%	0.60%
Hierarchical	3			1	4	3
%	1.67%			1.64%	1.72%	1.79%
Science/Technology		3	2		4	
%		1.85%	1.82%		1.72%	
Religion					2	
%					0.86%	
Time			1			
%			0.91%			
Agriculture		3				
%		1.85%				
Food						
%						
Law and Order						
%						
Fantasy		1				
%		0.62%				
Miscellaneous	6	6	5		9	10
%	3.33%	3.70%	4.55%		3.86%	5.95%
TV/Entertainment						
%						

Hague	Grayling	Clegg	Cable	Davey	Huhne	Total Labour	Total Tories	Total Lib Dems
1648	1853	5145	2187	2548	1940	12225	13463	11820
89	86	244	130	81	100	513	576	555
18.52	21.55	21.09	16.82	31.46	19.40	23.83	23.37	21.30
15	3	17	6	12	3	51	48	38
16.85%	3.49%	6.97%	4.62%	14.81%	3.00%	9.94%	8.33%	6.85%
5	10	14	3	1	7	26	50	25
5.62%	11.63%	5.74%	2.31%	1.23%	7.00%	5.07%	8.68%	4.50%
	3							3
	30.00%							0.52%
12	6	29	13	10	16	43	82	68
13.48%	6.98%	11.89%	10.00%	12.35%	16.00%	8.38%	14.24%	12.25%
1		2	2		1	7	7	5
8.33%		6.90%	15.38%		6.25%	1.36%	1.22%	0.90%
7	1	17	5	5	3	14	45	30
58.33%	16.67%	58.62%	38.46%	50.00%	18.75%	2.73%	7.81%	5.41%
		1	1	1		4		3
		3.45%	7.69%	10.00%		0.78%		0.54%
4	4	8	5	4	12	18	27	29
33.33%	66.67%	27.59%	38.46%	40.00%	75.00%	3.51%	4.69%	5.23%
	1						3	
	16.67%						0.52%	
3	3	7	6	2	3	54	33	18
3.37%	3.49%	2.87%	4.62%	2.47%	3.00%	10.53%	5.73%	3.24%
1		2	2		1	19	17	5
33.33%		28.57%	33.33%		33.33%	3.70%	2.95%	0.90%
14	17	48	22	11	26	99	101	107
15.73%	19.77%	19.67%	16.92%	13.58%	26.00%	19.30%	17.53%	19.28%
6	12	29	18	9	19	52	50	75
42.86%	70.59%	60.42%	81.82%	81.82%	73.08%	10.14%	8.68%	13.51%
		5	3	2	3	14	9	13
		10.42%	13.64%	18.18%	11.54%	2.73%	1.56%	2.34%
8	5	14	1		4	31	42	19
57.14%	29.41%	29.17%	4.55%		15.38%	6.04%	7.29%	3.42%
						2		
						0.39%		
		3	1		2	5	2	6
		1.23%	0.77%		2.00%	0.97%	0.35%	1.08%
3	1	4		2	1	7	11	7
3.37%	1.16%	1.64%		2.47%	1.00%	1.36%	1.91%	1.26%
							2	
							0.35%	
4		30	1	2	1	20	19	34
4.49%		12.30%	0.77%	2.47%	1.00%	3.90%	3.30%	6.13%
4	7	9	4	1	11	24	23	25
4.49%	8.14%	3.69%	3.08%	1.23%	11.00%	4.68%	3.99%	4.50%
12	13	31	36	11	14	79	101	92
13.48%	15.12%	12.70%	27.69%	13.58%	14.00%	15.40%	17.53%	16.58%
11	18	36	25	14	7	68	53	82
12.36%	20.93%	14.75%	19.23%	17.28%	7.00%	13.26%	9.20%	14.77%
1	1	1	1	1		6	9	3
1.12%	1.16%	0.41%	0.77%	1.23%		1.17%	1.56%	0.54%
2	1	2	3			4	10	6
2.25%	1.16%	0.82%	2.31%		1.00%	0.78%	1.74%	1.08%
1	1	2	4	1	1	5	6	8
1.12%	1.16%	0.82%	3.08%	1.23%	1.00%	0.97%	1.04%	1.44%
1							3	
1.12%							0.52%	
						1		
						0.19%		
					2	3		2
					2.00%	0.58%		0.36%
		3	1	3	1			8
		1.23%	0.77%	3.70%	1.00%			1.44%
		2						2
		0.82%						0.36%
						1		
						0.19%		
1	5	7	4	5	4	17	25	20
1.12%	5.81%	2.87%	3.08%	6.17%	4.00%	3.31%	4.34%	3.60%
				5				5
				6.17%				0.90%

'Arab world on tenterhooks. Israel on alert' (Miliband); 'Massive debt. Social breakdown. Political disenchantment' (Cameron). Osborne and Johnson both use contrast to produce witty epithets: 'The iron chancellor has turned into the plastic prime minister' (Osborne); 'John Wayne in their rhetoric, Woody Allen in their actions.' (Johnson).

It will be interesting to see whether the coalition between Liberal Democrats and Conservatives leads to any changes in linguistic styles. . . .

Chapter Three

The Art of Persuasion

Successful democratic politicians . . . advance politically only as they placate, appease, bribe, seduce, bamboozle, or otherwise manage to manipulate the demanding and threatening elements in their constituencies.

Walter Lippmann, 1955[1]

How many times were you seduced today? Chances are you don't know the answer. As far as advertising men are concerned, you're not supposed to know. Their job is to arouse you without you suspecting it. This very day, every time you looked at a TV commercial or an ad in print, you very probably were being sexually assaulted by devices your conscious mind cannot detect.

Dr Wilson Bryan Key, *Subliminal Seduction*, 1973

Politicians are sounding like strippers to me
They keep sayin' (but I don't wanna hear it)
'Ooh babe you want me, ooh babe you want me, ooh babe you want me.
Well you can get this lap-dance here for free.'

Pharrell Williams and Chad Hugo, *Lap-Dance*, N*E*R*D*

Most speeches try to persuade an audience of something, whether it is Steve Jobs persuading MacWorld that the iPhone is the best smartphone on the market, Barack Obama persuading a Democratic convention that he is their best hope for the future or Michael Moore persuading us that the Iraq War was the most disastrous decision in history. The whole world is a marketplace for ideas. We are all of us only as powerful as our persuasive skill. Business power comes from convincing consumers that we have something they want. Personal power comes from an ability to win hearts and minds. Political success comes from being able to grow small grass-roots groups into major national movements. The tragedy of Gordon Brown's career was that he discovered far too late that real power came not from winning the keys to Number Ten but from the ability to cajole, convince and carry. This was what gave Tony Blair his exceptional power. It's also what took David Cameron from rank outsider in a race to lead the 'nasty party' to leader of the most popular political party in the May 2010 general election and prime minister.

As speechwriters, we must understand the essential elements of persuasion: it is the persuasive power of the speech that gives it its whole strength. Fortunately, we are all blessed with a degree of innate persuasive ability. We have this from the moment we are born, when we scream for our mother's milk. This continues throughout our lives, as we charm our way into jobs or relationships.

The key to persuasion can be summed up in two simple words: *audience focus*. We all know this is an essential part of persuasion in our personal lives, flattering and fudging our way through all sorts of situations. But when we are writing speeches, we seem to throw this out of the window. Instead, we revert to a Brit-abroad approach to communication, based on a misguided belief that, if we keep shouting loud enough, sooner or later, our message will get through.

But persuasion is about seduction, not assertion. This is true whether we are selling double-glazing or making an intervention in a House of Commons debate. That's why audience research is so crucial. We should have a clear picture of our audience in our minds all the time we are writing. The clearer the picture, the easier the writing. This doesn't need to be a major research project – even just a few minutes brainstorming very quickly produces valuable insights that will inform the persuasive strategy.

This chapter sets out an easy-to-follow four-step model of persuasion which will cover even the most hostile of audiences.[ii]

Audience insight	Speaker response	Rhetorical techniques
Uninterested, distracted	Grab and hold attention	Verbal/physical 'wake up' calls
Cynical, sceptical	Secure acceptance	Flattery, mimicry, empathy
Rejection and resistance	Win agreement	Anchoring, smoothing, critical mass
Apathy and laziness	Motivate action	Rewards and punishments, role models

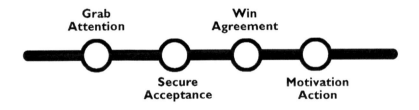

Step One: Grabbing and Holding the Audience's Attention

Attention is crucial to any communication activity: if no one is listening, why bother communicating at all? That is why TV stations pump up the volume when the ads come on. It is why catchy songs blast out of the radio. And it is why, if you are backpacking, scamsters yell for your attention when you get off a bus. Some speechwriters make the mistake of thinking they don't need to bother trying to capture the audience's attention because

they are physically captive. Of course, this is true in one sense, but the audience can and will depart mentally at any point if we don't make the effort. The speaker must compete fiercely for the audience's attention. He must be more interesting than where they're going on holiday and what they're having for dinner. He must be more enticing than the vibrating iPhones in their pockets.

The trick here is to think of the speech as a series of signs, not words. Some signs say 'wake up', e.g. a dramatic pause, a modulating voice, a surprising statement, a story or a joke. Others say 'go to sleep,' e.g. a monotonic voice, a slouched posture, endless platitudes, jargon or the hum of a PowerPoint projector. If we want our speech to be effective, we must send our audience utterly unambiguous 'wake up' signs at the beginning of the speech and at regular intervals throughout.

First, at the beginning of the speech. This is the moment when audiences are usually at their most alert and therefore most susceptible to persuasion. Sadly, it is also often the time when most speakers want to curl up in a ball and die, which is why so many take the entirely rational step of issuing as many 'go to sleep' signs as they can (looking down at their feet, mumbling, saying nothing even remotely interesting). This is fine if we don't mind our audience taking forty winks during our speech. But 'Honky Tonk Women' does not start with the Rolling Stones tuning up. *A Tale of Two Cities* does not open with long, flowery descriptions of London and Paris. An effective speech should lunge out and grab the audience by the throat.

Jacobus Van Dyn is not a name that will be familiar to most readers. But, during the 1960s, he was a legend of Speaker's Corner in Hyde Park, renowned for his extraordinary appearance (he was covered in tattoos), his shady activities (he was constantly in and out of prison) and his unique method of grabbing attention. This is a transcript of one of his speech openings:

> Well now, ladies and gentlemen, when a man's in the park, the first thing he's gotta do is get an audience . . . and to get an audience in Hyde Park, you gotta use psychology. And, when you use psychology, you gotta apologize to the people in front of you because you don't want to give them a scare. Now what I'm gonna do . . . it's gonna make my voice a little bad, but I'm forced to do it . . . is to give a yell, and I'm gonna try and do it. Now I want you to see for yourselves what psychology does. Just come up a bit ladies and gentlemen. Don't be afraid of me. I ain't Oscar Wilde . . . LADIES AND GENTLEMEN . . . AAAAAAAGGGGHHHHH! Now that's all you gotta do . . . here they are . . . you'll be all right.[iii]

There is a myriad of ways to achieve the same effect without ripping our speaker's larynx. Our speaker might relate a startling statistic, killer quotation or revealing reference. He can ask a challenging question, pose a puzzle or tell a story. He can take a show of hands or do anything else that reinforces the audience's view that it is they who are the most important people in the room. Hypnotists often do this at the beginning of shows, getting everyone to stand up. This is a clever persuasive trick, creating the illusion that the hypnotist is empowering the audience whilst actually underlining his own authority.

We should try to create a sense of occasion, even going a little over the top. Audiences will always forgive a little hyperbole at the beginning of a speech. If the speaker doesn't think it matters, why should the audience care? Steve Jobs opened the iPhone launch at MacWorld in 2007 saying, 'We're going to make some history together today.' Steve Ballmer, Microsoft's CEO, described the launch of Vista as the 'biggest launch in software history'. A good speech should sound momentous from the start, as with Barack Obama's, 'They said this day would never come. . . .' Queen Elizabeth II's, '1992 is not a year I shall look back on with undiluted pleasure', Abraham Lincoln's 'Four score years and seven years ago. . . .'[iv] or Neil Kinnock's, 'I am happy to report that we are definitely in the last month of Thatcherism.'[v] Start with a bang, not a whimper. Make them care.

Many speechwriters swear that the best way to start a speech is with a story, particularly in inspirational, motivational or social speeches. Ted Kennedy began his 2009 eulogy for John F. Kennedy Junior saying: 'Once, when Bill Clinton asked John what he would do if he went into politics and was declared president, he said, "I guess the first thing is call up Uncle Teddy and gloat." I love that, it was so like his father.' Many business speakers begin speeches by telling their rags-to-riches stories. Like Richard Branson:

At sixteen, it seemed highly unlikely that I would have the opportunity to rub shoulders with a band as great as the Rolling Stones, or even fly around the world in my own jumbo – or nearly make it around the world in my own hot air balloon for that matter. My business education has come from trying and succeeding – and even from trying and failing.[vi]

Or Jeff Bezos, Amazon's founder:

> In the spring of 1994, I came across a startling statistic: web usage was growing at 2,300 per cent a year. I had never seen anything grow so fast, and I don't think many people had, except for perhaps in a Petri dish. So the question was: what's the first best product to sell online . . . I picked books.[vii]

Audiences also like to feel they have something to grapple with, so it is often good to expose a conflict at the beginning of the speech. Hamlet's 'To be or not to be,' exposed the whole theme of his speech in six words. Our conflict might be, 'Do we invest in China or do we not?' If the issue is more layered, we might present a whole list of conflicts, as Iran's Supreme Leader Mahmoud Ahmadinejad did in his now-notorious speech calling for Israel to be wiped from the map:

> We need to examine the true origin of the issue of Palestine. Is it a fight between a group of Muslims and non-Jews? Is it a fight between Judaism and other religions? Is it the fight of one country with another country? Is it the fight of one country with the Arab world? Is it a fight over the land of Palestine?

Speakers can also use physical signs to grab the audience's attention. Some speakers have natural presence. Boris Johnson's untidy hair and dishevelled suit guarantee him attention when he enters a room. So do Andrew Rawnsley's red socks. Or Martin Bell's white suits. Many professional public speakers deliberately don unusual clothes like lurid bow-ties, colourful suits or bright make-up to stand out.

Other speakers opt for a more thespian approach. One of the most powerful speakers I have seen in recent years was Lord Levy. I saw him deliver a fundraising speech for City Academies at the height of the 'cash for honours' scandal when he was being pilloried on the front pages. This made his presence electrifying in any case, but he ramped up the current to the max. He walked to the stage very slowly. When he reached the lectern, he paused for a full ten seconds before looking up and saying quietly: 'Yes, there's a national scandal. Yes, I'm at the centre of it. Yes, people are calling for my head. But I'm not complaining. I'm not suffering. I'm not really troubled. Not like the people we're here to help tonight. Like the poor black kid in Stepney who. . . .' He then went on to tell a story, the first of many emotionally charged stories he told in his speech. It was a breathtaking performance. Had I had a million pounds in my pocket, I would have sponsored a City Academy there and then.

The speaker might also pull a stunt of some kind. Richard Branson launched Virgin Digital by hologram in 2005, beamed direct from Necker Island. Nissan's CEO, Carlos Ghosn, has begun speeches by driving a car on to the stage. I once saw Dave Stewart from the Eurythmics open a speech on creativity by telling everyone that he had placed an imaginary sweet under their chair. He asked them to reach for it, put it in their mouths and taste it. This stunt drew everyone in and successfully underlined the theme of his speech: that we all possess powerful imaginations.

It is not just the opening of the speech that matters: we must fight for attention throughout the speech. This does not mean continually holding their attention; on the contrary, we should expect our audience to drop off from time to time. The average speaker talks at around 120 words a minute whilst the average audience member's mind processes information at a rate of around 700 words a minute. This means that, for every word we say, five are passing through our audience's minds. Our audience just will think of other things from time to time: that's a fact. So it is not only fine to let them drift off for short periods, it is to be commended as considerate, provided we remember to reel them back in with something good later on. This could be a good statistic, a rhetorical device or a story. It could be a new direction in the argument, a quotation or a joke. It could be a physical action – the speaker could walk about the stage, raise his voice or shift his tempo.

Speeches need padding: like life, they should contain ups and downs. A song like 'Help' by The Beatles maintains interest not by being high octane the whole way through but through its variety: the spectacular chorus sounds all the more explosive because it is set against the psalm-like verse. My rule of thumb is to lob a grenade at the audience every two or three minutes.

The end of our speech represents another natural peak in our audience's attention. A strong peroration brings together the strongest soundbites, strongest metaphors and strongest arguments in one big, shattering oratorical orgasm. Churchill tells us how it's done:

> The climax of oratory is reached by a rapid succession of waves of sound and vivid pictures. The audience is delighted by the changing scenes presented to their imagination. Their ear is tickled by the rhythm of the language. The enthusiasm rises. A series of facts is brought forward, all pointing in a common direction. The end appears in view before it is reached. The crowd anticipate the conclusion and the last words fall amid a thunder of assent.

Step Two: Securing Acceptance

We all constantly judge people we meet. We might pretend we don't, but it is simple human nature. We look at them, compare them against what we know, process that information through a complex system of classification and decide whether they can be trusted or not. This happens when we meet someone in person and it happens when we see someone at the podium.

As speechwriters, we must ensure that our speaker passes these tests. We must extinguish any cynicism or scepticism and secure what Cicero called *captatio benevolentia*, the goodwill of the audience. We must show the audience that the speaker is on their side. In film, they use lighting, visual props and music to

differentiate the good guys and the bad guys. A similar process takes place in speech-making and, as speechwriters, we have an equally dizzying array of tricks up our sleeve.

We can *flatter* the audience. Everyone likes being told they are great. There's no quicker way to warm an audience to our speaker. We should make them feel important; reinforcing the idea that it is they who are the stars of the day and our speaker who has the walk-on part. At all costs, we must avoid the impression (sadly so frequently given) that our speaker is just breezing in and out, another engagement in another day. So, *don't* brush over what the conference is about, *don't* allow your speaker to inadvertently mispronounce the names of fellow speakers and *don't*, for God's sake, allow your speaker to say 'I'm delighted to be in Rotherham' when he is actually in Rochester. If the speaker appears genuinely happy to be there, it will put everyone else at ease.

Flattery has long been a crucial aspect of rhetoric. Socrates said, 'It is not hard to praise the Athenians to an Athenian audience.'[viii] Flattery was one of the main features in the first recorded speech, a speech by a political adviser called Korax in Sicily in 467 BC.[ix] A contemporary witness recorded:

> Coming into the assembly, where all the people had gathered together, he began first to appease the troublesome and turbulent element among them with obsequious and flattering words . . . After this he began to soothe and silence and to speak as though telling a story. . . . He contrived to persuade the people just as he used to persuade one man.[x]

It sounds like a Bill Clinton speech!

We can *mimic* the audience. Mimicry is often the first technique of spies, diplomats, therapists and others involved in the professional business of persuasion. A diplomat might spot someone at a reception and discreetly start mirroring their actions: lifting their drink, touching their nose, playing with their hair at the same time they do. The other person's antennae will be alerted; eventually their curiosity will be roused to the extent that they will feel compelled to initiate conversation.

A speech is a different proposition – a speaker cannot mimic all of his audience's actions at once, but he can mimic their language. Many groups have a unique dialect. Dialect is a helpful way of identifying alliances and allegiances, working out who's in and who's out. By mimicking our audience's dialect, even very discreetly, our speaker can subtly suggest he is 'one of them'. A quick dip into Internet chat rooms reveals a group's unique dialect, for instance, the somewhat pompous tone of traditional Tories, the archaic language of trade unions or the unremitting jargon of management consultants. Our dialect should match our audience. If our speaker were addressing an audience of soldiers, BNP members or Mafia capos, we would probably do well to pepper our speech with profanities, but such language might not go down so well in the House of Lords.

Tony Blair, David Cameron and Bill Clinton all display a chameleon-like ability to imitate their audiences. It is a crucial element of their charm, although at times they have all gone too far. Tony Blair, in particular, got caught out a couple of times as he switched a little too swiftly between Fettes English and Estuary English.

If a speaker is not keen to imitate his audience's dialect, he should at least take care to ensure that he doesn't use a dialect that will actively wind them up. This is what happens when health ministers lecture nurses about 'practice based commissioning' or business ministers address entrepreneurs about 'productivity drivers.' It generates hostility and positions the audience against the speaker.

We should *empathize* with our audience. No-one minds having their views played back to them; in fact, most people rather like it. We feel better disposed to people who reinforce our own feelings. If we have just moaned to someone and they reply, 'So, you're feeling a bit let down at the moment,' we nod enthusiastically and say, 'Exactly!' However, if they reply with, 'Oh, you won't guess who I bumped into the other day,' we feel ignored. An even graver error is to try to replay someone's views and get it wrong, which can really inflame matters. The best approach is to address the disagreement, deal with it as honestly as you can, and then swiftly move on.

We should build up *common ground* with our audience. It is amusing to watch older people find common reference points with younger audiences. In 2004, Bono, then aged forty-four, began a commencement address to the students of the University of Pennsylvania saying, 'My name is Bono and I am a rock star. Don't get me too excited because I use four letter words when I get excited.'[xi] Two years later, Jodie Foster rapped lines from Eminem's 'Lose Yourself' complete with hip-hop jabs: 'You better lose yourself in the music, the moment, you own it, you better never let it go, you only get one shot, do not miss your chance to blow, this opportunity comes once in a lifetime yo'.

There are less nauseating ways to establish common ground. One simple way is to use the first person plural (i.e. 'we', 'us' and 'our') instead of the first person singular (i.e. 'I', 'me' and 'my'.) The use of 'I' and 'we' provides a wonderful insight into a speaker's state of mind, showing where they consider their real alliances to be.

Audiences are subconsciously always very aware of where the 'them and us' boundaries lie, far more so than the speaker. If they believe the speaker is pitching himself against them, it can make them terribly defensive. If someone says, 'We all need to be more responsible with our money,' it feels far less aggressive than if someone says, 'You all need to be more responsible with your money.'

Larry David, a notoriously hostile stand-up comic, addressed his audiences as 'you, people', deliberately emphasizing his perceived superiority for comedic effect. Barack Obama, in contrast, uses the first person plural almost twice as often as the first person singular. And when Barack Obama says 'we' you get the sense he is speaking on behalf of the whole of humanity. When Gordon Brown said 'we' (i.e. 'we have taken difficult decisions'), you actually got the feeling he meant 'I'. I saw Brown say, 'We gave independence to the Bank of England' dozens of times, yet this was a decision he took almost entirely alone. He wasn't speaking to me at all.

Hillary Clinton expertly exploited the first person plural in an address to the United Nations World Conference on Women in 1995.

This is a coming together, much the way women come together every day in every country. We come together in fields and in factories. In village markets and supermarkets. In living rooms and board rooms. Whether it is while playing with our children in the park or washing clothes in a river or taking a break at the office cooler, we come together and talk about our aspirations and concerns. And, time and again, our talk turns to our children and families.

Humour can also prove an excellent icebreaker, *provided* that our speaker is one of the few, fortunate people who can deliver a gag. If he can, he's in a very small minority. Most can't, and it's not pleasant to watch a speaker have a tumbleweed moment in front of a thousand people. No responsible speechwriter would ever risk that happening. If we are sending a speaker on to the stage with a joke, it must be a sure-fire hit, otherwise it is game over. Alternatively, it can be helpful as an insurance policy to line up three or four short jokes in rapid succession: that way, if one of them is a stinker, all is not lost.

Another way to build common ground with the audience is through *identification of a common enemy*. We understand and define ourselves partly in relation to what we are not. This technique works particularly well with party conferences or any other gatherings of disparate and fragmented audiences: they can be united through their opposition. It can be a group of people that the speaker defines himself against (e.g. the French), an institution ('the Tories are vermin'), a company ('I came by Virgin Railways'), an ideology ('Why is everything changing') or a trend (e.g. 'I hate these new fangled computers!').

Step Three: Winning Agreement

It's not easy to win people's agreement. Most people don't like being told that they're wrong. Instead, they prefer having their views reinforced. This is why people generally buy newspapers that reflect, rather than challenge their views (you don't get many left wing liberals reading the *Daily Mail* for provocation). For the speechwriter, this presents a dilemma. It means we must avoid confronting our audience too directly; instead, we should try to present the illusion of agreement, even when we are completely at odds. The way to achieve this is through framing. We should position our proposition so that it appears to sit comfortably with everything else that exists and matters in our audience's world: their backgrounds, their values, their social networks, their existing opinions. There are a number of ways we can do this.

We should create an illusion of *critical mass*. People don't like to feel isolated from their peers. We can cite opinion polls, quote supporters, share anecdotes or produce any other form of social proof to show that people agree with us. Courtney Love attempted to create a sense of critical mass behind her call for musicians to dump the major record labels and go independent in a speech in 2000: 'I'm just the tip of the iceberg. I'm leaving the major label system and there are hundreds of artists going to follow me. Here, take my Prada pants. Fuck it. Let's do our real jobs.'[xii]

Most people want to *go with the flow*. Provided we can establish our speaker as leader of the group dynamic (which he automatically is as the speaker), we can lead our audience towards the most absurd opinions. In the film *The Yes Men*, two pranksters went around the world giving speeches, supposedly on behalf of the World Trade Organization, but issuing the most obscene and outrageous suggestions. They suggested that the solution to third world poverty was to feed Africa faeces piped directly down from American toilets. Supposedly intelligent audiences nodded along with these outlandish suggestions. William Hazlitt called this 'the bystander effect'[xiii] – people will stand to one side whilst even the most repugnant acts are taking place because they assume that, if something is wrong, someone else will challenge them. However, invariably, as we are all too scared to break off from the crowd and run the risk of looking stupid, nobody does. This goes some way to explaining what happened in Nazi Germany. 'The greater the number of judges, the less capable must they be of judging.'

We should make our proposition *go with the grain* of history. I think of this as *smoothing*. Any suggestion can appear to run with the grain of history, provided we start from the right point. Again, it comes down to framing. Christopher Reeve neatly demonstrated this in a speech on disability rights when he said, 'This past century has accomplished two civil rights movements. First the rights for blacks and Hispanics. . . . The second was equality for women. But there remains one *huge* minority that is still terribly discriminated against. And that population is the disabled population.'[xiv] A speaker who was opposing Christopher Reeve's argument might frame the argument differently: 'Disabled people were not given rights in the nineteenth century, they were not given rights in the twentieth century and nor should they be given rights now.' When a referendum on British membership of the euro seemed imminent, the two camps clashed bitterly about the wording of the question. The pro-euro camp wanted: 'Do you think Britain should continue the process of gradual integration with Europe by joining the European single currency?' The eurosceptics preferred: 'Do you think Britain should scrap the pound?' Both sides understood the importance having history on their side.

Our propositions will appear far more attractive if they are anchored deep within our audience's values and beliefs.

Our identities are complex constructs, comprising different levels of conviction. It is like a swimming pool. At the bottom of the pool are our values, which are deeply felt and tend to be fixed and enduring, based on factors like upbringing, schooling or nationality. Every group has different values. When Saddam condemned the US army as 'beer swilling, pork eating, gun toting, whore using infidels' it was perceived as a terrible insult by his Muslim followers because it offended their values. However, to an audience of Mafia capos, this could have been a compliment.

At the top of the pool lie our opinions. Our opinions are far more transitory and up for grabs. Although the press promotes most issues in the public sphere as fierce battles, the truth is that most people don't actually care about most issues. A twenty/eighty rule exists. Whether you are talking about joining the euro, abolishing the House of Lords or adopting nuclear energy, just twenty per cent will feel strongly about the issue one way or the other whilst the other eighty per cent couldn't care less (although they might rapidly express an un-thought-through opinion or something they have overheard, if asked).[xv] Academic research bears this out. And it is anecdotally true on all sorts of issues. The only exception is the odd divisive issue such as Iraq where the nation splits sharply in two.

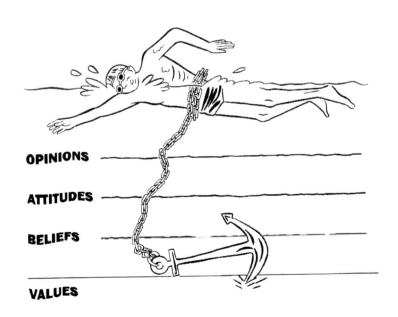

If we try to change our audience's values we will, to sustain the swimming pool metaphor, quickly get out of our depth and sink. That's why successful speakers never challenge an audience's values. Instead, they anchor their argument deep within the audience's values and use this to shift opinions. Basically, we connect the target opinion to a deeply held value. We link something they don't care about to something they do. This is what Ronald Reagan did in his famous 1983 'Evil Empire' speech. He anchored his anti-communism argument deep in American religious values by arguing that communism was fundamentally unholy, using satanic references and conjuring up images of 'dark forces'. To underline the point, he delivered the speech before an audience of evangelists. This was a smart strategy. After all, capitalism and communism, for all the fuss, are little more than different economic approaches. Why should anyone care about them? But by elevating it into a holy struggle between good and evil, Reagan guaranteed their attention and support. He presumably calculated that, though Americans don't care about economic theories, they do care about God. He was right.

British politicians have also used anchoring. Tony Blair's whole approach for New Labour was based on promoting 'traditional values in a modern setting'. The more modern and right wing his reform proposals, the deeper the argument would be anchored in old Labour values. The more ambitious the extension of markets in health and education, the more ubiquitous the accompanying references to Nye Bevan and Tony Crosland. Likewise, when Gordon Brown made a major speech on liberty, prefiguring his forty-two days detention plan, he cited libertarians such as George Orwell in his favour.[xvi] Orwell himself would surely have appreciated the irony of being subjected to such Orwellian treatment.

Any argument can be connected to any value; it scarcely matters if there is an actual connection. In the Second World War, a campaign to promote war bonds led with the message: 'Save Freedom of Speech, Buy War Bonds.'[xvii] The two issues were not remotely connected but, because they ran alongside one another, people assumed there was a link. Bagley, a character in the film, *How to Get Ahead in Advertising*, explained the strategy:

> Shall I tell you why people buy hydrogen bombs? Because they're not like the bombs people used to use in wars. We use an added ingredient in bombs these days. It's called peace. Our warheads are stuffed to the brim with it. And we're years ahead of the competition, of course, because the Russians don't put any peace in theirs.[xviii]

Much of David Cameron's repositioning of the Conservatives was based on *appealing to values*. This was crucial. In the 1980s, the Tories had seemed at odds with the nation's values after comments such as Norman Tebbit's 'on your bike' or Norman Lamont's 'price worth paying'. Cameron moved the message back into the mainstream by clearly repositioning the party back on the side of the angels. Great communications thinkers like George Lakoff argue that the political parties who spend the most time speaking to values are far more likely to poll better because they are far more likely to reflect people's true priorities. This places the right wing at a natural advantage, because they tend to focus more on how people feel anyway, whilst the left focuses on what government can do. He argues that left-wing parties spend far too much time talking about initiatives that most audiences simply don't care about, whilst right-wing parties spend more time talking about deeply held values and emotions. Our audience might not care about Section 336 of the Companies Act but if they care deeply about freedom and democracy then our challenge is to show them that Section 336 is good for freedom and democracy. We achieve that simply by mentioning the two together.

Another persuasive technique is *triangulating*. This is when we position our proposition between two polarized extremes to make our speaker seem more moderate and reasonable. Most people believe that they are moderate and reasonable so they tend to agree with opinions that appear moderate and reasonable. Tony Blair was a great fan of this approach, as demonstrated here, in a speech on foreign policy: 'Britain does not have to choose between being strong with the US, or strong with Europe . . . Britain can be both. Indeed . . . Britain must be both; we are stronger with the US because of our strength in Europe; we are stronger in Europe because of our strength with the US.'[xix] Here he is again in a speech to the European Parliament: 'The issue is not between a "free market" Europe and a social Europe, between those who want to retreat to a common market and those who believe in Europe as a political project. This . . . is a mindset I have fought against all my political life.'[xx] Triangulating sat very well with Blair's politics, as with other politicians who believed in Antony Giddens' 'Third Way' philosophy – indeed the whole Third Way was arguably triangulation taken to an extreme.

If we don't think our speaker can realistically find agreement, either because opinions are too polarized or he lacks political credibility or confidence, he might, in desperation, resort to fudging. This is when we create a message that is so blurred and nebulous that people can read anything they want into it. Ambiguity is a useful technique for speechwriters. This is because different people can hear the same message in different ways. As Morris Halle said, 'XXXXXX can mean six vowels to a poet, six roses to a gardener or six steps to a dancer.'[xxi] That's why Tony Blair's 'tough on crime, tough on the causes of crime' worked so well. The right heard it as a tough law and order call; the left heard it as an expression of sympathy for the plight of the poor souls who are plunged into crime by an uncaring society. Many other soundbites from the early New Labour years were also fudges, including on the euro ('In principle, we favour joining the euro. In practice, the five tests must be met') and the economy ('economic efficiency and social justice are two sides of the same coin'). People heard them either way depending on their persuasion. It explains, at least in part, how New Labour managed to amass such a broad coalition.

In recent years, ambiguous messaging has featured at the heart of two major election campaigns. In Britain, in 2005, we had Michael Howard's, 'Are you thinking what we're thinking?' In America, in 2009, they had Barack Obama's, 'Yes, we can.' Both of these lines were utterly open to interpretation. People could project whatever they wanted onto them. This was almost certainly not accidental. Jon Favreau said in an interview that the reason he and Obama settled on the line 'They said this day would never come' for the Iowa speech was because they 'knew that it would have multiple meanings to multiple people . . . Barack and I talked about it, and it was one that worked for the campaign.'[xxii]

Step Four: Motivating Action

The ultimate test of a speech's success is whether it actually changes people's behaviours; whether it persuades someone to vote for a new party or buy a new product. It is notoriously difficult not only to persuade someone, but to confirm in them that persuasion, as Machiavelli observed in *The Prince*, but it can be done.

We should construct our speech around a robust framework of rewards and punishments. It should be clear to our audience that if they do what we want, they will go to heaven; if they do not, they will go to hell. Or, as Aristotle put it more prosaically, 'The orator must establish the expediency or harmfulness of a proposed course of action; if he urges its acceptance, he does so on the ground that it will do good; if he urges its rejection, he does so on the ground that it will do harm.'[xxiii]

The heaven and hell scenario might sound extreme but the drama is not out of place in a speech. The peroration of William Gladstone's great 'Midlothian Address' illustrates the lengths to which this can be stretched: 'I have spared no effort to mark the point at which the roads divide – the one path which plunges into suffering, discredit and dishonour, the other which, slowly perhaps, but surely, leads a free and a high minded people towards the blessed ends of prosperity and justice, of liberty and peace.'

When we are constructing our heaven and hell, our heaven should be a bright, glorious, beautiful place where all our audience's deepest needs will be met; hell should be a dark, cold, wicked place where none of their needs will be met. To get down to the nitty gritty of what this might mean in practice, we might look back at Abraham Maslow's 'Hierarchy of Basic Human Needs'. Maslow was a Brooklyn psychologist who identified that every human being has five basic human needs. They work in a hierarchy, so that once one need is met we start worrying about the next one up the list. So we want to ensure we are healthy; then we check we are safe; then we start looking for love; then we build up our self esteem; and finally we look to grow as people (what Maslow called self actualization).

Maslow's needs are frequently used by advertising agencies to develop marketing strategies. Calls to buy consumer products are anchored within deeply felt needs. No one really needs a BMW or

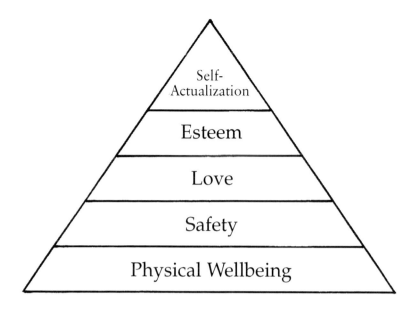

a chocolate bar. But, by saying, 'Buy this BMW and your self esteem will grow' or 'Eat this chocolate bar and your need for love will be met,' they induce the same powerful urge to act as if it were some primeval instinct.

The same principle holds true in speeches.

The deeper down Maslow's hierarchy you anchor your argument, the more compelling your case will be and the more powerful the reaction it will provoke in the audience. For many years, the case for investing in science has been based on appealing to people's deep fears of ill-health. This is why scientists have constantly been said to be on the brink of discovering cures for cancer, diabetes and Alzheimer's, from Harold Wilson's 'White Heat of Technology' speech in 1963 to Tony Blair's 'Science Matters' speech in 2003. The moral issues involved in exploiting such deep fears were examined in an episode of the *West Wing*. President Bartlett, preparing his State of the Union address, asked, 'Why can't I just say we'll cure cancer in ten years?'[xxiv] Toby, his Communications Director, replied, 'It would be seen as a political ploy.' President Bartlett relented and dumped the idea. Gordon Brown either received no such advice or had no such scruples: in his 2008 conference speech, he announced that, over the next decade, Britain would 'lead the way in beating cancer.'[xxv]

Politicians also play on people's need for safety and security. Such appeals have been particularly prevalent tactic in recent years as the last government made the case for ID cards, the extension of the period for detention without trial and the invasion of Iraq. It is the appeal of our times. And it is successful because the popular consciousness is so stuffed full of terrifying images to draw upon: from bombs falling in Baghdad to the Twin Towers tumbling down in Manhattan. We live in a climate of fear so it is only natural that fear is the first-response emotional appeal, even though that then becomes self-perpetuating.

Businesspeople are more likely to play on people's need for love or esteem, particularly when they are promoting lifestyle or aspirational products. Steve Jobs is the master of this method: he launches his products as if they are sex toys, using the language, actions and expressions of someone who is physically aroused. When he launched the first Apple Macintosh computer in 1984, he used sensual metaphors, slowly and carefully unzipping the computer and bringing it to life. When he launched the iPhone in 2008, he caressed it seductively, whispering sweet-nothings into its microphone.

Many speeches also play to people's hopes. Most people are fundamentally optimistic so they will readily agree with anyone who tells them things will get better. Bill Gates played to aspirations in a Commencement Speech at Harvard University in 2007:

I hope you will come back here to Harvard thirty years from now and reflect on what you have done with your talent and your energy. I hope you will judge yourself, not on your professional accomplishments alone, but on how well you have addressed the world's deepest inequities . . . on how well you treated people a world away who have nothing in common with you but their humanity.

Summary

- Audience: get to know your audience, analysing them with the same care and precision as a doctor would a patient, knowing what they think, how they feel and what motivates them.
- Aim: set a clear and realistic aim for your speech, carefully isolating the specific thought, emotion or behaviour you want to change and building your speech from there.
- Attention: send your audience powerful 'wake up' signs at the beginning, end, and when you are sending messages you want them to remember.
- Acceptance: use flattery, mimicry, humour and empathy to make the audience warm to your speaker.
- Agreement: frame your argument so that your proposition appears to go with the grain of history, public opinion and your audience's existing values and beliefs.
- Action: motivate your audience through constructing a system of rewards and punishments.

Case study

I have selected Johnnie Cochran's closing speech in the O.J. Simpson trial to illustrate the techniques in this chapter. This was surely one of the most outrageously audacious, yet devastatingly successful persuasive speeches of the twentieth century. It seemed like an open and shut case. O.J. had been charged with the murder of his estranged wife, Nicole Simpson, and her friend, Ronald Goldman. The victims' blood was found all over O.J.'s car and clothes. His footprints were all over the crime scene. When the police moved in to speak with him, he fled. There seemed little doubt of his guilt. But Johnnie Cochran's masterful oratory and dulcet delivery ensured his acquittal. In terms of persuasive precedent, the only comparable example was 'case of the bloody knife' in *Blackadder*:

I remember Mattinburg's most famous case, the case of the bloody knife. A man was found next to a murdered body, he had the knife in his hand, thirteen witnesses had seen him stab the victim and, when the police arrived, he said, 'I'm glad I killed the bastard.' Mattinburg not only got him off, but he got him knighted in the New Year's Honours list, and the relatives had to pay to have the blood washed out of his jacket.[xxvi]

Edited extract of Johnnie Cochran's closing speech in the trial of O.J. Simpson, 27 September 1995

You are empowered to do justice. You are empowered to ensure that this great system of ours works.

Listen for a moment, will you please. One of my favourite people in history is the great Frederick Douglass. He said, shortly after the slaves were freed, 'In a composite nation like ours, as before the law, there should be no rich, no poor, no high, no low, no white, no black, but common country, common citizenship, equal rights and a common destiny.'

This marvelous statement was made more than 100 years ago. It's an ideal worth striving for and one that we still strive for. We haven't reached this goal yet, but certainly, in this great country of ours, we're trying.

From the very first orders issued by the LAPD so-called brass, they were more concerned with their own images, the publicity that might be generated from this case, than they were from doing professional police work. That's why this case has become such a hallmark, and that's why Mr Simpson is the one on trial.

But your verdict in this case will go far beyond the walls of Department 103 because your verdict talks about justice in America and it talks about the police and whether they are above the law. And it looks at the police perhaps as though they haven't been looked at very recently.

Remember I told you, this is not for the naive, the faint of heart or the timid. . . .

So it seems to us that the evidence shows that professional police work took a backseat right at the beginning. Untrained officers trampled and traipsed through the evidence. And it was interesting because the prosecution didn't agree with that at the beginning but later on in this trial we heard Mr Goldberg talking to witnesses use my words – 'traipsing through the witness scene'. That scene there at Bundy. He used our words because they understood. We knew what we were talking about. We were able to demonstrate it through the videos.

They delayed routine procedures in notifying the coroners. They didn't call the criminalists out on time. And yes, they allowed this investigation to be infected by a dishonest and corrupt detective. They did that in this case. And they might try to back away from that all they want. But that's very important, as you're going to see, to this case and the resolution of my client's innocence.

Because of their bumbling, they ignored the obvious clues. They didn't pick up paper at the scene with prints on them. Because of their vanity, they very soon pretended to solve this crime and we think implicated an innocent man. And they never, they never ever looked for anyone else. We think, if they'd done their job like we have done, then Mr Simpson would have been eliminated early on.

And so this case is not – let me say this at the outset – it is not about attacking the Los Angeles Police Department. We're not anti police in making these statements. You're not anti police. We all need the police. I just said, we have so much crime in this country we need the police.

But what we need, what we must demand, what all of us should have, are honest, effective, non-biased police officers. Who could demand less? Can any of you say that's not what we should have? Like the defining moment in this trial: the day Mr Darden asked Mr Simpson to try on those gloves and the gloves didn't fit. Remember these words: if it doesn't fit, you must acquit. And we're going to be talking about that throughout.

So, to summarize, if you take the witnesses that we presented, who stand unimpeached – unimpeached – and if you are left with dogs starting to bark at 10.35 or 10.40 – 10.40, let's say – and we know from the most qualified individuals – Henry Lee and Michael Badden – this was a struggle that took from five to fifteen minutes, it's already 10.55. And remember the thumps were at 10.40 or 10.45. O.J. Simpson could not be guilty. He is then entitled to an acquittal.

Now we've talked to you and you've heard from the court and my colleagues talked to you about this whole idea of circumstantial evidence. Now I want to talk to you a little more about that now. We've shown you the incredible evidence that it would be impossible: O.J. could not, would not and did not commit these crimes. And where you have a circumstantial evidence case, this becomes very, very important. The prosecution then must disprove our timeline beyond a reasonable doubt.

And if they don't? You must acquit.

Analysis of Johnnie Cochran speech
Audience
Cochran took great care to get his audience right. As defence attorney, he had influence over their selection. The original jury pool comprised five Caucasians, three African Americans, two Hispanics and two Asians. Cochran rejected them. The final jury comprised nine African Americans, two Caucasians and one Hispanic.

Aim
Cochran's aim was very simple. He needed to persuade the jury there was a reasonable doubt in the prosecution's case. There is nothing in Cochran's speech that does not directly contribute to this aim.

Attention
Cochran used rhetorical devices to ensure his key messages burnt on to the jurors' memories. There was the rhyming contrast, 'If it doesn't fit, you must acquit', repeated as a refrain throughout the speech, to show the simplicity of the defence. There was a repetitive

rule of three, 'O.J. could not, would not and did not commit these crimes', that made the defence appear certain and final.

Acceptance

Cochran flatters the jury by highlighting their power ('You are empowered to do justice'). He takes pains to associate himself with Frederick Douglass, one of the great nineteenth-century anti-slavery campaigners ('One of my favourite people in history is the great Frederick Douglass'). His rhyming style and sing-song delivery subconsciously connects him with the tradition of black preachers in the US.

He unites the jury in a common hatred of the Los Angeles Police Department. He demonizes the LAPD, using a range of rhetorical devices. He uses the metaphor of disease ('they allowed this investigation to become infected'), pejorative language ('they trampled and traipsed through the evidence') and smears ('professional policework took a back seat').

However, he is ultimately forced to resile from this line of argument, 'This is not about attacking the Los Angeles Police Department. We're not anti police in making these statements. You're not anti police. We all need the police.' This qualification is necessary. Without a police force, society crumbles: the jury would not have wanted that on their conscience.

Agreement

Cochran's defence was weak and based almost entirely on fallacies. The only time that he attempts to deconstruct the prosecution's case, he actually winds up supporting their hypothesis! Read this section again. 'If you are left with dogs starting to bark at 10.35 or 10.40 – 10.40, let's say – and we know this was a struggle that took from five to fifteen minutes, it's already 10.55. And remember the thumps were at 10.40 or 10.45.' Cochran's timeline does not disprove the prosecution's scenario at all; he actually shows the prosecution's case was feasible: a five minute struggle that started with the dogs barking at 10.35 would have concluded with the thumps at 10.40. But most of the jury will not have noticed the deception. Instead, they will most likely, have been left slightly bewildered by the confusing mass of times spun out at them, and finally only alighted upon Cochran's thumpingly confident final assertion: 'O.J. Simpson could not be guilty. He is then entitled to an acquittal.'

Cochran anchored his appeal for O.J.'s innocence deep within the long struggle for black justice in America. After quoting Frederick Douglass's desire for 'common country, common citizenship, equal rights and a common destiny' he says, 'This marvellous statement was made more than 100 years ago. It's an ideal worth striving for and one that we still strive for. We haven't reached this goal yet, but certainly, in this great country of ours, we're trying.' The suggestion was that, if the jury believed in the struggle for equality in America, then they had to find O.J. not guilty. As Robert Shapiro, one of O.J.'s lawyers, later conceded, 'Not only did we play the race card, we dealt it from the bottom of the deck.'

Cochran's speech also includes some subliminal messaging. In the opening passage, when he quotes Douglass, he says, 'In a composite nation like ours, as before the law, there should be no rich, no poor, no high, no low, no white, no black.' It may just be that by repeating the word 'no' six times within the space of twelve words, he wanted to impress on the jury the word 'no'.

Action

Cochran's speech is based around two powerful emotional appeals. First, he appeals to pride, invoking Frederick Douglass, implying they held Douglass's legacy in their hands. 'You are empowered to do justice . . . This is not for the naive, the faint of heart or the timid . . . What we need, what we must demand, what all of us must have are honest, effective, non-biased police officers. Who could demand less? Can any of you say that's not what we should have? . . . You must acquit.' Second, he appeals to shame on the grounds of the LAPD's bungling, and what that represents in our society: 'This case will go far beyond the walls of Department 103 because your verdict talks about justice in America and it talks about the police and whether they are above the law. And it looks at the police perhaps as though they haven't been looked at very recently.'

Chapter Four

The Art of Argument

I'm fed up with the Punch and Judy politics of Westminster, the name calling, backbiting, point scoring, finger pointing. We won't play politics with the long term future of this country.

David Cameron's acceptance speech on becoming Tory Party leader, 6 December 2005

I will absolutely hold up my hands and say this is a promise I have been unable to deliver.

David Cameron on the *Today* programme, 2008[i]

A chapter on the art of argument may seem superfluous in a book about speechwriting – after all, a speech is inherently one-way communication. But, to succeed, a speech must create the *illusion* of an argument. By mimicking the style, sound and structure of an argument, we make our speech more credible and more effective – for three good reasons. First, because the audience wants to act as arbiter, so by presenting them with a fair argument we give them the illusion of control. Second, because we are used to understanding issues through polarized perspectives: traditionalist versus modernist; progressive versus conservative; right versus left, so by replicating this approach our argument is more likely to fit in with our audience's usual way of thinking. Third, by recreating the impression of an argument, our speech appears more thought-through: we are naturally more trusting of apparently interactive reasoning, just as we are instantly suspicious of anyone who pounds, preaches and polemicizes.

There are all sorts of ways to mimic an argument. Cicero's suggested speech structure (see page 63) provides one off-the-shelf method. If we don't want to download an entire structure, we can simply mimic the features of a regular argument in particular passages, adopting a 'call and response' strategy (e.g. 'There are those that said . . .' 'To them, I say . . .'). The important thing is that, throughout the whole speech, we air both sides and appear to do so fairly, resisting the temptation to reduce our opponent's argument to an absurdity or straw-man (i.e. one that is so weak that it is easy to knock down). It's just not necessary. We have enough advantages: we control the argument, we frame the issue, we lead the debate. The risk of landing a cheap shot is that it damages our speaker's credibility by making him appear uncharitable and mercenary.

This chapter is based around the three essential elements of an argument, Aristotle's golden triangle of ethos, pathos and logos. It is these elements that determine who wins an argument. Audiences make up their minds based on a mix of intuition, emotion and analysis; or head, heart and gut. We must work out where the strengths and weaknesses in our argument lie and develop our argumentative strategy accordingly.

Ethos: Appeals From Character

Character is a vital element in settling arguments. Audiences often decide with whom they agree based on whom they believe. This is why John Humphreys and Jeremy Paxman often smear their interviewees instead of focusing on the issue, it is why matters of character like sleaze and scandal invariably rise to the fore in general elections and it's also why Tony Blair believed he could win a referendum on the euro: because key figures in the 'yes' camp (Tony Blair, Gordon Brown, Michael Heseltine, Kenneth Clarke) were, at that time, far more trusted than those in the 'no' camp (Margaret Thatcher, Iain Duncan Smith, William Hague, William Cash). Blair presumably calculated that, as each side would make the same claims – more jobs, cheaper goods and lower interest rates – the final judgement would come down to trust.

Character is particularly important in speeches. Aristotle said, 'We believe good men more fully and more readily than others.'[ii] Quintilian said, 'No man can be a good orator unless he is a good man.'[iii] Speeches are like windows into a speaker's soul. We can't help but allow our true character and feelings to come through, either through what we say, how we say it or how we act. I always thought it was incredibly revealing when Robin Cook began his resignation statement saying, 'This is the first time in twenty years that I have addressed the House from the backbenches. I must confess that I had forgotten how much better the view is from up here.' I thought he unwittingly revealed the pleasure he derived from looking down on people – something he had a terrible reputation for in private.

Ancient Greek society had clear rules about what constituted good character: good sense, good morals and good will.[iv] Today, it is not such a precise science: society is more fragmented and notions of character are more blurred. Different audiences reach different conclusions. The do-gooder who shines in church on Sunday morning might not come across so well down the pub on a Friday night. Some might regard an old Etonian talking about yachts as an unspeakably decent fellow whilst, to others, he might seem a prat. So, appeals to ethos must be rooted in knowledge of our audience's taste but, basically, we want our speaker to stand tall whilst his opponent appears small.

Establishing our speaker

We can establish ethos through association, connecting our speaker with someone we know the audience will admire. By carefully selecting appropriate quotes, references, anecdotes or stories, our speaker can enhance his credibility, sharing in the magic dust of e.g. Obama, Branson or Cameron. Quotes should not be selected randomly. A quote sends a signal about our speaker's politics, allegiances and values. The right quote can redeem a speaker; the wrong one can condemn him. Some audiences might appreciate a quote from Adam Smith; others might prefer Karl Marx. It's often smart to quote an authority unconnected with our speaker: that makes him look rounded.

We can establish *ethos through analogy*. Analogies provide an insight into a speaker's character, his ways of thinking and frames of reference. If he says, 'This is like the first meeting between Lennon and McCartney' he shows levity and a taste for pop culture.

If he says, 'This is like the first meeting between Watson and Crick' he suggests knowledge and seriousness. Such analogies can be used deliberately to soften or sharpen a message, to strengthen or diminish an image.

We can establish *ethos through metaphor*. Terms like 'heroic feat' or 'herculean endeavour' plant pictures that will grow in our audience's mind whilst they look at our speaker, hopefully establishing connections. One of the most powerful metaphors is the metaphor of 'leader as father': if our speaker adopts a patriarchal tone it can enhance his authority whilst reducing our audience to children, thereby making them more susceptible to persuasion.

We can establish *ethos through experience*. Speakers often resort to this under duress, when they are defending themselves from character attack. Nelson Mandela said in his treason trial: 'I hold a Bachelor's Degree in Arts and practiced as an attorney in Johannesburg for a number of years.'ⁿ In Britain, politicians often draw on family experiences to enhance their credibility: Hazel Blears talked about her brother, the bus driver, to impress working class audiences; others have talked about members of their family who were entrepreneurs to build credibility with business audiences. Any assertions should not seem like isolated boasts but like threads through the natural fabric of the speech (e.g. 'We talked about this when I was working at the Royal Society.')

We can establish *ethos through knowledge*. Again, subtlety is the key. It's about leaving behind impressions, rather than actual information. This is what Gordon Brown did when he issued one of his statistical blitzkriegs: no one remembers the stats, but we do remember he is a man of knowledge.

We can establish *ethos through authority*. Our speaker might directly or indirectly invoke the authority of his office. Tony Blair played this card regularly during the run-up to the Iraq War. Typical lines heard from Blair included: 'There are times in this job when you must make difficult decisions,' or 'This is what the intelligence services are telling me as prime minister.' These lines reminded us of his authority whilst simultaneously generating sympathy for his predicament. This technique should be used sparingly. Society is less deferential now and some audiences instinctively reject appeals from authority.

We can establish *ethos through appearance*. The clothes our speaker wears might seem incidental but they also send signals. These can be exploited, provided we remember that different clothes have different connotations for different audiences. A city audience might respond well to a pinstripe suit, a charity audience less so. The speaker's voice can also establish ethos. To many Labour supporters, John Prescott's thick northern accent represented the authentic sound of the movement, even though some right-wing commentators sneered.

We can establish *ethos through assertion*. This is what Tony Blair did when he was under attack for accepting a 1 million pound donation from Bernie Ecclestone on behalf of the Labour Party. He famously responded that he was a 'pretty straight kind of guy'. We can only deploy this strategy a limited amount of times. Often, when someone flashes a toothy smile and says, 'trust me', it achieves precisely the opposite effect. Demosthenes had sage advice: 'to talk . . . about oneself . . . is so vulgar and so offensive . . . I shrink from it . . . [But I will] remind you of a few things that I have said on former occasions.'[vi]

We can also establish *ethos by re-framing*. Ronald Reagan achieved this during the Iran-Contra affair. He turned the table on his critics, making his admission of duplicity into a virtue.

A few months ago, I told the American people I did not trade arms for hostages. My heart and my best intentions still tell me that's true, but the facts and evidence tell me it is not. Now what should happen when you make a mistake is this: you take your knocks, you learn your lessons, and then you move on. That's the healthiest way to deal with a problem . . . You know . . . You've made plenty of mistakes, if you've lived your life properly. So you learn. You put things in perspective. You pull your energies together. You change. You go forward.[vii]

This 180 degree revolution was executed with aplomb. He had been the kid caught with his hand in the biscuit tin. He once again became the moralizing parent.

President Mahmoud Ahmadinejad of Iran also turned a difficult situation around when he addressed Columbia University in 2006. The host had launched a vicious personal and political attack on him in his introduction. President Ahmadinejad responded with quiet equanimity: 'At the outset, I want to complain a bit about the person who read this political statement against me. In Iran, tradition requires that when . . . a person invites us to be a speaker, we actually respect our students and the professors by allowing them to make their own judgement. . . .' According to the next day's *Washington Post*, the students spontaneously burst into applause.

Some speakers need to worry more about their ethos than others. Some professions, politics and the ilk, are particularly tainted, just as some audiences are particularly cynical. We should consider our audience's preconceived ideas. Most audiences already have fixed ideas about people's characters based on what they have said and done in the past. In a piece of academic research, a group of black and white students in Chicago were told that, 'X ... has said that African Americans must stop making excuses and rely much more on themselves to get ahead in society.' The respondents were then given different names for whom X might be. Some were told it was George Bush, others Jesse Jackson, others Ted Kennedy. They were then asked whether they agreed with that statement. The findings showed that the students' views varied wildly depending on who they believed had said that statement and whether they had agreed with them previously. In other words, they listened to the messenger, not the message.[viii] That is why ethos is so crucial.

Attacking the ethos of our opponent

As well as building up our speaker's ethos, we can also *attack the ethos of our opponent*. This strategy may be morally dubious but it is such a prevalent part of argument it's impossible to ignore. It also features regularly in public discourse, from Kinnock's attacks on

Thatcher to Richard Branson's broadsides against Lord King of British Airways to the demonizing of the World Trade Organization and International Monetary Fund by NGOs. Even if we have no intention of using these techniques ourselves, we should at least understand them. They may well be used against us.

'Doing a hatchet job' requires we throw all the previous strategies into reverse. So we could undermine someone's ethos by association ('well, we would expect this from a friend of Jonathan Aitken'), by metaphor ('he's throwing his toys out of the pram'), by knowledge ('he just doesn't get it'), by authority ('when you're in opposition you can get away with saying things like this') or by analogy ('it's like being savaged by a dead sheep').

In the Second World War, as you would expect, Hitler and Churchill constantly attacked one another's ethos. In a speech to the Reichstag in 1941, Hitler said, 'What does [Churchill] care for the lives of others? What does he care for culture? . . . [His actions] are symptomatic of a paralytic disease or of a drunkard's ravings. . . . For over five years, this man has been chasing around Europe like a madman in search of something that he could set on fire.'[ix] Churchill shot back with similar invective, presenting Hitler as a megalomaniac madman.

Many political character attacks highlight an opponent's inexperience. Lloyd Bentsen slapped down Dan Quayle during the 1988 vice presidential debate with the immortal, 'Senator, I served with Jack Kennedy. I knew Jack Kennedy. Jack Kennedy was a friend of mine. Senator, you're no Jack Kennedy.'[x] In the 2008 Democratic primaries, Hillary Clinton struck a blow on Barack Obama: 'I have a lifetime of experience that I will bring to the White House. Senator John McCain has a lifetime of experience that he'd bring to the White House. And Senator Obama has a speech he gave in 2004.'[xi] Gordon Brown attacked David Cameron in his 2008 party conference speech with, 'This is no time for a novice' – widely interpreted as a further veiled attack on possible challenger David Miliband. More amusing epithets are often lobbed around in the House of Commons, such as Michael Foot's glorious put-down of

Norman Tebbit as a 'semi house-trained polecat'.

A decision to attack character should be considered carefully. It is one of the most dangerous decisions someone in public life can make, if for no other reason than that it frequently results in retaliatory fire. This was a recurring feature of Gordon Brown's career: his constant recourse to character attacks generated phenomenal animosity and was deemed, even by his strongest supporters, to be a weakness. The following ignominious exchange between Gordon Brown and the *Daily Mail* sketch-writer, Quentin Letts, illustrates the umbrage that can surface:

Quentin Letts: Following on from your disgusting statement earlier that journalists don't take terrorism seriously can I ask whether in yesterday's meetings. . . .

Gordon Brown: Um, I didn't say that by the way actually.

Quentin Letts: Yes, well that was certainly what I understood. In yesterday's meetings. . . . [The prime minister smirks patronisingly at this point.] It is a serious matter! It is a disgusting suggestion! [Prime minister pulls a serious face.] In yesterday's meetings, that ministers had with MPs, in all those meetings, were civil service note-takers present [the prime minister bursts out laughing] and will those notes be available under FoI, in case we choose to believe those rather than you?

Gordon Brown: I don't think with all your great and extensive knowledge of the political system, I don't think you assume that at every meeting between a Member of Parliament and a government minister there's always a civil service note-taker. That is not the case.

Instead of launching full-blooded character attacks, we might heed Sir Humphrey Appleby's words of wisdom: 'The first step . . . to rubbish someone [is] to express your fullest support ... After all, you must first get behind someone before you can stab them in the back.'

Pathos: Emotional Appeals

Emotion is the *primus inter pares* of Aristotle's holy trinity. As Cicero wrote, 'Men decide far more problems by hate or love or lust or rage or sorrow or joy or fear or illusion or some other inward emotion than by reality or authority or any legal standard.'

Emotions operate within diametrically opposite but complementary pairs: hope and fear; anger and pity; shame and pride. Many speakers play these opposites off one another within the same speech, using the juxtaposition to obtain maximum impact. So they might stir someone's fear before offering hope, incite anger before generating pity, provoke shame before rousing pride.

Priming

An emotional appeal can begin even before a speaker reaches the podium, through *priming* – putting our audience in the right emotional mood. There are a number of ways an audience can be primed. When an audience is marched into a room in uniform lines, subjected to loud music and flashing lights, they are being put into a submissive state of mind which makes them more susceptible to persuasion. Their individuality is reduced and they're converted into a malleable mass. Control over their environment is a precursor to controlling their minds. It might sound sinister, but it has also been the foundation of public speaking for centuries, from Caesar to Cameron: it's only the technology that has changed. In the eighteenth century, John Wesley used incense, candles and crucifixes. Today, Steve Jobs uses technology, lasers and a big Apple logo. The principles are identical.

There can be a danger in over-exciting the audience. This was what happened with Neil Kinnock's infamous Sheffield rally in the 1992 election. Kinnock became metaphorically drunk on the excitement and energy in the room. He lurched over the podium like a rock star shouting, 'Alright!' This drove the audience in the room crazy, but to the audience outside it looked like a cross between a Bruce Springsteen gig and the Nuremberg rallies. Labour lost the subsequent election.

Priming is particularly big in the US where huge time, effort and money are invested into perfecting the lighting, scenery and backdrops for American presidential rallies, evangelical meetings and major corporate product launches. It's taking off in Britain but it doesn't need to be massively complex or over-elaborate. There are frequently just minor steps we can take to create the right atmosphere: it could be showing a video, playing music as people are coming in or putting up a picture of someone who might inspire the audience.

Different emotional appeals

We must be clear which emotions we are seeking to activate.

We can *play to people's hopes*, e.g. 'imagine how things could be', 'look to the future' or 'you can have everything you want (if only you do everything we want)'. Modern communications gurus such as Frank Luntz (who advises the US Republican Party and the British Conservative Party), Aaron Sorkin (writer of the *West Wing*) and George Lakoff (an eminent Professor of Linguistics) strongly advocate appeals to hope because it plays to people's innate if irrational sense of optimism and self-confidence. Barack Obama and David Cameron both based their campaigns on appeals to hope: Obama, with his legendary 'Yes we can' calls; Cameron, with his cry that, 'We can get a great NHS. . . . We can get great schools. . . . We can get safer streets.'

The flip side of playing to hopes is *playing to people's fears*. The threat could be veiled or explicit, ranging from a 'who knows what might happen' to 'these people want to kill us'. Frightened people are easy to manipulate which is why the climate of fear is now omnipresent. The character Bagley, in the film *How to Get Ahead in Advertising*, describes the essence of advertising as 'throwing a brick through someone's window, then knocking on the door and asking if they want to buy a burglar alarm'. This sums it up: you create a problem, blow it out of all proportion and then offer up the solution. This technique has been deployed by all sorts of politicians in pursuit of all sorts of goals, but perhaps none so infamously as Enoch Powell: 'As I look ahead, I am filled with foreboding; like the Roman, I seem to see "the River Tiber foaming with much blood".' Rear Admiral Chris Parry painted a similar picture more recently when, speaking about new security threats, he warned of 'reverse colonization . . . like the Fifth Century Roman Empire facing the Goths and the Vandals'.

We can appeal for pity, e.g. 'poor me' or 'how could you do that after all I've been through'. Cherie Blair appealed for pity after her links with a convicted fraudster were exposed: 'I am juggling a lot of balls in the air. And sometimes some of the balls get dropped.' Princess Diana appealed to people's hunger for love when she said: 'Hugging has no harmful side effects. If we all play our part in making our children feel valued, the result will be tremendous. There are potential huggers in every household.'[xii] Charlton Heston appealed for pity following his struggles against political correctness:

> When I told an audience last year that white pride is just as valid as black pride or red pride or anyone else's pride, they called me a racist. I've worked with brilliantly talented homosexuals all my life. But when I told an audience that gay rights should extend no further than your rights or my rights, I was called a homophobe. I served in World War Two against the Axis powers. But during a speech when I drew an analogy between singling out innocent Jews and singling out innocent gun owners, I was called an anti-Semite.[xiii]

We can play to people's anger. This might involve rousing hatred against an institution, ideology or group of people. Anger is often provoked in the run-up to wars. Pope Urban II roused the Christians to fight in the Crusades by stirring them in hatred of this 'race utterly alienated from God . . . invading Christian lands . . . by sword, pillage and fire . . . committing heinous crimes'. Adolf Hitler, Osama Bin Laden and George W. Bush have also appealed to anger using the same techniques of hyperbole, hysteria and disease/vermin metaphors.

Another emotion *we can play to is pride or patriotism.* This is often based around personalizing a company, institution or country, e.g. 'Remember that great British fighting spirit' or 'Our company will never give in.' It is hard to resist a patriotic appeal because, by implication, anyone who resists is a traitor or weak. Most audiences like having their pride roused for the same reason we like having our hopes lifted: we feel we are entitled to it! Most people are far prouder than they have any right to be. A study of Harvard students showed that eighty-three per cent believed their academic performance was above the university average. A successful speaker can harness this misjudged pride and turn it to his advantage.

The British National Party appeals to patriotism. Nick Griffin spewed up some Churchillian rhetoric after winning his party's first seats in the European Parliament:

Tonight has shown that the mettle of the men and women who created the British Empire, who fought like lions in the furthest corners of the globe, who sacrificed like Titans in Flanders, who endured the Blitz and who stormed the beaches of Normandy, is still alive. The British lion [has been] awoken, and its roar will now be heard throughout the world.[xiv]

More mainstream politicians play to patriotism in a more understated manner, recognizing the nuances in British pride. Blair struck the right note in his resignation speech, 'This country is a blessed nation. The British people are special. The world knows it. In our innermost thoughts, we know it.' In the film *Love, Actually*, Hugh Grant parodied Blair: 'We may be a small country but we're a great one, too. The country of Shakespeare, Churchill, the Beatles, Sean Connery, Harry Potter. David Beckham's right foot. David Beckham's left foot, come to that.'

The flip side of appealing to pride is *appealing to shame*. Such appeals are commonly found in charity speeches, religious sermons or calls to duty. Oxfam and Greenpeace appeal to shame with pictures and images of global destruction. Religious preachers appeal to shame by citing examples of abominable behaviour. Even the most positive politicians sometimes appeal to shame, for example, Obama: 'Let us resolve that we will not leave our children a world where the oceans rise and famine spreads and terrible storms devastate our lands.'[xv]

One final point: when we are writing emotionally, we should write emotionally. The language of emotion is very different from the language of logic. A credible emotional appeal should comprise the kind of incoherency that is characteristic of mental agitation. We shouldn't be afraid of our speaker going a little over the top because that is what speakers do naturally when their emotions are roused.

We can magnify, amplify and escalate; muddle our thoughts and mix our metaphors; ramp it up and raise the stakes. As the Roman rhetorician Longinus wrote, 'In real life we often see a man under the influence of rage . . . begin a sentence and then swerve aside . . . being borne with quick turns by his distress, as though by a shifting wind.'[xvi] The speaker must also raise his performance to match the emotion of the speech. I remember seeing David Beckham making a speech in support of England's 2018 World Cup bid; he repeatedly said how passionate he was about it, but because it was delivered in a peculiar, ultra-flat monotone, it failed to convince.

Defusing the emotion in our opponent's argument

Our speaker should take great care if he is arguing with an emotional opponent, particularly if he is intending to respond with logic; this is like responding to a nuclear bomb with a pea-shooter. The greatest mistake a speaker can make is to ignore emotion, particularly when that is clearly dominant. There is nothing more infuriating than expressing deep emotion, only to have someone respond with Spock-like logic. This was the mistake Haringey Council made after Peter Connolly died under their supervision. They responded to intense public anger by showing a PowerPoint presentation on how they had surpassed their performance targets. Their graphs and charts may have been right, but they missed the mood and made the Council look callous.

Gordon Brown made the same mistake speaking about the same incident during prime minister's questions. He read dispassionately from a pre-prepared script and then accused the Conservatives of playing party politics with the issue. David Cameron responded furiously, throwing his own notes to one side: 'Look. Let's be honest. This is a story about a seventeen-year-old girl who had no idea how to bring up a child. It's about a boyfriend who couldn't read but could beat a child. And it's about a social services department that gets a hundred million pounds a year and can't look after children. That's what this is about.'[xvii] She wasn't seventeen or anything like it, but who cared. The emotion trumped the facts and always will. As the saying goes, you can forget what a speaker says but you will never forget how they made you feel.

The best approach is to acknowledge that a debate is emotional from the off. By acknowledging the emotion, it might just be possible to rein it in, or even guide it elsewhere. For instance, you could shame an audience for being so swayed by anger, rather than reason (e.g. 'we need a debate with less heat and more light').

Logos: Logical Appeals

The third step in the art of argument is the *use (and abuse) of logic*. People disagree about the importance of logic in argument. Peggy Noonan, Ronald Reagan's ex-speechwriter, says it is the most crucial part. However even Aristotle emphasized that it was only the *illusion* of logic that mattered, as have many subsequent writers, from Quintilian to Macaulay. I reside firmly within the latter camp.

There are two different types of knowledge: hard and soft knowledge. Hard knowledge is based on absolute certainty or scientific fact (such as water equals two parts hydrogen to one part oxygen, or 1 + 1 = 2). With hard knowledge, every link in the logical chain is rock solid, proved beyond doubt. Soft knowledge is based upon extrapolative reasoning and is consequently often stuffed with missing logical links and fallacies. Most political debate is based on soft knowledge, almost by definition: it is the lack of certainty that throws it open to dispute.

There are a number of ways to enhance the logic or illusion of logic in our speaker's argument, whilst subtly undermining the appearance of logic in his opponent's case.

Enhancing the logic in our speaker's case

The easiest way to construct a logical argument is to *start from a premise* and build up from that. The beauty of this, from the speechwriter's point of view, is that we can locate that starting point wherever we wish. It is completely arbitrary. What's more, the premise doesn't, strictly speaking, even need to be accurate. In fact, the premise is sometimes the best place to dispose of the weakest parts of our argument because they are often beyond scrutiny: listeners often assume a premise to be true simply because it is the premise. Jonny Cochran's defence of O.J. Simpson revolved around the clinching argument: 'If it doesn't fit, you must acquit.' This assertion was based on the false premise that the glove had not fit; the glove had actually fit, but O.J. made a meal of putting it on in front of the jury, giving Cochran grounds to infer it hadn't.

However, for all the skulduggery that is possible, the best place to start an argument is from a credible, compelling, critical premise. The stronger our audience agree with it, the more powerful our argument will be. This is why so many great American speeches – from the Gettysburg Address to Martin Luther King's 'I have a dream' – start from the premise that 'all men are created equal', from the American Declaration of Independence.

The argument is therefore simple:

1. American Declaration said all men are created equal.
2. But all men are not being treated equally.
3. We therefore need to redress this.

Once we have established our premise, the argument can be advanced in all sorts of ways. We can *argue from knowledge*, producing an array of facts, stats and figures. This is the Gordon Brown way. We can *argue from authority*, invoking the authority of our own post or quoting the view of someone else of authority. A monarch might make such an appeal. We can *argue from probability*, setting out a likely sequence of events under different scenarios. This is the Bill Gates, Stephen Hawking or scientist's approach. We can *argue from experience*, setting out the lessons of history as might a statesman-like character in the mould of Ken Clarke or Paddy Ashdown. We can *argue by analogy* – the Bill Clinton method. Whichever approach we take, the overall effect should feel like a snowball rolling down a hill, steadily growing in size, scale and speed before knocking our opponents off their feet.

Tony Blair made the case for war in Iraq in three successive statements to the House of Commons between September 2002 and March 2003. He knocked down his opponents' arguments like skittles, even though we know now that many of his own arguments were bogus, based on faulty reasoning. His argument came from every direction.

He argued *from knowledge*: 'As the dossier sets out . . . there were up to 360 tonnes of bulk chemical warfare agents, including one and a half tonnes of VX nerve agent; up to 3,000 tonnes of precursor chemicals; growth media sufficient to produce 26,000 litres of anthrax spores; and over 30,000 special munitions for delivery of chemical and biological agents.'

He argued *from authority*: 'This is what they are telling me the British prime minister and my senior colleagues. The intelligence picture they paint is one accumulated over the past four years. It is extensive, detailed and authoritative. I know that there are some countries or groups within countries that are proliferating and trading in WMD, especially nuclear weapons technology. I know there are companies, individuals, some former scientists on nuclear weapons programmes, selling their equipment or expertise . . . I know there are several countries – mostly dictatorships with highly repressive regimes – desperately trying to acquire chemical weapons, biological weapons or, in particular, nuclear weapons capability.'

He argued *from probability*: 'Read not just about the 1 million dead in the war with Iran; not just about the 100,000 Kurds brutally murdered in northern Iraq; not just the 200,000 Shia Muslims driven from the marshlands in Southern Iraq; not just the attempt to subjugate and brutalize the Kuwaitis in 1990 which led to the Gulf War. Read about the routine butchering of political opponents; the prison 'cleansing' regimes in which thousands die; the torture chambers and hideous penalties supervised by him and his family and detailed by Amnesty International. Read it all and again I defy anyone to say that this cruel and sadistic dictator should be allowed any possibility of getting his hands on more chemical, biological or even nuclear weapons.'

He argued *from experience*: 'Look at Kosovo and Afghanistan. We proceeded with care, with full debate in this House and when we took military action, did so as a last resort.'

He argued *from opposition*: 'And if he refuses to co-operate – as he is refusing now – and we fail to act, what then? Saddam in charge of Iraq, his WMD intact, the will of the international community set at nothing, the UN tricked again, Saddam hugely strengthened and emboldened – does anyone truly believe that will mean peace?'

He argued *by analogy*: 'We can look back and say: there's the time, that was the moment; for example, when Czechoslovakia was swallowed up by the Nazis – that's when we should have acted. But it wasn't clear at the time.'

The whole argument was underpinned with two strong emotional appeals. The now-notorious appeal to fear was: '[Saddam Hussein] has existing and active military plans for the use of chemical and biological weapons, which could be activated within 45 minutes.' The appeal to pride was based on personalizing the House of Commons and activating associations with Churchill and Hitler: 'This is the time for this House . . . to give a lead, to show that we will stand up for what we know to be right, to show that we will confront the tyrannies and dictatorships and terrorists who put our way of life at risk, to show at the moment of decision that we have the courage to do the right thing.'

It is interesting that both the pro-war and anti-war lobbies argued from history, but where the pro-war lobby used the Second World War as their point of reference, the anti-war lobby used Vietnam. This leads us neatly on to the importance of framing.

Framing

One of the speechwriter's great strengths is the control he wields over the audience's perspective. We can increase and decrease the salience of certain aspects, blurring some whilst putting others in sharp focus. Framing can predispose the audience to even the most surprising viewpoints. Take the film *The Silence of the Lambs*. Thomas Harris deliberately placed Hannibal Lecter in a frame that would make the audience feel conflicted. Lecter's cultured pursuits of classical music and painting contrasted sharply with the thieving, cheating, duplicitous guards and his obscene, name-calling, semen-throwing cell-mates. We are led to sympathize with Lecter, until he bites someone's cheek off! Perspective is crucial: through framing, as Hitler wrote in *Mein Kampf*, 'people can be made to see paradise as hell and to consider the most wretched sort of life as paradise'.

In speeches, we have complete control over the frames of debate. We determine the issue that is under discussion and can shift it around 180 degrees to suit our argument as we wish, as Roosevelt did when he was mobilizing support for US involvement in the Second World War: 'This is not a fireside chat on war. It is a talk on national security.'[xviii] By shifting the frame, he turned a distant, irrelevant skirmish into a direct, immediate threat to national security. Tony Blair pulled a similar trick during the Iraq war: 'This is not a battle between the United States of America and terrorism but between the free, democratic world and terrorism.'

Different perspectives can establish different allegiances and alliances in our audience's minds. Screenwriters and broadcast journalists often deliberately show us a situation from a particular point of view to predispose us to sympathy. The same principles follow in a speech. A populist business leader will speak from the perspective of his customers. A populist politician will speak from the perspective of the electorate.

By shifting the perspective, we can vastly improve our argument. For instance, if we are told that a new cancer drug killed ninety per cent of people in tests, we feel very differently than if we are told it has saved fifty out of 500 lives. A report that shows unfavourable customer service findings will produce very different reactions from a story about one very happy customer.

We can label the topic under debate. The label of a debate often makes people instinctively pick sides before they've weighed up the evidence. President Bush's 'War on Terror' instantly put his opponents at a disadvantage because the frame implicitly put dissenters on the same side as terrorists. Look at the different reactions that are created by the terms 'pro choice' or 'pro life', 'inheritance tax' or 'death tax', 'tax cuts' or 'tax relief'. In the UK, many policy programmes have been named to deflect criticism. It is hard to argue with an education policy titled 'Every Child Matters' or a labour market strategy called 'Full and Fulfilling Employment'. It isn't always handled so adroitly though. When Gordon Brown announced his 'Next Stage Review' of the NHS, he put in the title everything that characterized government's mishandling of the NHS: constant interference, never-ending reviews and bungling bureaucrats.

Fallacies

Fallacy comes from the Greek verb *sphal*, which means 'to cause to fall'. When we use fallacies we are looking to trip our audience up by introducing a false connection, a misrepresentation or a deception. There are dozens of different fallacies. Broadly, they fall into the following groups.

The first set of fallacies involves *smearing*: playing the man and not the ball. A speaker might undermine someone by referring to an instance when they've failed in the past, e.g. 'I won't take any lessons in economic management from the man who. . . .' They might mispronounce or mis-state an opponent's name to subtly introduce negative associations, as President Bush Senior did with Saddam Hussein (calling him 'SAD-dam'). Gordon Brown tainted the Liberal Democrats by referring to them as the 'Liberal Party' which denied them the positive connotations of the word 'democrat', whilst emphasizing the more pejorative term 'liberal', e.g. liberal upbringing, liberal education and so on. You can use abusive analogies ('it's like explaining something to Winnie the Pooh') or abusive metaphors ('he's bumbling along'). A speaker might even smear someone by actively insisting that he would never stoop so low (e.g. 'I'm not even going to mention his personal life, which would be extremely unfair.')

Post Hoc Ergo Propter Hoc

The second set of fallacies revolves around creating *false connections*. If people hear something alongside something else, they often assume the two are connected. This is known as *cum hoc ergo propter hoc*, meaning 'with this, therefore because of this.' The most famous example of this technique in action (or over-action) was when President George W. Bush continuously referred to 11 September and Iraq in the same breath, thereby planting the idea of a causal connection between the two (a 2002 opinion poll showed that sixty-six per cent of Americans believed that Saddam Hussein was involved in the Twin Towers attack[xix]). People also assume a causal connection if they hear something after something else, for instance, 'We've trebled health spending. Cancer deaths are down by twelve per cent.'

Alliteration helps lock unrelated ideas even tighter together, e.g. 'Brussels Bureaucrats', 'Mad Muslims', 'Boom and Bust'. Forcing connections is fundamental to the arts of propaganda (e.g. 'Alexander the Great') and advertising: any ad man who links his brand with a generic product has discovered the golden goose (e.g.

'Pears Soap'). For such labels to stick, they require constant repetition: Alastair Campbell is reported to have said that it is only when people are sick of hearing something that your message is beginning to get through.

The third set of fallacies involves *misrepresenting your opponent*. A speaker can reduce his opponent's position to an absurdity: for instance, suggesting that, because he won't vote for forty-two days detention, he is effectively supporting terrorists. He might reduce his argument to a straw man. He can reduce a complex dilemma into a false choice, for instance, 'The real issue here is whether we remain members of the European Union.' Another technique is to disprove a single part of the other side's case and then use that to suggest that all must be wrong.

The fourth set of fallacies is based around *misleading*. A speaker can throw a red herring into the argument. He can disorientate his opponent, changing the issue with such bewildering rapidity he's impossible to catch, like a rabbit zigzagging across a field. He can force his opponent's attention somewhere new, even achieving this whilst explicitly claiming that he is not: e.g. if you say 'don't look over there' the first thing someone will usually do is look over there. Low-balling is another possibility: starting from an indisputable proposition and then slowly moving up from there, as many salespeople do e.g. starting with 'Do you agree that you deserve the best?' and ending with, 'And how would you like to pay for this double-glazing?' Pejorative language can lead people a certain way, as when Mrs Merton asked Debbie McGee what attracted her to 'the millionaire, Paul Daniels'. Language can also turn the tables on an issue, as when Sir Ian Blair brazenly claimed Jean Charles de Menezes's killing arose from a 'shoot to protect' policy. General points can be used to make a specific assertion, e.g. 'The Tories are always wrong. Therefore they must be wrong on this.' Or a specific point can be used to 'prove' a general assertion, e.g. 'The Tories were wrong on Black Wednesday. Therefore they must be wrong now.'

The fifth set of fallacies is based around *laying it on thick*. The speaker can blind the audience with science ('That ignores Professor

Halpern's work in the Seventies'), seduce them with flattery ('Someone of your intelligence couldn't fail to see this. . . .') or overwhelm them with hyperbole ('This is really, really, really important'). He can raise the stakes ('I will find it impossible to work with you unless you agree with me'), become over-emotional ('You never understand me'), or failing this, he might just keep repeating his argument ever louder and more persistently until finally the audience submits.

There is a danger inherent in all of these techniques: if the speaker is caught using debating tricks, not only does his logic collapse, so does his character.

Undermining our opponent's argument

When we are undermining our opponent's argument, it is like a game of Jenga: by destabilizing just a couple of blocks, we can very quickly bring the whole thing crashing down.

We can attack the premise of our opponent's argument. This strikes at the very bottom. In Anita Roddick's celebrated 2002 Trading Without Principles speech, she challenged the whole stated purpose of the World Trade Organisation when she said that instead of 'serving the many' it was protecting a privileged few, thereby knocking out its whole *raison d'être* with a single shot.[xx]

We can attack the *deductions* in our opponent's case. We shouldn't assume something is logical just because it appears so, as illustrated by the classic syllogism: a) a cat has four legs; b) a dog has four legs; c) therefore a cat is a dog. Test each link in the logical chain. Point out the weaknesses. Invite the audience to consider what those weaknesses mean for the rest of their argument.

We can attack the conclusions our opponent has reached. Some of the areas we might challenge include:

a) whether the right thing is being done;
b) whether it is being done by the right person;
c) whether it is being done at the right time;
d) whether it is being done for the right reasons;

e) whether it is being done in the right way;

f) whether it is being done in the right place;

g) whether it is going to achieve the right effects.[XXI]

There is bound to be a weakness in one of these.

There is an episode of *Yes Minister* that dissects Sir Humphrey's techniques for smashing down Hacker's proposals.

Tom: His objections will come in five stages. First of all, he'll tell you that your administration is very new and that there are lots of things to be getting on with.

Jim: Told me that this morning.

Tom: Eh, quite. Then if you still persist whatever your idea is he'll say something like, 'Er . . . yes, minister. I quite appreciate the intention. Certainly something ought to be done but are you sure this is the right way to achieve it?'

Jim: I must make a note of this.

Tom: Now, if you are still unperturbed, he will shift his ground. He will shift from telling you how to do it to when you should do it. You know, I mean he'll say, 'Now, minister. This is not the right time, for all sorts of reasons.'

Jim: What? And he expects ministers to settle for that?

Tom: Well, lots do. And if you don't he'll simply say that the policy has run into difficulties.

Jim: Such as?

Tom: Technical, political, legal. Now legal are the best sort because he can make these totally incomprehensible and, with any luck, this stalling technique will have lasted for about three years and you'll know that you're at the final stage when he says, 'Now, minister. We're getting very close to the run up to the next general election. Are you sure you can get this policy through?'

Attacks on our opponent's argument should be plotted with the same care and precision as we would construct our own case: aim at their most vulnerable spot and don't allow them subsequent wiggle-room. That was the mistake made by the 'Stop the War' Coalition: as soon as Bush and Blair declared the war over, the central pillar of their campaign collapsed.

Summary

- A good speech should sound not like a monologue, but a dialogue, mimicking the sound of two people in discussion.
- Arguments come down to three things: intuition, emotion and reason – gut, heart and head – or, as Aristotle put it, ethos, pathos and logos.
- Good character can be demonstrated by experience, assertion, association, metaphor or anecdote.
- Emotional appeals should be directed according to the emotional state of the audience: hope or fear, pride or shame, passion or anger.
- Logic, or the illusion of logic, can be illustrated either through deductive reasoning, framing or fallacies.

Case study

I have selected the forum speeches in Act III Scene Two of Shakespeare's *Julius Caesar* to illustrate the techniques in this chapter. Shakespeare was a master in the art of rhetoric, writing 31,959 speeches in thirty-seven plays[xxii] and possessing a knowledge of its techniques that would rival many modern professors of classics. *Julius Caesar* was, in my view, his greatest political work, a deep exploration into the dark side of rhetoric.

The forum scene is an exposition of rhetoric at its finest. Shakespeare carefully constructed two speeches which perfectly contrasted two very different styles of rhetoric from the two central characters: Brutus, the conspirator, and Mark Antony, the Caesar loyalist. Brutus's speech is noble, magnificent and glorious, comprising appeals to character and patriotism and laden with rhetorical flourish. Antony's speech is far more subtle and sophisticated: whilst he appears honourable, his whole speech is based upon deception. So he declares that he is not questioning Brutus's integrity, he then challenges Brutus's integrity. He declares that he is not trying to prove Brutus wrong, he then proves Brutus wrong. He declares that he is not there to praise Caesar, he then praises Caesar. He confesses it has all been a trick in a final aside to the audience, 'Mischief, thou art afoot, Take thou what course thou wilt!'

Extract from Julius Caesar, Act III, Scene Two, William Shakespeare

Brutus
Romans, countrymen, and lovers! Hear me for my
cause, and be silent, that you may hear: believe me
for mine honour, and have respect to mine honour, that
you may believe: censure me in your wisdom, and
awake your senses, that you may the better judge.
If there be any in this assembly, any dear friend of
Caesar's, to him I say, that Brutus' love to Caesar
was no less than his. If then that friend demand
why Brutus rose against Caesar, this is my answer:
– Not that I loved Caesar less, but that I loved
Rome more. Had you rather Caesar were living and
die all slaves, than that Caesar were dead, to live
all free men? As Caesar loved me, I weep for him;
as he was fortunate, I rejoice at it; as he was
valiant, I honour him: but, as he was ambitious, I
slew him. There is tears for his love; joy for his
fortune; honour for his valour; and death for his
ambition. Who is here so base that would be a
bondman? If any, speak; for him have I offended.
Who is here so rude that would not be a Roman? If

any, speak; for him have I offended. Who is here so
vile that will not love his country? If any, speak;
for him have I offended. I pause for a reply.

Antony

Friends, Romans, countrymen, lend me your ears;
I come to bury Caesar, not to praise him.
The evil that men do lives after them;
The good is oft interred with their bones;
So let it be with Caesar. The noble Brutus
Hath told you Caesar was ambitious:
If it were so, it was a grievous fault,
And grievously hath Caesar answer'd it.
Here, under leave of Brutus and the rest –
For Brutus is an honourable man;
So are they all, all honourable men –
Come I to speak in Caesar's funeral.
He was my friend, faithful and just to me:
But Brutus says he was ambitious;
And Brutus is an honourable man.
He hath brought many captives home to Rome
Whose ransoms did the general coffers fill:
Did this in Caesar seem ambitious?
When that the poor have cried, Caesar hath wept:
Ambition should be made of sterner stuff:
Yet Brutus says he was ambitious;
And Brutus is an honourable man.
You all did see that on the Lupercal
I thrice presented him a kingly crown,
Which he did thrice refuse: was this ambition?
Yet Brutus says he was ambitious;
And, sure, he is an honourable man.
I speak not to disprove what Brutus spoke,
But here I am to speak what I do know.
You all did love him once, not without cause:

What cause withholds you then, to mourn for him?
O judgment! Thou art fled to brutish beasts,
And men have lost their reason. Bear with me;
My heart is in the coffin there with Caesar,
And I must pause till it come back to me.

First Citizen
Methinks there is much reason in his sayings.

Second Citizen
If thou consider rightly of the matter,
Caesar has had great wrong.

Third Citizen
Has he, masters? I fear there will a worse come in his place.

Fourth Citizen
Mark'd ye his words? He would not take the crown;
Therefore 'tis certain he was not ambitious.

First Citizen
If it be found so, some will dear abide it.

Second Citizen
Poor soul! his eyes are red as fire with weeping.

Third Citizen
There's not a nobler man in Rome than Antony.

Fourth Citizen
Now mark him, he begins again to speak.

Analysis
Brutus's primary appeal is based on character: 'Believe me for mine honour and have respect to mine honour that you may believe.' He

inflates his character further by referring to himself in the third person.

He appeals to two emotions: pride and fear. First, he appeals to the mob's pride in being Roman. He puts the fact that they are Roman before all else ('Romans, countrymen and lovers!'); Antony starts with the more seductive friends. He defends the murder as an act of patriotism ('Not that I loved Caesar less, but that I loved Rome more'). His second emotional appeal is based upon fear. His manner is bullying from the start: 'Hear me for my cause, and be silent, that you may hear.' When he invites dissenters to come forward, there is a thinly veiled threat: 'Who is here so base that would be a bondman? If any, speak; for him, have I offended. Who is here so rude that would not be a Roman? If any speak; for him have I offended. Who is here so vile that will not love his country?' Given the audience knows that Brutus has Caesar's blood on his hands, it would have been a brave man that came forward.

The logic in Brutus's argument is weak. His argument is based on the false premise that Caesar was ambitious, which Antony smashes down. Brutus therefore works hard to create the *illusion* of logic, which he achieves with the rhetorical device of contrast. Brutus's speech is replete with contrasts, in fact more sentences are contrasts than not: 'As Caesar loved me, I weep for him, as he was fortunate, I rejoice at it; but, as he was ambitious, I slew him.'

Antony's whole approach is markedly different. Instead of telling the audience what to think, he plants seeds in their minds that grow a life of their own.

Antony doesn't assert his ethos. Instead, he hopes his reputation precedes him, which it does (one of the citizens says, 'There's not a nobler man in Rome than Antony.') He never once stoops so low as to impugn Brutus's integrity, even though the whole tenor of his argument fundamentally requires he does; instead, he repeatedly puffs up Brutus's character with the refrain, 'For Brutus is an honourable man', allowing the puncture to be inflicted by the audience via the logic.

Antony says he's not there to praise Caesar, but then, at two points in his speech, he forces the mob to look at the whole bloody affair from Caesar's perspective, transporting them straight into his coffin: 'The evil that men do lives after them; the good is oft interred with their bones; so let it be with Caesar. . . .' And later: 'O judgement! Thou art fled to brutish beasts, and men have lost their reason. Bear with me; my heart is in the coffin there with Caesar and I must pause till it come back to me.'

His logical argument is advanced cautiously, because he does not want to be seen to be openly sparking dissent: 'I speak not to disprove what Brutus spoke, But here I am to speak what I do know.' He then recalls he 'thrice presented' Caesar with a 'kingly crown' which he did 'thrice refuse', squarely contradicting Brutus's central claim that Caesar was ambitious.

The real-life Mark Anthony was said to possess unparalleled mastery of rhetoric. He spent many years studying rhetoric in Greece before fighting in Gaul with Caesar. Shakespeare could not have paid him greater tribute than through his expert craftsmanship of this scene. It is a true example of rhetorical wizardry.

Chapter Five

The Art of Story-telling

He needs to go with the crowds wanting more. He should be the star who won't even play the last encore. In moving toward the end he must focus on the future.

Leaked note from Philip Gould to Tony Blair, planning his departure from the world stage[i]

In every state mental hospital, there are people, classified as paranoid schizophrenics, who think they could save the world if they were only heeded. . . . But a rather large proportion of the population, especially a great number who hold, or aspire to, high political office . . . also think they could save the world if they were only heeded. Judging from the fruits of their efforts over many centuries of recorded history, they are no more likely to be either right or wrong than the schizophrenics.[ii]

Murray Edelman

All the world's a stage,
And all the men and women merely players

William Shakespeare, *As You Like It*

We all love a good story from childhood until the day we die. As Roland Barthes said, stories are the stuff of 'life itself'. As infants, we love bedtime stories. When we are older, we love novels, films and newspapers. On one level, stories are entertainment, but they also work on a much deeper level. It is through stories that we learn about ourselves and our place in the world. Stories can force us to confront unhelpful thought, emotional or behavioural patterns. This makes them powerful persuasive devices. Mothers tell children stories about nasty things that happen to kids who stay out past bedtime, because they know it will persuade their children to come home on time. Advertisers use stories to promote products, such as the long-running sagas of the Gold Blend couple or the Oxo family. Pyramid-sales companies tell stories about people going from nothing to owning Ferraris and million-pound country homes because they're proven to entice. Even psychotherapists use stories to help people confront traumatic issues from a safe distance: for instance, child psychotherapists might use Snow White to help children deal with the death of a parent or Cinderella to help with bullying.

Stories are essential to a good speech. Many of the greatest speakers – like Clinton, Blair and Obama – are great story-tellers. Some orators were such natural story-tellers that their whole lives almost evolved into legend, like Gandhi, King, and Mandela. There are many similarities between story-telling and speech-making: both derive from the oral tradition and both owe much to Aristotle (Aristotle's *Poetics* is the bible for story-tellers whilst his *Rhetoric* is the bible for speechwriters). Likewise, many great novelists make great speechwriters (e.g. John Steinbeck and Charles Dickens). Many speechwriters move into screenwriting. One of my old speechwriting colleagues now writes episodes of *The Fixer* and *Spooks*. One of Nixon's ex-speechwriters, Peter Binchley, left the White House to write the screenplay for *Jaws* (impudently, he even named Jaws' first victim, Kintner, after his White House boss!) Antony Jay, who penned *Yes Minister*, helped Margaret Thatcher with some of her speeches.

But what is a good story? I like the definition proposed by Robert McGee in his terrific book, *Story*, that, 'A good story revolves around a protagonist overcoming the forces of antagonism in order to reach the object of his desire.' This emphasizes the need for conflict. Conflict lies at the heart of a strong story. It is the conflict which makes the audience's ears prick up and demand resolution, whether we are talking about the good-versus-evil struggles of *Star Wars*, the class-based conflicts of *Lady Chatterley's Lover* or the man-versus-state conflict of *Nineteen Eighty-Four*. Without conflict, there is nothing. But before we get to exposing the conflict, we must first clearly establish the protagonist and make sure the audience cares about what they have to say.

Step One: Exposition of the Protagonist

We must establish the protagonist in our speech as efficiently and effectively as any screenwriter or novelist. The protagonist might be the speaker or the organization, the audience may know them or not: whichever, we must rapidly send the audience signs to show what they are about. For me, perhaps the best character exposition comes in the opening sentence of the late J.D. Salinger's *The Catcher in the Rye*:

> If you really want to hear about it, the first thing you'll probably want to know is where I was born, and what my lousy childhood was like, and how my parents were occupied and all before they had me, and all that David Copperfield kind of crap, but I don't feel like going into it, if you want to know the truth.

What an opener! We are instantly left with a clear, compelling picture of the principal character. We are gripped and want to know more.

The same effect can be achieved in the opening moments of a

speech, as Che Guevara demonstrated in a speech to the Cuban militia in 1960: 'Years ago, I began my career as a doctor. I dreamed of working indefatigably to discover something which would be used to help humanity.' Nelson Mandela conjured up a similarly powerful picture in his trial speech:

> In my youth in the Transkei, I listened to the elders of my tribe telling stories of the old days. Amongst the tales they related to me were those of wars fought by our ancestors in defence of the fatherland. I hoped then that life might offer me the opportunity to serve my people and make my own humble contribution to the freedom struggle.

In each case, we are given a clear picture of the character, we form an allegiance with them and are curious to see how their story unfolds.[iii]

Few people knew much about Sarah Palin when she accepted the Republican Party's nomination for the vice presidential candidature. In her 2008 acceptance speech, she very quickly projected a clear image of who she was:

> I had the privilege of living most of my life in a small town. I was just your average hockey mom, and signed up for the PTA because I wanted to make my kids' public education better. When I ran for city council, I didn't need focus groups and voter profiles because I knew those voters and knew their families too.

When thinking about how to project a speaker, it is worth remembering how rudimentary and one-dimensional most public images are, even for people who have been in the public eye for a long while: Gordon Brown is a dour Scot, John Prescott is a back-street fighter, David Cameron is a posh Etonian. Real life characters are far more complex than this but the public appreciate the accessibility, as do audiences for speeches. We might consider what kind of archetypal character our speaker could be: are they a helper, a warrior, a talker or a thinker? What character in a film are they?[iv] Imagining the Chief Scientific Adviser as the wily Doc from *Back to the Future* or Trevor Phillips as the intrepid Indiana Jones certainly opens the mind to some intriguing creative possibilities.

It will not always be the speaker that is the main protagonist within the narrative of our speech. Sometimes it may be the organization that he is representing or addressing. If so, we should personalize that organization: through personalization we open the possibility for rich emotional connections.

Step Two: Exploration of the Conflict

We should dramatically articulate the conflict that our protagonist is up against. He should appear burdened by this conflict and the speech should be his way of removing that burden. Many

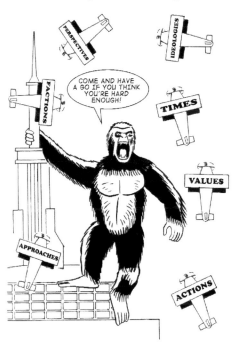

organizations shy away from exposing any form of conflict, either because of institutionalized Pollyannaism or they fear airing their dirty linen. Ultimately, provided we proceed sensibly and select an appropriate conflict in which our protagonist is clearly on the side of the angels, it should help both the leader and the organization. After all, addressing conflict is a strong sign of leadership, showing a desire for progress. He doesn't have to appear unprofessional or pugnacious.

There are a number of conflicts we might expose.

We can create a conflict with a group of people. Identifying, isolating and demonizing an enemy can boost an embattled leader and unite a fragmented audience. It stirs primeval instincts and can produce a fevered response. In extremis, this is what Orwell described in his 'two minute hate sessions' in *Nineteen Eighty-Four*: 'A hideous ecstasy of fear and vindictiveness, a desire to kill, to torture, to smash faces in with a sledgehammer seemed to flow through the whole group of people like an electric current, turning one even against one's will into a grimacing screaming lunatic.'[v]

Demonizing someone outside the room is a common political strategy. The phrase 'enemy of the people' has been used in speeches by Caesar, Nero, Adolf Hitler, Josef Stalin and George W. Bush. Audiences can be roused to hate even the most vulnerable groups.

In the 1980s, Margaret Thatcher attacked trade unions as 'the enemy within . . .'[vi] 'dangerous to our liberty . . . [a] scar against the face of our country ...' She did lasting damage to the whole trade union movement, to the extent that membership figures halved during her premiership.

In the 1990s, single mums became the new enemy of choice. In a now-notorious speech to the Conservative Party conference, Peter Lilley read out a 'little list' of people whom he wanted chucked out of Britain, parodying a Gilbert and Sullivan song. Top of the list were single mothers who become 'pregnant just to jump the housing queue'.[vii] Weeks later, John Redwood gave a similar speech, condemning young women who have babies, 'with no apparent intention of even trying a marriage or stable relationship with the father of the child'.[viii] The smears enabled swingeing cuts in single parent benefits to follow, politically unopposed. When David Cameron became leader, he declared the 'war on lone parents . . . over'.[ix]

Other minority groups have fallen into the firing line: the most recent victim being the Islamic community in the aftermath of 11 September. Politicians on all sides of the political spectrum gave incendiary speeches but perhaps the most surprising was Jack Straw's 2006 attack on Islamic women for wearing the veil. A week after he made this speech, I watched a drunk white woman verbally attack a woman in a burkha in a chip shop, telling her she was setting her children a terrible example by hiding her face. Her children looked on in shock. I have lived in the same part of London my whole life and never seen someone pick on a woman wearing a veil before. This shows how such speeches can shift attitudes, often sadly in the most pernicious way.

The conflicts in our own speeches may not be as stark or dramatic: we might be attacking Islamophobes, technophobes or Luddites. It doesn't matter, provided the conflict is there. But there are flip-sides: first, there is the risk that the group we are attacking retaliates; second, there is the risk that our attacks become self-fulfilling. Academics such as Murray Edelman have examined the reinforcing effect of language on social problems.[x] If young single mums are labelled spongers even when they're working hard, why should they bother? They might as well live off the state.

We might also create a *conflict between two possible courses of action.* This works particularly well in political speeches, or in any other situation where a speaker is weighing up two alternate possibilities. The perfect model of such a speech is Prince Hamlet's soliloquy in Shakespeare's *Hamlet*:

To be or not to be, that is the question;
Whether 'tis nobler in the mind to suffer
The slings and arrows of outrageous fortune,

Or to take arms against a sea of troubles,
And by opposing, end them.

This formula, 'to do this or not to do this,' has spawned many political speeches. Tony Blair's Iraq speeches asked whether it was right 'to stand British troops down and turn back; or to hold firm to the course we have set'. Gladstone's Midlothian Address asked, 'Is this the way, or is this not the way, in which a free nation, inhabiting these islands, wishes to be governed?' This formulation is only a rhetorical construct. The speaker will rarely truly expose his whole deliberative process for fear he looks overly laden with doubts and insecurities.

The 'to be or not to be' formula also works well in motivational or inspirational speeches. The point of deliberation in these speeches usually revolves around a speaker's moment of self-doubt leading up to their eventual epiphany. So, sportsmen talk about 'sink or swim' moments, adventurers talk about 'live or die' moments and CEOs talk about 'boom or bust' moments. Reformed alcoholics, born-again Christians and victims follow similar formats. George Best, Billy Graham and Christopher Reeve made some tremendously uplifting, life-affirming speeches. It creates terrific drama. I recently saw a great speech by Gill Hicks, who lost both of her legs in the 7 July bombings. She described how the bombing was a turning point. She realized how precious life was: her own life and the lives of others. She told how, ever since, she has done all she can to build a more compassionate world.

We can also examine *a conflict between two ideological positions*. Many great speeches emerged along these lines during the Cold War when speeches were used as weapons. In a February 1946 election speech, Stalin said it was capitalism that triggered the First and Second World Wars because the underlying cause of each was inequality. Churchill responded within weeks with his iron curtain speech. In the 1950s, the invective increased. President Eisenhower described Marxism as a 'hostile ideology, global in scope, atheistic in character, ruthless in purpose and insidious in methods'. By the

1980s, Ronald Reagan was using the metaphor of Star Wars to talk about the Cold War. Margaret Thatcher said that communism was, 'like terrorism, a menace that needs to be fought wherever it occurs'.

Even in this post Cold War age, there are many ideological differences that can still be explored in speeches. Many thought Blair's most brilliant speech was his 1999 conference speech against 'the forces of conservatism'. He argued it fell to Labour 'to liberate Britain from the old class divisions, old structures, old prejudices, old ways of working and of doing things. . . . To be the progressive force that defeats the forces of conservatism. For the twenty-first century will not be about the battle between capitalism and socialism but between the forces of progress and the forces of conservatism.' Alastair Campbell wrote in his diary that 'the forces of conservatism definitely gave it drama and definition.'[xi] Peter Hyman, the speechwriter who wrote it, thought it Blair's best speech ever.

We can also create *conflict between different policy objectives*. Recent political and business speeches have explored, amongst others, the tensions between economic growth and environmental protection, global co-operation and local autonomy, social cohesion and economic growth. The juxtaposition brings interest to the mundane. The ex-Labour leader John Smith made a speech the night before he died arguing that, 'social justice and economic efficiency are two sides of the same coin'. David Cameron addressed the same conundrum in a speech to the Google Zeitgeist conference more than a decade later, concluding: 'It's time we admitted that there's more to life than money, and focused not just on GDP but on GWB, general wellbeing.'[xii]

We can also *create a conflict between two different approaches*. Some Labour Party speeches compare the merits of pragmatic politics (epitomized by the trade union wing of the party) against ideological politics (epitomized by the Fabians). Bill Clinton also spoke about these different approaches, as does Hillary now: indeed, she used one of her first speeches as Secretary of State to argue that, 'Foreign policy must be based on a marriage of principles and pragmatism, not rigid ideology.'[xiii]

We can also *create conflict by using our speech to shoot down myths*. This makes our speaker appear strong and often attracts press interest. The inventor James Dyson has argued for Britain to wake from its creative sleep:

> The first thing we must do is divest ourselves of several lazy misconceptions ... that the eighteenth and nineteenth centuries were a golden age of manufacturing. They weren't. That Britain once led the industrial world. We didn't. That we are a nation of inventors. We're not. ... It's essential that we dump hoary old myths if we want to maintain our wealth, power and influence over the future.

Finally, if all else fails, we can always go for the ultimate conflict. We can start a rhetorical war. Liberal England was up in arms when George W. Bush declared a 'War on Terror' in 2001, saying it was impossible to launch a war against an abstract noun. But, in fact, Bush was only doing what many presidents before him had done.[xiv] Lyndon B. Johnson announced a 'War on Poverty'.[xv] Richard Nixon announced a 'War on Drugs'. Even Gerald Ford declared a 'War on Inflation', with a hyperbolic warning that inflation could 'destroy our country, our homes, our liberties, our property, and our national pride as surely as any well armed wartime enemy'. It's not just an American thing. Here in Britain, health ministers have launched wars against obesity, education ministers have launched wars against illiteracy and environment ministers have launched wars on waste. In fact, the only politicians who do not seem to like to talking about wars are those at the Ministry of Defence ... Who can blame them?

Step Three: Creating Something Worth Desiring

Of course, none of this conflict counts for anything unless we can clearly demonstrate to our audience that it is in pursuit of a worthwhile cause. Our speech needs some kind of 'holy grail' worthy of our speaker and audience's concern. Don't be afraid of shooting high! Many great speeches have been built on guts and gall, like King's glimpse of the Promised Land, Kennedy's promise to put a man on the moon and Blair's promise to abolish child poverty. The object of desire might be real or metaphorical, aspirational or concrete; the important thing is that there is a reason why our speaker cares so much.

Step Four: Story-telling Techniques

There are many story-telling techniques which can add colour and drama to our speeches.

We can *show not tell*. Ernest Hemingway claimed that his greatest story was just six words long: 'For sale. Baby shoes. Never worn.' The power of this story came from what was left unsaid: everybody could project what they wanted on to the story and take something different away. Audiences like being allowed to think for themselves instead of having someone else's views imposed. It is the difference between an audience that is active or passive. People love being able to use their imaginations. When we show, we give an audience room to think. When we tell, we simply hope they're going to listen.

The different methods are clearly demonstrated by Tony Blair (show) and Gordon Brown (tell) in the different ways that they addressed the Labour Party conference about the same issue of social mobility:

> Gordon Brown: 'It isn't levelling down but empowering people to aspire and reach ever higher. And to take advantage of all the opportunities of the global economy I want to unleash a new wave of rising social mobility across our country. For too long we've developed only some of the talents of some people – but the modern route to social

mobility is developing all the talents of all the people . . . helping those who are working their way up from very little and lifting up those in the middle who want to get on. It means supporting what really matters – hard work and effort and enterprise. This is not just the new economic necessity, it is the modern test of social justice and the radical centre ground we occupy and will expand.'[xvi]

Tony Blair: 'There is no more powerful symbol of our politics than the experience of being on a maternity ward. Seeing two babies side by side. Delivered by the same doctors and midwives. Yet two totally different lives ahead of them. One returns with his mother to a bed and breakfast that is cold, damp, cramped. A mother who has no job, no family to support her, sadder still – no one to share the joy and triumph of the new baby . . . a father nowhere to be seen. That mother loves her child like any other mother. But her life and her baby's life is a long, hard struggle. For this child, individual potential hangs by a thread. The second child returns to a prosperous home, grandparents desperate to share the caring, and a father with a decent income and an even larger sense of pride. They're already thinking about schools, friends she can make, new toys they can buy. Expectations are sky high, opportunities truly limitless.'[xvii]

The difference is clear. Blair's personal perspective is immediately more compelling than Brown's technocratic view. But, more importantly, Blair transports us straight into that maternity ward so we can almost see those mother's faces and hear the nurses clattering around. Brown's speech contains nothing so vivid, just a heap of abstract ideas and confused metaphors about 'not levelling down but reaching higher', 'unleashing a new wave of rising social mobility' and 'lifting those in the middle'. Any normal audience would be turned off by this kind of talk.

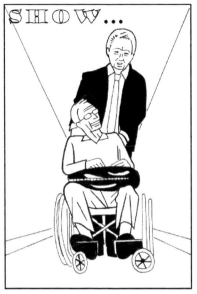

We can *soar and dive*, switching rapidly between global and personal perspectives: one second talking about a really big world issue – like climate change, globalization or poverty – and the next talking about its impact on a family in a village outside Nairobi, painting vivid, colourful and personal images. Sweeping between such extremes excites our audience. It can also be slightly bewildering, which compounds the persuasive effect, leading the audience to seek comfort and reassurance from the speaker. This is the late Anita Roddick soaring, diving and then soaring again:

> Every day, the gleaming towers of high finance oversee a global flow of two trillion dollars ... In the dark, cramped factories where people work for a pittance for twelve hour days without a day off. 'The workers are not allowed to talk to each other and they didn't allow us to go in the bathroom,' says one Asian worker in that garment factory. We have a world trade system that is blind to this kind of injustice.[xviii]

You can talk about issues on three levels: global, institutional or personal. A bad speech will typically spend around eighty per cent of the time addressing institutional issues, with just twenty per cent on the global and personal. It's best to turn this ratio on its head. Regard the institutional as a no-fly zone.

We can *magnify the importance of our issue.* Many of the so-called great speeches of the twentieth century were not about such grand issues as they appeared; often they concerned obscure differences of opinion about mundane aspects of economics or territory. They only appeared dramatic because they had been attached to sky-scraping issues of universal concern, such as freedom versus slavery, wisdom versus stupidity, the individual versus the state. So our speech shouldn't just be about introducing City Academies, it should be about whether children grow up free or enslaved. There's nothing morally wrong with this approach: we all habitually dramatize. Andrew Marr wrote in his book, *My Trade*:

> To work the alchemy, journalists reshape life, cutting away details, simplifying events, improving ordinary speech, sometimes inventing quotes to create a narrative that will work. It is not only journalists. Everyone does it. All the time. We hear a piece of gossip and, as we retell it, we improve it, smoothing away irrelevances and sharpening the point. We turn experiences of friends and relatives into bolder, more dramatic episodes than they really were.[xix]

We should tell our story in a way that will have meaning to our audience. If 200 factory workers were about to lose their jobs, they wouldn't care for complex arguments about economic nationalism and protectionism: their immediate concerns would be where the next pay cheque is coming from. Our argument must be relevant to the audience and grounded in terms they will understand. President Eisenhower took the trouble to explain defence spending in a way that would have most meaning for the American people:

> The cost of one modern heavy bomber is this: a modern brick school in more than thirty cities. It is two electric power plants, each serving a town of 60,000 population. It is two fine, fully equipped hospitals. It is some fifty miles of concrete highway. We pay for a single fighter plane with a half million bushels of wheat. We pay for a single destroyer with new homes that could have housed more than 8,000 people.[xx]

We can also use *stylistic devices* to heighten the drama, suggesting urgency and increasing tension. By removing connectives and shortening sentences, we create a breathless style, known as asyndeton. The Greek rhetorician, Demetrius, described the effect of asyndeton as, 'a vehement brevity, like men aiming blows in a close fight'. Quintilian said, 'Asyndeton is useful when we are speaking with special vigour because it at once impresses the details on the mind and makes them more numerous than they really are.'[xxi]

We should *get the pacing right*. A speech cannot be high octane all of the way through. Instead, it should reflect the vicissitudes of life, balancing light and shade. Sigmund Freud developed a term for this: he called it 'here and gone' after watching the sheer joy a baby gained from throwing a toy on a string out of his pram then pulling it back again. What this means for us speechwriters is that it is okay to be boring sometimes. It is a liberating notion: speeches can and should contain some padding. The padding helps the important bits stand out.

Geoffrey Howe's resignation speech to the House of Commons is regularly cited as one of the great speeches of the twentieth century. But, when you read it, a lot of it is actually quite dull, concerned with tedious European negotiations and technical aspects of the single currency. The crux of the speech comes in six knockout blows:

- Style and substance . . . are two sides of the same coin.
- My Right Hon friend the prime minister increasingly risks leading herself and others astray in matters of substance as well as of style.
- [She] seems sometimes to look out upon a continent that is positively teeming with ill-intentioned people, scheming, in her words, to 'extinguish democracy,' to 'dissolve our national identities' and to lead us 'through the back door into a federal Europe'.
- It was tragic to hear my Right Hon friend dismissing, with such personalized incredulity, the very idea that the hard ECU proposal might find growing favour among the people of Europe.
- It is rather like sending your opening batsmen to the crease, only for them to find, the moment the first balls are bowled, that their

bats have been broken before the game by the team captain.
- The time has come for others to consider their own response to the tragic conflict of loyalties with which I have myself wrestled for perhaps too long.

Geoffrey Howe's speech was 2,689 words long. But the heart of the speech lay in these 186 words. It was seven per cent killer argument, ninety-three per cent padding. When we are writing, it's best to start by plotting these six points; the rest will take care of itself.

We should never be afraid of telling stories in our speeches. Many great speakers regale their audiences with stories. When we tell a story, the mood in the room shifts perceptibly. It is like opening the audience's minds, leaving us free to pour in our ideas. Stories pack a much bigger punch than simple assertions.

Bill Clinton was the master of the story:

> The other day, the Mayor of Baltimore, a dear friend of mine, told me a story of visiting the family of an 18-year-old young man who had been killed on Halloween. He had a bunch of little kids along with him. He always went out with the little-bitty ones so they could trick-or-treat safely. And across the street from where they were walking on Halloween, a 14-year-old boy gave a 13-year-old boy a gun and dared him to shoot the 18-year-old friend he was walking with – and he shot him dead.[xxii]

This story had far more impact than if he'd recounted a pile of statistics on crime. Plus, by telling the story through the mouth of the Mayor of Baltimore, he gave the story more credibility: the Mayor acted as a legitimizing source.

Ronald Reagan used a similar technique in his Evil Empire speech:

> A number of years ago, I heard a young father, a very prominent young man in the entertainment world, addressing

a tremendous gathering in California. It was during the time of the Cold War, and Communism and our own way of life were very much on people's minds. And he was speaking to that subject. And suddenly, though, I heard him saying, 'I love my little girls more than anything.' And I said to myself, 'Oh, no, don't. You can't – don't say that.' But I had underestimated him. He went on: 'I would rather see my little girls die now, still believing in God, than have them grow up under Communism and one day die no longer believing in God.'

The story beggars belief but the legitimizing source means Reagan got away with it (just!).

Stories can also act as metaphors or analogies for situations that are either too complex or emotionally intense to address directly. Bishop Belo used a poignant analogy to illustrate the problems East Timor faced after the conflict:

Peter and John are friends. . . . Peter stole a bicycle from John, and then after three weeks Peter came to John saying, 'John let's talk about reconciliation.' And then John said, 'I don't think we need talk about reconciliation at the present moment until you bring back my bicycle. Where is my bicycle?' And Peter said, 'No, let us forget about the bicycle, let us talk about reconciliation.' And then John said, 'We cannot talk about reconciliation until my bicycle is back.' We cannot deal with reconciliation until the people who are victimized sit down around the table and talk about what happened first. The bicycle may be replaceable but the dead are not. We cannot go to a shop and buy back those people who are dead.[xxiii]

Franklin D. Roosevelt also told a story to persuade Congress they should help Britain in the Second World War:

Suppose my neighbour's home catches fire, and I have a length of garden hose four or five hundred feet away. If he can take my hose and connect it up with his hydrant, I may help him put out his fire. Now what do I do? I don't say to him before the operation, 'Neighbour, my garden hose cost me $15; you have to pay me $15 for it' . . . I don't want $15; I want my garden hose back after it is over.[xxiv]

Many speakers know the value of a good speech. One member of Richard Nixon's speechwriting team wearily commented, 'He needs the speechwriting team of Jesus and Aesop, with Matthew, Mark, Luke and John as staff assistants.'[xxv] But the story must be relevant and it must be credible.

For me, this story from Nick Clegg's 2008 Conference speech lacks credibility:

Angie, a middle aged mum, came to see me recently in my constituency. She said she was finding it difficult to sleep. She told me about that sinking feeling she gets at the supermarket checkout and the petrol pump. Counting down the days until her cheap mortgage deal ends. Switching down to just half an hour of heating in the morning because it's all she can afford. You know how it feels don't you?[xxvi]

Angie seems too one-dimensional to be credible. It needs embellishment; more human elements. It feels like a focus-group finding turned into a fictional character. Authentic stories are normally a bit more surprising or quirky than this. We should bear that in mind if we are making stories up. The risk in telling fake stories is we get found out. Tony Blair told the 1996 Labour Party conference:

I can vividly recall the exact moment that I knew the last election was lost. I was canvassing in the Midlands on an ordinary, suburban estate. I met a man polishing his Ford Sierra. He was a self-employed electrician. His dad always voted Labour, he said. He used to vote Labour too. But he'd bought his own house now. He'd set up his own business. He was doing quite nicely. 'So I've become a Tory,' he said. . . . In that moment, he crystallized for me the basis of our failure. . . .[xxvii]

This crude story supported Blair's point beautifully. But then the *Sun* carried out an extensive search to find Sierra Man. Despite huge publicity, and all the Sun's investigative resources, Sierra Man was never found. Maybe he'd just been a figment of Blair's imagination?

Summary

- Clearly establish the protagonist so that the audience cares about them.
- Establish a dramatic conflict.
- Create a clear object of desire that will enthrall our speaker and audience.
- Use story-telling techniques to increase the colour and drama of a speech.

Case study

The case study I have selected to illustrate the techniques in this chapter is David Davis's 2008 resignation speech. David Davis is well known as a political bruiser. He thrives on conflict. It is said that he would start a fight within thirty seconds even if left in a room on his own. True to form, Davis's speech is replete with conflicts and represented a genuinely surprising political development.

Extract from David Davis's resignation speech, 13 June 2008
The name of my constituency is Haltemprice and Howden. Haltemprice is derived from the medieval proverb meaning 'noble endeavour'. Up until yesterday I took the view that what we did in

the House of Commons representing our constituents was a noble endeavour because for centuries our forebears defended the freedoms of the British people – or we did, up until yesterday.

This Sunday is the anniversary of the Magna Carta, the document that guarantees that most fundamental of British freedoms, *habeas corpus*, the right not to be imprisoned by the state without charge or reason. Yesterday this House decided to allow the state to lock up potentially innocent citizens for up to six weeks without charge.

The counter-terrorism bill will in all probability be rejected by the House of Lords very firmly. What should they be there for if not to defend the Magna Carta? But because the impetus behind this is essentially political not security the government will be tempted to use the Parliament Act to overrule the Lords. It has no democratic mandate to do this since forty-two days was not in the manifesto. Its legal basis is uncertain to say the least. But purely for political reasons this government's going to do that.

In truth forty-two days is just one, perhaps the most salient example, of the insidious, surreptitious and relentless erosion of fundamental British freedoms.

We will have shortly the most intrusive identity card system in the world. A CCTV camera for every fourteen citizens, a DNA database bigger than any dictatorship has, with thousands of innocent children and a million innocent citizens on it. We've witnessed an assault on jury trials, that bulwark against bad law and its arbitrary abuse by the state, shortcuts for our justice system that make our justice system neither firm nor fair, and the creation of a database state, opening up our private lives to the prying eyes of official snoopers and exposing our personal data to careless civil servants and criminal hackers.

The state has security powers to clamp down on peaceful protests and so-called hate laws that stifle debate, while those who serve violence get off scot-free. This cannot go on, it must be stopped and for that reason today I feel it is incumbent on me to take a stand.

I will be resigning my membership of this House and I intend to force a by-election in Haltemprice and Howden. I will not fight it on the government's general record; there is no point repeating Crewe and Nantwich. I will fight it on my personal record. I am just a piece in this great chess game. I will fight it. I will argue this by-election against the slow strangulation of fundamental British freedoms by this government. That may mean I have made my last speech to the House, possibly. And of course that would be a cause of deep regret to me. But at least my electorate and the nation as a whole would have had the opportunity to debate and consider one of the most fundamental issues of our day. The ever-intrusive power of the state into our lives, the loss of privacy, the loss of freedom. If they do send me back here, it will be with a single, simple message. That the monstrosity of a law that we passed yesterday will not stand.

Analysis

In the opening paragraph, Davis clearly establishes his constituency of Haltemprice and Howden as the main protagonist. He presumably chose not to make himself the main protagonist ('I am just a piece in this great chess game'), to reduce the risk of charges of egotism. He personalizes his constituency through the Latin name which means 'noble endeavour'.

He then establishes no fewer than twelve conflicts within just 558 words:

- Noble endeavours versus political skullduggery
- Past versus present
- House of Commons versus House of Lords
- Freedom versus intrusion
- Democracy versus totalitarianism
- Davis versus government
- Davis versus voters of Haltemprice and Howden
- Duty versus sacrifice
- Davis versus Conservative Party
- State versus individual
- Government versus people

This is about one conflict every twenty seconds. In comparison, Ian Fleming based twenty-two James Bond films and novels, totalling more than 2 million words, around just fourteen recurring conflicts:[xxviii]

- Bond versus M
- Bond versus villain
- Villain versus woman
- Woman versus Bond
- Free world versus Soviet Union
- Great Britain versus non Anglo-Saxon countries
- Duty versus sacrifice
- Cupidity versus ideals
- Love versus death
- Chance versus planning
- Luxury versus discomfort
- Excess versus moderation
- Perversion versus innocence
- Loyalty versus disloyalty

Davis establishes a very clear prize that is at stake – freedom. He says the word freedom five times.

David Davis uses many other story-telling techniques. He magnifies the significance of the previous day's vote, connecting it to a thousand years of British history. He gives the story more colour by introducing the metaphors of gameplay ('great chess game'), murder ('slow strangulation') and personalization ('noble'). He also uses violent language, talking about the 'assault on jury trials', 'criminal hackers' and 'I will fight'. He also uses colourful language, talking about the 'insidious, surreptitious and relentless erosion of fundamental British freedoms'.

Chapter Six

The Art of Metaphor

You know I used to think the future was solid or fixed, something you inherited like an old building that you move into when the previous generation moves out or gets chased out. But it's not. The future is not fixed; it's fluid. You can build your own building, or hut or condo, whatever; this is the metaphor part of the speech by the way.

Bono, Commencement speech at Pennsylvania University, 2004[i]

Being good at metaphor is by far the most important gift for any writer. It is a sign of natural genius.

Aristotle, *Poetics*

Bill Gates once asked me, 'Could you make me more human?' I said, 'Being human is over-rated.' '[ii]

Mark J. Penn, Worldwide CEO of PR Firm, Burston Marsteller

All day long, tens of thousands of messages come hurtling at us like missiles. They hit us when we are at our least suspecting: on the bus, flicking through a magazine, watching the television or surfing the web. We can try to avoid them, but the most powerful get through regardless. They weave their way past normal sight, avoiding detection, bypassing rational scrutiny, striking deep into our unconscious minds. Metaphors are like the guided cruise missiles of communication. As speechwriters, we can use them to frame issues, prime audiences and enhance the credibility of speakers. They can heighten or reduce drama, legitimize or demonize groups, elevate the mundane to the sublime, convert the abstract to the concrete or reduce the powerful into the absurd.

Metaphor derives from the Greek word, 'to transfer'. When we use a metaphor, we transfer one idea to another. We ask our audience to believe that x = y. Generally we do so for the purposes of illumination. Metaphors originated in Ancient Greece: by using building metaphors – 'laying down the foundations', 'constructing the framework' or 'moving up another level' – it became easier for philosophers to discuss abstract issues. Today, phrases like 'credit crunch', 'housing bubble' and 'mortgage meltdown' make complex economic concepts easily understandable. When David Cameron said 'you can't drop democracy out of a plane at 50,000 feet and expect it to land in one piece' he made the abstract issue of governance sound like a bomb.

Metaphors also have phenomenal persuasive qualities. They allow us to speak directly to an audience's unconscious mind, putting them into particular moods without their knowledge. Hypnotists use metaphors to induce trances and implant suggestions.[iii] Advertisers use metaphors to make their products more enticing. Propagandists use metaphors of the 'nation as family' and 'the leader as father' to increase their power.

Adam Smith's metaphor about the 'invisible hand of the market' was a work of genius. Not only was it very vivid and illuminating, it also had a powerful persuasive effect. It countered the prime criticism of his laissez-faire economics: the view that markets might be efficient, but were cruel, callous and uncaring. By personalizing the market, he addressed this criticism in the audience's unconscious minds, if not directly. This was no accident, I'm sure. As well as being a great economist, Adam Smith also taught rhetoric at Glasgow University. Rhetoric has played a huge role in shaping economic discourse throughout the ages: the economists with the greatest gift in metaphor have been the economists whose views have endured the longest. Like Smith, David Ricardo and Karl Marx also made extensive use of metaphors in their works, particularly biological metaphors.[iv]

Metaphors are also killer devices in speeches. Many speeches have revolved around a single metaphor, from Harold Macmillan's 'wind of change', to Charles De Gaulle's 'flame of French resistance', to Prince Charles's 'monstrous carbuncle on the face of a much loved and elegant friend'.

However, perhaps the best metaphor of the twentieth century was Winston Churchill's 'iron curtain'. Again, this was a metaphor that worked on two levels: it illuminated and it persuaded. It was perfection both in its totality and its individual components. The iron implied coldness, the curtain implied darkness and the entire phrase bore theatrical connotations, leaving a suggestion of imminent drama (in Churchill's day, the phrase 'iron curtain' was commonly understood to refer to the fire safety curtain which came down on to the stage before and after a performance). All of these metaphors had currency throughout the Cold War, characterizing the moral values of the two sides (cold versus warm, darkness versus light, hard versus soft). The irony is that Churchill never even intended 'iron curtain' to be the main metaphor in the speech. He gave the speech a different title: 'The Sinews of Peace.'

Metaphors are sophisticated devices, but we all use them all the time without realizing. We use around six metaphors a minute.[v] My own research shows that on average politicians use a metaphor once every twenty-three words. Quintillian said that metaphors are 'natural' and 'often employed unconsciously'. It is because they are used unconsciously that they are so revealing: they open windows to our souls. If we speak about a plant being thirsty, it shows that we love a plant as if it were a human being. If we use war metaphors, it shows that we are confrontational. If we use gambling metaphors, it shows that we have a competitive streak.

As Lakoff has shown, some metaphors are common across society: for instance, the idea that arguments are wars (we 'shoot down' ideas or become 'entrenched'); ideas are containers (let's 'unpack' that, it has got 'holes in it'); welfare is weather (the 'clouds' are setting in, I'm feeling much 'brighter'); people are machines (he's going 'full steam', 'recharging his batteries'); and, conversely, machines are people (give the computer 'a rest', it needs a bit of 'love'). We talk about illnesses as wars, careers as journeys and relationships as flowers. Cicero said we should not be afraid to use metaphor more than any other rhetorical device 'because it is of the commonest occurrence in the language of townsmen and rustic alike.'[vi] Friedrich Nietzsche argued that there was little in the world that was not a metaphor, saying that it was only through metaphor we created meaning: 'When we speak of trees, colours, snow and flowers, we believe we know something about the things themselves, although what we have are just metaphors of things, which do not correspond at all to the original entities.'[vii] In fact, as

Professor Jonathan Charteris-Black has pointed out, much of twentieth century history can only be told through metaphors, most of which are explicitly designed to activate particular associations.

In this chapter, we explore different types of metaphors and the ways in which they can be used to advance ethos, pathos and logos. We also look at ways to select the right metaphor, as well as some of the risks of using metaphors.

Types of Metaphors

These are some of the more common sources of metaphor, with some clichéd examples of them in practice. I would urge you not to use any of these examples directly, but they will prove good starting points for brainstorms.

Art metaphors
- Theatre – it's curtains, he's waiting in the wings, preparing the stage
- Writing – turn the page, open a new chapter, dotting the i's
- Music – a chorus of approval, a grand crescendo, making overtures

Nature metaphors
- Climate – wind of change, stormy atmosphere, sunny disposition
- Landscape – bleak outlook, new horizon, scorched earth
- Plants – we're blooming, green shoots, planting seeds
- Trees – the root of the problem, branching out, low-hanging fruit
- Fire – a spark of an idea, a roaring success, fan the flames
- Water – ideas are flowing, clear water between us, making waves
- Night/day – a new dawn, sun setting, eleventh hour
- Seas – waves of approval, the tide has turned, what's been washed up

Experience metaphors
- Life/Death – last gasp of breath, the birth of a new project, kiss of life
- Sickness/Health – on its last legs, giving it a boost, picture of health
- Personalization/Depersonalization – the company is up and running, he's going full steam ahead
- Freedom/Slavery – unleashing the shackles, you have nothing to lose but your chains
- Cruel/Compassionate – a savage tax, a pernicious law, compassionate conservatism

Activity metaphors
- Religion – crusading zeal, we were crucified, the disciples
- War – keeping our powder dry, increasing our arsenal, retreating to the bunker
- Journeys – the path to freedom, at a crossroads, long and winding road
- Day to day experiences – toothpaste out of the tube, spilt milk, missed the bus
- Eating – I just need to digest that, unpalatable proposal, see how it goes down
- Sleeping – wake it up, put it to bed, the stuff of nightmares
- Seeing – it's a bit foggy, can we see more clearly, transparency
- Sport – around the track, back of the net, finishing line
- Gambling – there's a lot at stake, I'll take my chances, throw the dice

Man-made objects
- Construction – laying down foundations, building up, cementing
- Machines – building up steam, feeling a bit rusty, broken down
- Cars – the lady's not for turning, I have no reverse gear, shift in gear
- Container/suitcase – it's empty, it's got holes in it, let's unpack it
- Money – investing time, valuing people, building up credits

Finding Appropriate Metaphors

Different metaphors suggest different things. Nature metaphors suggest inevitability, art metaphors suggest freedom, journey metaphors suggest momentum. We should select metaphors that are appropriate to our speaker, his aim and the audience.

Different speakers habitually use different metaphors. Their choices provide an insight into their personalities. Digby Jones constantly uses Alan Partridge-esque 'back of the net' metaphors which support his image as 'one of the lads' but would not work well for a more statesmanlike figure. Tony Blair naturally uses metaphors of retribution and salvation that reinforce his pulpit preacher persona. Gordon Brown used conflict metaphors which suggested he saw politics as war. We should notice the kind of metaphors our speaker likes and then supply more of the same. However, if we deliberately want to reveal that the speaker has another side, we might toy with a new kind of metaphor. For instance, a nature metaphor could soften a hard image whilst a military metaphor could toughen up someone weak.

Different audiences prefer different metaphors. If we study our audience's past communications (e.g. websites, press releases or in conversation), their favourite metaphors will quickly become apparent. For instance, civil liberty groups habitually use the metaphor that authority means danger ('alarms ringing', 'siren sounds' and 'warning signs'), teachers use the metaphor that education equals freedom ('opening doors', 'releasing the shackles', 'freeing minds') and doctors and nurses speak about healthcare as a war ('fighting infection', 'weapons against cancer', 'being on the frontline'). Using the same metaphor as our audience demonstrates empathy. This is why doctors are encouraged to use the same metaphors as their patients. If a patient complains of a migraine and say it feels like they have their head stuck in a vice a good doctor will reply, 'Well, let's see if we can loosen that vice.'

We should beware of any metaphors that might offend our audience. Female audiences do not respond well to military metaphors, nevertheless, they remain the metaphor of choice for many male politicians, particularly Labour politicians.

Our metaphor should also match our aim. Our metaphor can help activate a particular emotion. So, for instance, if we are trying to make our audience afraid, we might use a sickness, death or war metaphor. If we are trying to get them to behave in a uniform fashion, we might use a machine metaphor.

A metaphor can also have more meaning if it is latched on to a topical story or event. During the Olympics, our speaker might talk about 'going for gold' or 'jumping the gun'. During the Grand National, our speaker might talk about 'falling at the first fence'.

Using Metaphors to Create Ethos, Pathos and Logos

Like so much else, metaphors can be used to promote each of Aristotle's big three.

Metaphors can be used to establish ethos. One metaphor that we all commonly understand is the metaphor that light equals good whilst darkness equals bad. We can use this in our speech to indicate who's the good guy and who's the bad guy. Similar techniques are used in film-making. For instance, in *The Sopranos*, light pours into the family home to show this represents the good side of Tony's life whilst the Bada Bing, his Mafia hangout, festers in darkness. The metaphor of warmth has a similar effect: we can talk about someone's warm words or their chill indifference.

Over time, some speakers will consciously use particular metaphors in order to build up their image. It was through metaphors that George W. Bush, Tony Blair and Margaret Thatcher transformed themselves from ordinary people into enduring, iconic images.

George W. Bush was 'the cowboy', complete with ten-gallon hat, swagger and snarls of 'Dead or alive' and 'You're either with us or you're against us.' It turned us off in Britain, but it was never aimed at us, instead it was aimed at the American people brought up on a diet of Cowboys and Indians. For them, it was bang on target. The image also suggested a perfect antidote to the wet, wooly liberalism of the Clinton years. The American people wanted someone to swagger into town and tell it like it was and Bush showed he was the man: first through metaphors, later through actions.

Tony Blair was the 'pulpit preacher' who offered Britain the chance to scrub itself clean after the sleaze-ridden Tory years. He used conviction rhetoric in his speeches over and over again. His sanctimonious style was redolent of an impassioned vicar. Despite Alastair Campbell's protestations that Blair didn't do God, this became an integral part of his image. At one stage, Jeremy Paxman actually asked him whether he was concerned he could be turning into *Private Eye's* parody of the Vicar of St Albion.[viii]

Thatcher's 'Iron Lady' was also the perfect image for the woman and the times, tackling concerns that a woman wasn't up to the job of PM. The image was a startling leap for the grocer's daughter, as she conceded herself in a 1976 speech: 'I stand before you tonight in my red chiffon evening gown, my face softly made up, my fair hair gently waving. The Iron Lady of the Western world? Me? A Cold War warrior? Well, yes.'

Through their use of metaphor, Thatcher, Bush and Blair all created iconic images. They all aroused strong feelings – for and against – but what is undeniable is that none of them ever lost an election. It is also interesting to note that, in each case, as their careers drew to an end, it became harder to work out whether it was the politician controlling the metaphor or the metaphor controlling the politician. Thatcher fell out of touch during her downfall years, with comments like, 'We will go on and on and on' and 'We have become a grandmother.' Bush and Blair also acknowledged that their images might have gone too far. In his resignation speech, Blair conceded, '1997 was a moment for a new beginning. . . . Expectations were so high, too high – too high in a way for either of us . . .'[ix] In a press conference towards the end of his Presidency, George W. Bush said, 'I think that in retrospect I could have used a different tone, a different rhetoric. Phrases such as 'bring it on' or 'dead or alive' indicated to people that I was, you know, not a man of peace.'[x]

Some people object to this kind of image-making in politics, but it has always been a feature of public life, from Ancient Egypt through Tudor England to twenty-first century America. People demand invincible leaders. There are readily understood metaphors for leader. The metaphor of the leader as shepherd of his people dates back to Ancient Egypt.[xi] Today, the most common metaphors are 'the country as a family' and 'the leader as father'. In 2008, a note from US communications guru Mark J. Penn to Hillary Clinton was leaked: he advised her that the American people would not tolerate the idea of 'the president as mother' but they would accept the idea of a woman playing the role of father.[xii] It caused uproar but no one suggested he was wrong.

Metaphors can also give ethos to countries, companies and organizations. If we talk about them as living, breathing beings, we make it more likely that people will care about them.

The metaphor of personalization is often used for countries during wars, to rouse a sense of patriotism. After all, on its own, a country is nothing more than a political construct. By personalizing the country, people can be motivated to give their lives. In the Second World War, Churchill used the metaphor of personalization more than any other. Through his metaphors, he made London a person ('London can take it'), Britain a person ('Britain stood in the gap. There was no flinching and no thought of giving in') and Germany a monster ('a monstrous tyranny, never surpassed in the dark, lamentable catalogue of human crime').[xiii] De Gaulle deployed a similar strategy when he spoke of, 'Outraged Paris! Broken Paris! Martyred Paris!' So, of course, did Hitler.

The metaphor of personalization is also used to give companies life. Again, companies are no more than legal structures. By personalizing them, directors can attract more loyalty. The metaphor of the BBC as 'Auntie', which makes her a senior member of the national family, places her beyond reproach. The British Army is also personalized through the idea of 'Tommy'. Many recent government advertising campaigns have been based around the metaphor of personalization, overcoming the negative perceptions of bureaucracy. Effective examples include the 'Tell Sid' campaign to privatize gas and, more recently, the Drugs Treatment Agency's 'Ask Frank' campaign.

Metaphors can also depersonalize groups of people. The press often does this, smearing groups they see as undesirable: so we are 'swamped' by immigrants (suggesting we're knee-deep in a bog) whilst union leaders are labelled 'union dinosaurs' (suggesting they should have died out thousands of years ago). Studies have shown that, in the run-up to genocides, the metaphor 'vermin' is often used: in Rwanda, the Hutu described the Tutsi minority as 'cockroaches' whilst in Hitler's Germany the Nazis described the Jews as 'rats'. A chilling recent study showed that the same technique is now being used in the Western press to talk about Al Qaeda, with words like 'hunt', 'trap', 'nest' and 'lair' featuring regularly.[xiv]

Metaphors can also be used to create pathos, putting our audience in a particular mood which directs their decisions. Research has showed that students who were presented with an identical perceived threat were far more likely to back a military intervention in response if the speaker used the descriptive metaphor of the Second World War as opposed to the metaphor of Vietnam.

George W. Bush used fire metaphors throughout his second inaugural address to deter dissent: 'We have lit a fire – a fire in the minds of men ... it burns those who fight its progress.' This message was designed to instil fear.

Harold Macmillan used a climate metaphor to talk about the spread of African nationalism ('the wind of change'). By using a climate metaphor, Macmillan suggested that African nationalism was unstoppable (because we all know that climate is unstoppable). Interestingly, the French, who were trying to hold back African nationalism, chose a different metaphor: that of the insurgents as vermin.

Metaphors can also be used to create logos, underpinning the logic of an argument. Jason Kay, the lead singer of Jamiroquai, once tried to argue that his musical style was constantly changing by comparing himself to a river, arguing that, if it stopped flowing, it would become stagnant. People are not rivers, but the analogy suggested his argument had a logic that didn't really exist. The image was so vivid it distracted from his unchanging style. And it also bolstered his environmental credentials.

In the 2010 general election, the Conservative Party habitually used nature metaphors. This helped to reinforce the logic of their argument for smaller government. We all instinctively understand that, left to its own devices, nature has a tendency to be wild and uncontrolled. The nature metaphor supported the argument for cuts: we know that every now and then you need to get the garden shears out.

The Perils of Metaphors

There are a number of potential traps in using metaphors.

We might inadvertently reveal our speaker's true feelings. Chris Parry, the former head of the Independent Schools Council, was forced to resign in 2008 after using inflammatory terms like 'Cold War' and 'Sectarian Divide' to describe relations between private schools and the state sector.[xv] He inadvertently revealed his true hostility to the state sector.

There is a risk we might create a metaphor that is so powerful it backfires against us. This is what happened with Tony Blair's 'I have no reverse gear',[xvi] when William Hague's riposte came, quick as a flash, 'Neither would I have a reverse gear if I had Peter Mandelson behind me.'

There is the risk we get carried away, either resorting to dead metaphors (like 'laying the foundations', 'creating a level playing field' or 'blue sky thinking'), hyperbole ('we're in the fast lane, overtaking the people on the middle lane, but we need to keep an eye on the fuel and oil gauge because otherwise we could grind to halt') or mixed metaphors. *Yes Minister*'s Jim Hacker was the master of the mixed metaphor, with corkers like, 'we're going to nail this leak', 'we're gritting our teeth and biting the bullet' and 'I have to stop this country going downhill by getting into the driving seat and putting my foot on the accelerator.' Don't obsess too much about mixing metaphors though; even Shakespeare muddled them occasionally: didn't Prince Hamlet talk about 'taking arms against a sea of troubles'?

George Orwell's first rule of writing was, 'Never use a metaphor, simile or other figure of speech which you are used to seeing in print.' Orwell was a hard taskmaster but what is beyond doubt is that you can't beat a strikingly original metaphor for impact. John Bright was a great Liberal orator of the nineteenth century. He made a speech to the House of Commons describing the massacres of the Crimean War: 'The Angel of Death has been abroad throughout the land. You can almost hear the beating of his wings.' The image was so striking that contemporary reports showed his fellow parliamentarians physically looked up, as if expecting a visible apparition.[xvii]

Summary

- Metaphors can help illuminate a point.
- They can also be used as powerful persuasive tools.
- Metaphors should be appropriate for the speaker, audience and aim.
- Metaphors can help create ethos, pathos or logos.
- We should beware the risks of mixing metaphors, using dead metaphors or letting our imaginations run away with us.

Case study

I have selected Barack Obama's Election Victory Speech, delivered in Grant Park, Chicago, on 4 November 2008, to illustrate the points made in this chapter. This was, in my opinion, the finest speech made so far in the twenty-first century. Obama's use of metaphor is exquisite.

Barack Obama's election victory speech, delivered in Grant Park, Chicago, 4 November 2008

If there is anyone out there who still doubts that America is a place where all things are possible; who still wonders if the dream of our founders is alive in our time; who still questions the power of our democracy, tonight is your answer.

It's the answer that led those who have been told for so long by so many to be cynical, and fearful, and doubtful of what we can achieve to put their hands on the arc of history and bend it once more toward the hope of a better day.

I was never the likeliest candidate for this office. We didn't start with much money or many endorsements. Our campaign was not hatched in the halls of Washington – it began in the backyards of Des Moines and the living rooms of Concord and the front porches of Charleston.

It was built by working men and women who dug into what little savings they had to give $5 and $10 and $20 to this cause. It grew strength from the young people who rejected the myth of their generation's apathy; who left their homes and their families for jobs that offered little pay and less sleep; from the not-so-young people who braved the bitter cold and scorching heat to knock on the doors of perfect strangers; from the millions of Americans who volunteered and organized, and proved that more than two centuries later, a government of the people, by the people and for the people has not perished from this earth.

This is your victory. The road ahead will be long. Our climb will be steep. We may not get there in one year, or even one term, but

America – I have never been more hopeful than I am tonight that we will get there. I promise you: we as a people will get there.

There will be setbacks and false starts. There are many who won't agree with every decision or policy I make as president, and we know that government can't solve every problem. But I will always be honest with you about the challenges we face. I will listen to you, especially when we disagree. And, above all, I will ask you to join in the work of remaking this nation the only way it's been done in America for 221 years – block by block, brick by brick, callused hand by callused hand.

This election had many firsts and many stories that will be told for generations. But one that's on my mind tonight is about a woman who cast her ballot in Atlanta. Ann Nixon Cooper is 106 years old.

She was born just a generation past slavery; a time when there were no cars on the road or planes in the sky; when someone like her couldn't vote for two reasons – because she was a woman and because of the color of her skin.

Tonight, I think about all that she's seen throughout her century in America – the heartache and the hope; the struggle and the progress; the times we were told that we can't and the people who pressed on with that American creed: yes, we can.

At a time when women's voices were silenced and their hopes dismissed, she lived to see them stand up and speak out and reach for the ballot. Yes, we can.

When there was despair in the Dust Bowl and depression across the land, she saw a nation conquer fear itself with a New Deal, new jobs and a new sense of common purpose. Yes, we can.

When the bombs fell on our harbor and tyranny threatened the world, she was there to witness a generation rise to greatness and a democracy was saved. Yes, we can.

She was there for the buses in Montgomery, the hoses in Birmingham, a bridge in Selma and a preacher from Atlanta who told a people that, 'We Shall Overcome.' Yes, we can.

A man touched down on the moon, a wall came down in Berlin,

a world was connected by our own science and imagination. And this year, in this election, she touched her finger to a screen and cast her vote, because after 106 years in America, through the best of times and the darkest of hours, she knows how America can change. Yes, we can.

This is our chance to answer that call. This is our moment. This is our time. Thank you, God bless you, and may God bless the United States of America.

Analysis

Obama uses metaphor to establish his character (ethos). The line, 'Our climb will be steep. We may not get there in one year, or even one term, but America . . . I promise you: we as a people will get there,' echoes one of Martin Luther King's most famous speeches: 'I've looked over, and I've seen the Promised Land! I may not get there with you, but . . . we as a people will get to the promised land.' This establishes ethos by association. Obama used these associations so frequently throughout his campaign that after a while, he seemed almost indistinguishable from King, giving him instant credibility and recognizability. Madonna does the same thing by dressing up as Marilyn Monroe or Greta Garbo; by adopting a ready-made image she provides her audience with a pre-prepared, pre-packed personality. When Obama won the Democratic nomination, the British *Sun* newspaper actually showed a picture of Obama alongside the King quote: 'I had a dream.'

Obama also uses metaphor to reinforce the logic of his argument. By using the story of Ann Nixon Cooper as a metaphor for American history, he helped argue that America could change. It would have had a rather different effect if he had told the story through the eyes of a soldier who had served in Vietnam, Afghanistan and Iraq. The audience would have believed Obama's argument was hopelessly flawed.

Obama uses metaphor to rouse people's emotions. His plea that we should put our 'hands on the arc of history and bend it once

more toward the hope of a better day' invites the audience to consider the power and possibilities of collective action. When he says, 'the road ahead will be long', he reinforces his leadership credentials: it pitches him clearly at the front of the line with the American people behind him.

Chapter Seven

The Craft of Editing

A scrupulous writer, in every sentence that he writes, will ask himself at least four questions, thus: What am I trying to say? What words will express it? What image or idiom will make it clearer? Is this image fresh enough to have an effect? And he will probably ask himself two more: Could I put it more shortly? Have I said anything that is unavoidably ugly?[i]

George Orwell

There is no more important element in the technique of rhetoric than the continual employment of the best possible word. . . .[ii]

Broadly speaking, the short words are best, and the old ones are the best of all.[iii]

Churchill, 'The Scaffolding of Rhetoric'

Editing is one of the hardest parts of the writing process. It is the time when we must wave goodbye to those beloved words and phrases that have become like friends and family to us over the preceding days or weeks. We must cut them away, often to replace them with no more than white space. But there is no room for compassion: we must ruthlessly remove anything that stands between our text and our audience's comprehension.

At the editing stage, much text will disappear or change dramatically. My rule of thumb is that a 5,000 word draft can easily be hacked into 1,500 words of pithy text: it is usually only on the fourth or fifth edit that the copy starts looking really lively. A good test can be to underline all the separate points in the text. Strong copy will usually contain around seven separate points every fifty words. Dull text might contain just three or four points across the same length. *The Economist* or the *New Yorker* are great examples of sharp writing. If it's not too scary, read your own speech alongside one of these magazines and compare.

If you find it really hard to delete your beloved words, you can always store the discarded sections somewhere else for safe keeping. I often do this, dumping everything I delete in a 'cutting room floor' file, which I check over at the very end, to see I haven't hacked out anything unmissable. I rarely have.

It is often best to leave a decent interval between writing and editing. It is then easier to see what sections should go, because you are viewing the text more dispassionately without recent memory of the time invested!

There are a few standard things to look out for when editing.

Bits to Cut

- Any repetitive or unnecessary sections. Many early drafts will, on inspection, be found to make the same point a number of different ways.
- Any hesitancies or qualifications, e.g. 'I think', 'I believe', 'it seems' and 'I am of the opinion that' are usually unnecessary: it is self-evident that the speaker believes or thinks them if he is saying them.
- Any unnecessary introductory phrases along the lines of, 'I

would like to tell you about' or 'let me begin by saying'. The audience knows you want to tell them this – that's what you are doing.

- Any sections where your pen has run away with you – excessive flourish or description. Remember the old adage: 'adverbs and adjectives rarely add anything'.

- Any sections which have been foisted on you by some bureaucratic part of your organization but which have little meaning or relevance for either speaker or audience.

- Any poor taste jokes. Trevor Phillips was forced to apologize after beginning a speech with a story about the Queen Mother's colostomy bag.

- Any potentially offensive sections. I have written many speeches on equality issues in the past. In equality, everything can offend someone. I was told that I could never just write about gay people, it always had to be 'lesbian, gay, bisexual and transgender people', so that no one felt excluded. I was also once told that I could not describe a speech to a women's group as a seminar because that word derived from 'semen'.

- Any sections that we have plagiarized or borrowed. The reason for this is simple. If our speaker is high-profile, we will get caught.

In 1988, Joe Biden, the current vice president of America gave a speech asking: 'Why is it that Joe Biden is the first in his family ever to go to a university? Why is it that my wife who is sitting out there in the audience is the first in her family to ever go to college? Is it because our fathers and mothers were not bright?' This was a great passage and would have made it straight into the speech anthologies had it not been an almost direct lift from a speech by Neil Kinnock years earlier: 'Why am I the first Kinnock in a thousand generations to be able to get to university? Why is Glenys the first woman in her family in a thousand generations to be able to get to university? Was it because all our predecessors were 'thick'?'[iv] Biden was forced to stand down from the race after the similarities were revealed.

More recently, in 2003, the Canadian prime minister, Stephen Harper, made a speech about Iraq: 'That is the ultimate nightmare which the world must take decisive and effective steps to prevent. Possession of chemical, biological or nuclear weapons by terrorists would constitute a direct, undeniable and lethal threat to the world, including to Canada and its people.' This was extraordinarily similar to a speech by John Keating, the Australian prime minister: 'That is the ultimate nightmare which the world must take decisive and effective steps to prevent. Possession of chemical, biological or nuclear weapons by terrorists would constitute a direct, undeniable and lethal threat to Australia and its people.' Harper's speechwriter was sacked afterwards.

Bits to Replace

- Jargon. The Local Government Association has created a list of 100 banned words that it is trying to purge from speeches and articles, including such gems as beacon, bottom up, cascading, contestability, framework, localities, multidisciplinary, pathfinder, risk based, subsidiarity, transformational and value added. Douglas Hurd created a banned list when he was Ted Heath's private secretary: it included words like productivity. Maybe your organization would benefit from a banned list?
- Long-winded sections, e.g. replace 'we are embarking on a process of engagement' with 'we are talking'.
- Over-ornate words, e.g. replace 'utilize' with 'use' and 'endeavour' with 'try'.
- Weasel words – so called because they suck the meaning out. Replace 'it is our intention to aim to strive towards' with 'we will' or, at worst, 'we aim to'.
- Badly organized sentences. Make sure sentences are built around strong verbs and conclude strongly (never end with a proposition, e.g. 'this is a crime he was guilty of').
- Any words which our speaker will struggle to read. George W. Bush said 'nucular' instead of nuclear; I once wrote for someone who said 'orff' instead of 'off' and someone else who pronounced 'data' to rhyme with 'garter'.
- Clichés or tired metaphors. Try to move beyond the first idea that came to your mind and opt for something with a little more sparkle and originality.
- Replace words you over-use with something more intriguing. We all have a proclivity to certain words. You can identify your own word demons by preparing a word cloud. Just paste your text in to www.wordle.net and the computer does the rest.

Bits to Improve

If we are being really fastidious, we could look hard at every word and ask if it is really the best we can use. Each word works on at least two levels: first, there is the literal meaning, i.e. what it denotes; then, there are the connotations, i.e. what it suggests. By selecting a word with suitable connotations and meaning, we create a double-barrelled weapon. For instance, when Tony Blair said that, 'nuclear power is on the agenda with a vengeance', he gave the issue character and drama, making it clear that he was not going to back down again.

Words with childhood connotations can subtly undermine opponents. For instance, by saying that they are doing things 'willy-nilly' or 'throwing their toys out of the pram', we subtly suggest that they are children and reinforcing the idea that we are adults. The famous, if sinister, 1970s book, *Games People Play*, argues that in any situation we play one of three roles – child, adult or parent. We should bear this in mind when we are making speeches. The speaker should never appear like the child.

A word's sound can also suggest different moods. When Trevor Phillips spoke about 'society sleepwalking to segregation', the susurration produced a soporific effect that perfectly supported the message. Generally, syllables based around the letters l, b, y, p and s are soft and soothing (e.g. 'of the people, by the people, for the people'). The letters k, g, t and d, meanwhile, are harder and more aggressive (e.g. when Churchill said 'blood, toil, tears and sweat', the repetition of the hard letter t sounded like shots from a gun). Of course, there are exceptions to these rules but they are worth considering. Branding experts are wise to these tricks, which is why so many brand names now have inoffensive sounds, like Olay. Only two of the world's top 100 brands are based around hard consonants – Nokia and IKEA, both Scandinavian companies where different rules apply. Even drug dealers seem wise to the sensitivities: crack cocaine is hard, whilst marijuana sounds soothing!

If we cannot find the right word, we can ask around – most people love being asked to help. Failing that, we can check a thesaurus. There are many wonderful pictorial thesauruses available online these days that will draw up all sorts of whizzy diagrams suggesting possible alternatives. If we *still* can't find the right word, perhaps we should make one up. It's a great way of generating press interest and giving our speaker a reputation for originality. Some of the options include:

- Building from a suffix. For instance, creating a '-gate' for a scandal (e.g. Drapergate); a '-mania' for a fad (e.g. Beatlemania); an '-ista' for a devotee (e.g. Cameronista); or a '-meister' for an expert (e.g. Spinmeister). We can turn a subject into an '-ology', a process into an '-ization', and a belief into an '-ism'.
- Building from a prefix. For instance, using an 'eco-' to indicate we're going green (e.g. eco-shopping), a 'cyber-' to show technological know-how (e.g. cyber-warfare), a 'Mc-' as

shorthand for cheap, mass produced, global products (e.g. McJobs, McMafia) and an 'uber-' to turn anything into a superlative (e.g. 'uber-competitive').

• Using word modifiers, like 'creep' (jargon creep), 'fascist' (health fascist) or 'porn' (eco porn').[v]

• Mixing two existing words, as Shakespeare did in Hamlet with 'climature' (a mix of climate and temperature) or George Harrison did in the Beatles' film, *Help*, when he said 'grotty' (a mix of grotesque and rotten).

Check the Argument Hangs Together

We should check the draft back against first principles to see if it is doing what was intended. Is the balance right – between logic and emotion, speaker and audience, depth and levity? What impressions, images and ideas linger? How can they be improved? Is the speech the right length (most speakers speak at around 120 words per minute, so a five-minute speech should be around 600 words)?

We should honestly assess whether the argument, as a whole, is stacking up. It is sometimes only by writing a speech that flaws in a policy are exposed. This was what happened in 1968 when Lyndon B. Johnson was writing a speech about Vietnam. The speech was supposed to announce more troops to Vietnam. But, as he went through draft after draft, he realized he just couldn't make the policy stack up; in the end, he changed the policy. The final speech announced the withdrawal of US troops and that he would not be seeking re-election as president.

Check the Style is Right

Our style should suit our speaker. Most speakers today have a plain, colloquial style of speaking, quite unlike the nineteenth century. This is partly a response to technological change. Radio, television and the Internet all brought speakers closer to their audiences meaning they need to be calmer and more conversational.

Our style should suit our content. For instance, if we are talking about simplifying regulations, we should use simple words. If we are talking about an emotional subject, the speech should have that jerky, forceful feel that is characteristic of emotional speaking.

Our style should suit the occasion. Speeches to Parliament should generally be sober, serious and statesmanlike, with careful, precise language and a deferential tone. Speeches to award ceremonies should be short, breathless and have the appearance of surprise and spontaneity (so it would be acceptable to go off on tangents, as this would create the illusion of authenticity). Speeches at product launches should be filled with enthusiasm and energy (so it would be OK to speak in a hyperbolic style). After dinner speeches should be long and winding, like a raconteur's tale, taking the assembled diners on a journey that helps their food go down gently.

Check the Speech with Colleagues

We should check our speech with colleagues, but without risking it suffering a death by a thousand cuts. President Eisenhower said: 'I used to write speeches for MacArthur . . . and one thing I know: if you put ten people to work on a speech, they'll kill anything in it that has any character.'[vi] As soon as you give way to committees, any sparks of originality vanish. The other possibility is that loads of people pile in asking you to refer to their pet projects. You need to resist most of these calls; otherwise you wind up with a shopping list, not a speech. Remain true to your original vision. As Steve Jobs says to his designers, 'Focus means saying no. Stay focused. Don't allow feature creep.' One of the most effective techniques I have used to clear a speech is to get all of the key advisers around the table at once, with everyone reading the draft together and sharing thoughts as they arise. This means problems are quickly identified and resolved. It also reduces the risk of people pursuing their own narrow agendas.

Working with the Speaker

Some speakers are not always forthcoming with meaningful feedback. William Waldegrave worked as a speechwriter to Ted Heath and told how one draft he submitted was returned with the simple comment: 'This will not do.' There was no further guidance to what was right or wrong![vii] We should fight to get them involved. In the days running up to a major speech, I will usually submit a new draft every evening so that the speaker can flick through it and twist a word here or a paragraph there. By ping-ponging the speech back and forth, the draft gets better and better.

Summary

- Editing is hard but you must be ruthless.
- Remove anything unnecessary, incomprehensible or dangerously offensive.
- Invest time finding the best possible word.
- Do a final check that the speech is fit for purpose.

Case Study

I began this chapter with a quote from Orwell, and I will end with one. These are his six rules for writing.

George Orwell's six rules for writing, from 'Politics and the English Language' (Horizon, vol. 13, no. 76, April 1946, pp. 252-65)

a) Never use a metaphor, simile or other figure of speech that you are used to seeing in print.

b) Never use a long word where a short one will do.

c) If it is possible to cut a word out, always cut it out.

d) Never use the passive where you can use the active.

e) Never use a foreign phrase, a scientific word or a jargon word if you can think of an everyday English equivalent.

f) Break any of these rules sooner than say something outright barbarous.

Chapter Eight

The Craft of Soundbites

It was amazing the cry that went up from the audience at this
remark! Wasn't it the rhythm of the words? Change the order
and nothing remains. . . .[1]

> Cicero, De Oratore

If you can't convince them, confuse them.

> Harry Truman

'Hug a hoody.' 'The people's princess.' 'Tough on crime, tough on
the causes of crime.' No sooner were these phrases uttered than
they entered the lexicon. Today, they can still be heard being
bandied around by pundits, politicians and the public alike in pubs,
parties and Parliament. Some phrases just have a phenomenal
ability to march into our heads and colonize our brains.

It is no accident. These phrases are based on simple rhetorical
figures that have been around for thousands of years. The Ancient
Greeks called them *schemata lekseos*. The Ancient Romans called
them *figurae elocutionis*. Now, these rhetorical devices can be found
in newspaper headlines, advertising copy and campaigning
slogans. They are part of our culture. We instinctively use them
whenever we are talking about anything that matters. Cab drivers,

polemicists and barstool preachers litter their speech with rhetorical devices unconsciously. We need to transfer these tricks from the personal to the professional. This chapter shows you how to do that.

Some principles about using rhetorical figures:

First, work on them carefully. These are the sections of our speech that the audience will notice, the press will report and people will remember. We should therefore work on them far more carefully than the other sections of the speech. It took two years, several pens and dozens of formulations before John F. Kennedy finally settled on the legendary, 'Ask not what your country can do for you, ask what you can do for your country.'

Second, different speakers prefer different rhetorical tricks. George W. Bush loved contrast: 'We want him dead or alive'; 'You're either with us or you're against us'. Gordon Brown had a penchant for alliterative pairs: 'boom and bust'; 'listen and learn'; 'challenge and change'. Nick Clegg is wont to using contrast: 'The more they talk, the more they sound the same.' We should get to know our speaker's favourite soundbites and supply him with formulations that fit. If a phrase does not sound natural for him, it will damage his credibility.

Third, our rhetorical device should support our aim. Rhetorical devices are mimetic and can be used to subtly support our argument. Quintillian said: 'It is as ridiculous to hunt for [rhetorical] figures without reference to the matter in hand as it is to discuss dress and gesture without reference to the body.' For instance, if we want to suggest our argument is so simple a child could understand it, we might use a childlike rhyme, e.g. 'If you can't do the time, don't do the crime', 'If the glove don't fit, you must acquit' or 'It's my way or the highway.'

Fourth, only use rhetorical figures sparingly. The more rhetorical devices are wielded, the more their power wanes. What's more, you risk inadvertently creating the impression your speech is all spin and no substance.

Whilst researching this book, it has become clear that different

rhetorical devices achieve different effects. Rhetorical devices that have a strong logical structure (such as contrast and the rule of three) can help support the impression of a logical argument. Those rhetorical devices that purport to provide an insight into the speaker's state of mind (such as repetition, imagery or asyndeton) can help support emotional arguments. Rhetorical devices that seem to emerge from deep within the speaker (such as personal statements) can help support arguments from character.

Rhetorical Devices That Advance Logical Arguments (Logos)

These include some of the best-known rhetorical devices such as contrast, the rule of three and question/answer formulations. The logical structure creates the illusion of logic in the argument. This technique can therefore conceal all sorts of wicked fallacies.

Contrasts work on a number of levels. We naturally understand things in twos.[ii] We naturally define things in relationship to what they are not.[iii] And our senses are naturally heightened when faced with symmetrical form.[iv] So, the key for us as speechwriters is to find points of contrast, comparison or conflict rather than simply stating a one-dimensional point of view.

We can create an outright contrast between two opposites (antithesis):

- 'To be or not to be.' (Shakespeare)
- 'You're either with us or you're against us.' (George W. Bush)
- 'Where there is discord, may we bring harmony.' (Thatcher)

We can make comparisons:

- 'One small step for man – one giant leap for mankind.' (Neil Armstrong)
- 'Twice as fast at half the price.' (Steve Jobs on the iPhone)
- 'The death of one man is a tragedy; the death of a million is a statistic.' (Josef Stalin)
- 'The masses are more likely to fall victim to a big lie than a small one.' (Adolf Hitler)
- 'Aggression anywhere in the world is a threat to peace everywhere in the world.' (George W. Bush)

We can state what our position is not, before correctly saying our real position (*correctio*):

- 'This is not the end. It is not even the beginning of the end. But it is perhaps the end of the beginning.' (Winston Churchill)
- 'Not Flash. Just Gordon.' (Labour Party slogan)
- 'If you can't make it good, at least make it look good.' (Bill Gates)

We can create a phrase reversal (*chiasmus*):

- 'The government of business is not the business of government.' (Nigel Lawson)
- 'He would, wouldn't he.' (Mandy Rice Davis)
- 'Fair is foul and foul is fair.' (Macbeth)

Or we can develop a soundbite where each half is of equal length:

- 'Science without religion is lame, religion without science is blind.' (Einstein)
- 'If you want anything said, ask a man. If you want anything done, ask a woman.' (Thatcher)
- 'What's mine is yours, what's yours is mine.' (Anon)

There are a few general rules about comparing and contrasting.

The shorter the sentence, the more powerful it will be, like bullets firing out of a gun:

- 'Dead or alive.' (George W. Bush)
- 'Put up or shut up.' (John Major)
- 'In office, not in power.' (Norman Lamont)

The longer the soundbite, the greater the impression of grandeur:

- 'Liberty without learning is always in peril. Learning without liberty is always in vain.' (John F. Kennedy)
- 'The government of the United States is not the champion of freedom, but the perpetuator of exploitation and oppression.' (Che Guevara)

The symmetry of the structure can also conceal a tautology:

- 'We must succeed or else we fail.'

Rhyming contrasts enhance this effect, creating an even greater illusion of simplicity:

- 'Thrive, not just survive.' (Tony Blair)

As does an element of repetition:

- 'There can be no whitewash at the White House.' (Richard Nixon)

The rule of three (tricolon) leaves an impression of finality. The rule of three can involve an element of repetition: 'One realm, one people, one leader' (Hitler). Sometimes, it can be based upon repetition of a single word (known as *epizeuxis*), e.g. 'Education. Education. Education.' (Tony Blair). It also features in comedy, 'Englishman, Irishman, Scotsman' or 'Infamy! Infamy! They've all got it in for me!' The rule of three also often opens speeches, most famously with Marc Antony's 'Friends, Romans, Countrymen' and Obama's inaugural address: 'I stand here today humbled by the task before us, grateful for the trust you have bestowed, mindful of the sacrifices borne by our ancestors.'

Puzzle/solution formulations are two-part dramatic constructions. They can sound a bit pantomime-like so tend to suit more thespian-style speakers. The first part of the construction poses a puzzle (implicit or explicit), whilst the second provides resolution, e.g. 'Are we going to stand for this? Like hell we are.' Margaret Thatcher was a great fan of this technique, as three of her most famous quotes demonstrate:

- 'The Russians said I was an Iron Lady. They were right. Britain needs an Iron Lady.'
- 'There is no such thing as society. There are individual men and women. And there are families.'
- 'To those waiting with bated breath for that favourite media catchphrase, the u-turn, I have only one thing to say: You turn if you want to. The lady's not for turning.'

Peter Mandelson imitated Thatcher's style in his 2009 Labour Party conference speech: 'Tony said our project would only be complete when the Labour Party had learned to love Peter Mandelson. I think perhaps he set the bar too high. Though I am trying my best.'

Churchill used this style to show his power: '[The French] told their prime minister, "In three weeks, England will have her neck wrung like a chicken." Some chicken! Some neck!' Bevan used it to create humour: 'This island is made mainly of coal and surrounded by fish. Only an organising genius could produce a shortage of coal and fish at the same time' and 'Well, we know what happens to people who stay in the middle of the road. They get run over.'

Alliteration implies a natural connection between the alliterated words. It often features in campaign slogans, e.g.

- 'Power to the People.'
- 'Black is Beautiful.'
- 'Ban the Bomb.'

Alliterative pairs have also produced titles for many famous speeches, including:

- 'The bullet or the ballot.' (Malcolm X)
- 'The People's Princess.' (Blair)
- 'Hug a Hoody.' (Cameron)

In the nineteenth-century campaign against slavery, William Wilberforce spoke of slavery's 'brutishness and barbarity' whilst Pitt the Younger described it as an 'incurable injustice'. Alliteration can also be used to build a rhythm, e.g. 'pay any price, bear any burden' (J.F.K.).

Rhymes convey an illusion of simplicity:

- 'All the way with L.B.J.' (The Democratic Party)
- 'Coal, not dole.' (The Miners)
- 'Fight for the right to party.' (The Ravers)

- 'If you can't do the time, don't do the crime.' (Anon)
- 'If the glove don't fit, you must acquit.' (Jonny Cochran)

Rhetorical Devices That Advance Emotional Arguments (Pathos)

The second group of rhetorical devices provide an insight, or purport to provide an insight, into our speaker's state of mind. These techniques are best used to provoke emotional reactions because the speaker is usually the chief mood-maker within the room and his mood can prove infectious. These devices are mostly based upon stylistic techniques.

Repetition is self-explanatory. It creates the impression that the speaker is utterly fixated on the matter in hand. The word or clause that is repeated should be the most important point in the sentence, the one we want to emphasize. Often, it will be a verb. The repeated section can feature at the beginning or end of the sentence.

Anaphora is when the repeated section appears at the beginning of the sentence or successive phrases. It works particularly well at the beginning if the speaker wants to emphasize that he is the main protagonist, e.g. 'We shall fight on the beaches. We shall fight on the landing grounds. We shall fight in the fields and in the streets. We shall fight in the hills. We shall never surrender' (Churchill). Or Martin Luther King's:

I have a dream that one day on the red hills of Georgia the sons of former slaves and the sons of former slave owners will be able to sit down together at the table of brotherhood. I have a dream that one day even the state of Mississippi, a desert state sweltering with the heat of injustice and oppression, will be transformed into an oasis of freedom and justice. I have a dream that my four little children will one day live in a nation where they will not be judged by the colour of their skin but by the content of their character.

Epistrophe is when the repeated sections feature at the end of successive phrases. This works best when the speaker wishes to appear passive or powerless, as in the following examples:

- 'The white man sent you to Korea, you bled. He sent you to Germany, you bled. He sent you to the South Pacific to fight the Japanese, you bled.' (Malcolm X)
- 'There is no negro problem. There is no Southern problem. There is no Northern problem. There is only an American problem.' (Lyndon B. Johnson)

Anadiplosis is when the repeated word or phrase features at the end of one sentence and the beginning of the next. This makes possibly unconnected events appear connected, e.g.:

- 'Isolation breeds insecurity. Insecurity breeds suspicion and fear. Suspicion and fear breed violence.' (Zbigniew Brzezinski)
- 'Get up, stand up. Stand up for your rights.' (Bob Marley)
- 'Fear leads to anger. Anger leads to hate. Hate leads to the dark side.' (Yoda in *Star Wars*)

There are other stylistic writing techniques which can convey particular emotions.

Asyndeton removes all connecting words, creating a sense of breathlessness. Examples include:

- '*Veni. Vidi. Vici.*' (Caesar)
- 'We shall pay any price, bear any burden, meet any hardships, support any friend, oppose any foe.' (John F. Kennedy)
- 'Kuwait was crushed. Its people brutalized.' (George W. Bush)

Polysndeton is the opposite technique, when unnecessary connecting words are introduced to deliberately slow the text down, creating the impression we have time on our hands.

Hyperbole demonstrates our speaker is so wildly enthusiastic that he has lost grasp of reason: 'National Socialism would not be worth anything if it . . . did not secure the rule of the superior race over the whole world for at least one or two thousand years.' (Hitler).

Enallage is deliberately muddling language to imply a disordered mind:

- 'It was the *Sun* wot won it.' (the *Sun*)
- 'You pays your money and you take your chances.' (Tony Blair)
- 'We woz robbed.' (Anon.)

We can *paint pictures* with metaphors, analogies or similes. This suggests that our speaker's imagination has been sparked:

- 'The kaleidoscope has been shaken. The pieces are all in flux. Soon they will settle again.' (Blair)
- 'Suspicions amongst thoughts are like bats amongst birds.' (Francis Bacon)
- 'If I have seen further than others, it is by standing on the shoulders of giants.' (Isaac Newton)

Rhetorical Devices that Advance Arguments from Character (Ethos)

The third group of rhetorical devices seem to provide an insight into the character of the speaker; in other words, they establish ethos.

A simple truth that is based around plain monosyllabic language suggests our speaker sees things in a strikingly straightforward manner, e.g:

- 'They said this day would never come.' (Obama)
- 'In the name of God! Go!' (Cromwell)
- 'This is it.' (Michael Jackson)
- 'Peace for our time.' (Chamberlain)

A deeply *personal statement* which goes beyond cultural norms suggests the speaker attaches great passion to the issue, for example, when John Prescott apologized to the Labour Party conference after a sex scandal: 'In the last year I've let myself down. I've let you down.' Or when Nelson Mandela said: 'It is an ideal which I hope to live for, and to see realized. But my Lord, if needs be, it is an ideal for which I am prepared to die.' Or when Edward VIII confessed: 'I have found it impossible to carry the heavy burden of responsibility and to discharge my duties as King without the help and support of the woman I love.' Or when Neville Chamberlain said: 'You can imagine what a bitter blow it is to me that all my long struggle to win peace has failed.'

Twisting clichés makes a speaker sound lively, a slightly non-conformist character, e.g:

- 'Cool Britannia.' (New Labour)
- 'The Queen of People's Hearts.' (Princess Diana)

Summary

- Rhetorical devices highlight important parts of the speech.
- Different rhetorical devices produce different effects.
- Contrast and the rule of three support logical arguments; repetition and hyperbole support emotional arguments; plain, simple truths support character arguments.
- Rhetorical devices should only be used sparingly or their impact is reduced.

Case Study

I have selected David Cameron's 2009 speech to the Conservative Party conference to illustrate the techniques in this chapter. Cameron has a gift for soundbites and this was one of his most important speeches: the last before a general election, the pressure on to prove his readiness to become prime minister.

Edited extract of David Cameron's speech to the Conservative Party conference, 8 October 2009

We all know how bad things are, massive debt, social breakdown, political disenchantment. But I want to talk about how good things could be. There is a steep climb ahead. But the view from the summit will be worth it.

When I stood on that stage in Blackpool four years ago it wasn't just to head up this party. It was to lead this party and change it. Look what we've done. More women candidates, campaigning on the environment, the party of the NHS.

But for me and Samantha this year will only ever mean one thing. When such a big part of your life suddenly ends nothing else matters. It's like the clocks have stopped ticking. And as they slowly start again, weeks later, you ask yourself: do I really want to do this?

I love this country and the things it stands for. That the state is your servant, never your master. That there is such a thing as society; it's just not the same thing as the state. That there is a 'we' in politics, and not just a 'me'. This is my DNA: family, community, country. They are what I'm in public service to protect, promote and defend.

There are children growing up in Britain today who will never know the love of a father. Children who will never start a business, never raise a family, never see the world. Children who will live the life they're given, not the life they want. I want every child to have the chances I had. But we won't help anyone unless we face up to some big problems. The highest budget deficit since the war. The deepest recession since the war. Social breakdown. Political disillusionment.

Labour say that to solve the country's problems, we need more government. It is more government that got us into this mess. Why is our economy broken? Because government got too big, spent too much and doubled the national debt.

Why is our society broken? Because government got too big. Why are our politics broken? Because government got too big. Not everything Labour did was wrong. Devolution; the minimum wage; civil partnerships. These are good things that we will keep.

But this idea that for every problem there's a government solution, for every issue an initiative, for every situation a czar.... It ends with them making you register with the government to help out your child's football team. With police officers punished for babysitting each other's children. With laws so bureaucratic and complicated even their own Attorney General can't obey them.

We are not going to solve our problems with bigger government. We are going to solve our problems with a stronger society. Stronger families. Stronger communities. A stronger country. In that fight, there's one person this party can rely n. He's the man who has dedicated himself to the cause of social justice, Iain Duncan Smith.

The clearest sign of big government irresponsibility is the enormous size of our debt. The longer we leave it, the worse it will be. The longer we wait for a credible plan, the bigger the bill. The longer we wait, the greater the risk to the recovery. The longer we wait, the higher the chance we return to recession. The more we wait, the more we waste on the interest we're paying on this debt.

Next year, Gordon Brown will spend more money on interest than on schools. The progressive thing to do is to get a grip on the debt. Cutting back on big government is not just about spending less. Getting our debt down means getting our economic growth up. Let's be clear where growth will come from. Not big government, but new businesses, new industries, new technologies.

I get enterprise. I worked in business for seven years. Self-belief is infectious and I want it to spread again throughout our country. In Britain today, there are entrepreneurs everywhere – they just don't know it yet.

Britain is a great place to live. But there is a dark side as well. Poverty, crime, addiction. Failing schools. Sink estates. Broken homes. It's not just that big government has failed to solve these problems. Big government has all too often helped cause them. Just think of the signals we send out. To the family struggling to raise children: 'Stay together and we'll give you less; split up and we give you more.' To the young mum working part time, trying to earn something extra for her family: 'From every extra pound you earn we'll take back 96 pence.' Thirty years ago this party won an election fighting against ninety-eight per cent tax rates on the richest. Today I want us to show even more anger about ninety-six per cent tax rates on the poorest.

Labour still think that they are the ones who will fight poverty. When we announced our plan to Get Britain Working you know what Labour called it? 'Callous.' Excuse me? Who made the poorest poorer? Who left youth unemployment higher? Who made inequality greater? No, not the wicked Tories . . . you, Labour. You're the ones that did this to our society. So don't you dare lecture us about poverty. You have failed and it falls to us, the modern Conservative Party to fight for the poorest who you have let down.

Society begins at home. Responsibility starts at home. It's about what we all do. It's about our culture. And it's about our society. We give our children more and more rights, and we trust our teachers less and less. We've got to stop treating children like adults and adults like children. The more that we as a society do, the less we will need government to do. There are 2 million children in Britain growing up in homes where no one works. We have got to turn it around. If you really cannot work, we'll look after you. But if you can work, you should work and not live off the hard work of others.

My family owes so much to the National Health Service. When you're carrying your child to A and E in the middle of the night and don't have to reach for your wallet it's a lot better than the alternative.

We will never change the idea at the heart of our NHS. But that doesn't mean the NHS shouldn't change. It has to change because for many people, the service isn't good enough.

The fault lies with big government. Labour have tried to run the NHS like a machine. But it's not a machine full of cogs. It is a living, breathing institution made up of people – doctors, nurses, patients.

We're going to give the NHS back to people. That's why we can say this is the party of the NHS now, today, tomorrow, always.

The instinct to protect the people we love is so strong. Nearly two years ago it was that instinct that drove Fiona Pilkington to do something desperate. When I first read her story in the paper I found it difficult to finish the article. It's one of the saddest things I've ever read. It is about a breakdown of all the things that are meant to keep us safe. A breakdown of morality in the minds of those thugs. A breakdown in community where a neighbour is left to utter misery. And a breakdown of our criminal justice system. Every part of it, the police, the prosecution services, the prisons . . . is failing under the weight of big government targets and bureaucracy.

We cannot rebuild social responsibility from on high. But the least we can do, the least we can do, is pledge that a Conservative government, will reform the police, reform the courts, reform prisons.

To build a responsible society we need to teach our children properly. I come at education as a parent, not a politician. When I watch my daughter skip across the playground to start her first term in year one, I want to know that every penny of the education budget is following her. But it's not just about money. It's about values.

Family, community, country. In recent years we've been hearing things about our country we haven't heard for a long time. Britishness is not mechanical, it's organic. It's an emotional connection to a way of life, an attitude, a set of institutions. Make these stronger and our national identity becomes stronger.

We don't care who you are or where you're from, if you've got something to offer then this is a place you can call home. To be British is to be generous. To be British is to be sceptical. To be British is to have an instinctive love of the countryside.

But if you care about our country, you've got to care about the health of our institutions. Our parliament used to be a beacon to the world. The expenses scandal made it a laughing stock. We apologized to the public, paid back the money and published all our expenses online.

It's your community and you should have control over it. It's your money and you should know what's being done with it. It's your life and the people who make political decisions should answer to you.

But this is not over. We need to redistribute power.

Family, community, country. The problems we face are big and urgent.

Rebuilding our broken economy ... because unless we do, our children will be saddled with debt for decades to come. Mending our broken society ... because unless we do, we will never solve those stubborn social problems that cause the size of government to rise. Fixing our broken politics ... because unless we do, we will never reform public services ... never see the strong, powerful citizens ... who will build the responsible society that we all want to see.

You can never prove you're ready for everything that will come your way as prime minister. I've seen what happens when you waste your mandate obsessing about the twenty-four hour news cycle. That was Blair. And I've seen what happens when you turn every decision into a political calculation. That was Brown.

So I won't promise things I cannot deliver. But I can tell you that in a Conservative Britain: if you put in the effort to bring in a wage, you will be better off; if you save money your whole life, you'll be rewarded; if you start your own business, we'll be right behind you; if you want to raise a family, we'll support you; if you're frightened, we'll protect you; if you risk your safety to stop a crime, we'll stand by you; if you risk your life to fight for your country, we will honour you.

We will reward those who take responsibility, and care for those who can't. So if we cut big government back and rebuild responsibility, then we can put Britain back on her feet. Yes it will be a steep climb. But the view from the summit will be worth it. Let me tell you what I can see. I see a country where more children grow up with security and love. I see a country where communities govern themselves. I see a country with entrepreneurs everywhere, bringing their ideas to life. I see a country where it's not just about the quantity of money, but the quality of life. I see a country where you're not so afraid to walk home alone. I see a country where the poorest children go to the best schools not the worst, where birth is never a barrier.

No, we will not make it if we pull in different directions. But if we pull together, come together, work together – we will get through this together.

And when we look back we will say not that the government made it happen . . .

. . . not that the minister made it happen . . .

. . . but the businesswoman made it happen . . .

. . . the police officer made it happen . . .

. . . the father made it happen . . .

. . . the teacher made it happen.

You made it happen.

Analysis

David Cameron's speeches are stuffed to the brim with rhetorical devices but they are used with purpose. He seems to have a regular five-step sequence for constructing arguments.

Step One: Description

When he is unpacking an issue, David Cameron uses the rhetorical device of asyndeton, combined with the rule of three:

- 'Massive debt, social breakdown, political disenchantment.'
- 'Failing schools. Sink Estates. Broken homes.'
- 'Poverty, crime, addiction.'

He uses the same combination when he wants to convey the impression of pace:

- 'More women candidates, campaigning on the environment, the party of the NHS.'
- 'Devolution, the minimum wage, civil partnerships.'

Sometimes he adds repetition or alliteration:

- 'New businesses, new industries, new technologies'; 'the police, the prosecution services, the prisons'.
- 'For every problem, there's a government solution; for every issue, an initiative, for every situation, a czar.'
- 'It's your character, your temperament and your judgement.'
- 'If we pull together, come together, work together.'
- 'Stronger families. Stronger communities. A stronger country.'

He also tends to follow Mark Antony's example of starting his three at the most local or personal point ('Friends, Romans, Countrymen') and building out from there ('Families. Communities. Country').

Step Two: Show emotion
David Cameron uses repetition to demonstrate strength of feeling:

- 'There are children growing up in Britain who will never know the love of a father. Children who will never start a business. Children who will live the life they're given, not the life they want';
- 'Why is our economy broken? Because government got too big. . . Why is our society broken? Because government got too big. . . Why are our politics broken? Because government got too big. . . .'
- 'Who made the poorest poorer? Who left youth unemployment higher? Who made inequality greater?'
- 'It's your community and you should have control over it. . . . It's your money and you should know what is being done with it. It's your life and the people who make political decisions should answer to you.'
- 'To be British is to be generous. To be British is to be sceptical. To be British is to have an instinctive love of the countryside.'

This use of repetition makes it feel as if he's thumping his fist on the lectern with every repetition.

He is not afraid to make deeply personal statements that provide an insight into his emotional state:

- 'For me and Samantha this year will only ever mean one thing. When such a big part of your life suddenly ends nothing else matters. It's like the world has stopped turning and the clocks have stopped ticking.'
- 'When you're carrying your child in your arms to Accident and Emergency in the middle of the night and don't have to reach for your wallet it's a lot better than the alternative.'
- 'When I first read [Fiona Pilkington's] story in the paper I found it difficult to finish the article. It's one of the saddest things I've ever read.'
- 'When I watch my daughter skip across the playground to start her first term in year one, I want to know that every penny of the education budget is following her. . . .'

The single largest burst of applause for the speech came after a fierce defence of Tory values, a defence that seemed to encapsulate Cameron's detoxification of the Tory brand: 'Don't you dare lecture us about poverty. You have failed and it falls to us, the modern Conservative Party to fight for the poorest who you have let down.'

Step Three: Establish logic
David Cameron builds logical arguments (or the impression of logical arguments) through the rhetorical device of contrast. The contrasts create the impression that he sees things very clearly, in polarized terms, and arrives at simple judgements:

- 'The state is your servant never your master. There is such a thing as society, it's just not the same thing as the state. There is a "we" in politics and not just a "me".'
- 'The longer we leave it, the worse it will be. The longer we wait, the bigger the bill. The more we wait, the more we waste.'
- 'We give our children more and more rights, and we trust our

teachers less and less. We've got to stop treating children like adults and adults like children. The more that we as a society do, the less we will need government to do.'

He occasionally constructs *question/answer* formulations, which inject some pantomime-like drama to the proceedings: 'In that fight, there's one person this party can rely on. He's the man who has dedicated himself to the cause of social justice ... Iain Duncan Smith.'

Step Four: Demonstrate character
To show his good character, Cameron uses metaphor and dialect.

He explicitly rejects the metaphor of 'government as machine', which he claims characterizes Labour's misguided approach. Instead, he opts for the metaphor of personalization:

- 'Labour have tried to run the NHS like a machine. But it's not a machine full of cogs. It is a living, breathing institution made up of people – doctors, nurses, patients.'
- 'Britishness is not mechanical, it's organic. It's an emotional connection to a way of life, an attitude, a set of institutions.'

Cameron's personalization metaphor spawned the title of the speech, 'Putting Britain back on her feet'.

He uses two other metaphors: 'Yes it will be a steep climb. But the view from the summit will be worth it.' The combination of journey and landscape metaphors activates memories of Obama and even the Messiah, particularly when combined with the quasi-religious dialect he occasionally lapses into:

Let me tell you what I can see. I see a country where more children grow up with security and love. I see a country where communities govern themselves. I see a country with entrepreneurs everywhere, bringing their ideas to life. I see a country where it's not just about the quantity of money, but the quality of life. I see a country where you're not so afraid to walk home alone. I see a country where the poorest children go to the best schools not the worst, where birth is never a barrier.

The following section also sounds very biblical:

If you put in the effort to bring in a wage, you will be better off. If you save money your whole life, you'll be rewarded. If you start your own business, we'll be right behind you. If you want to raise a family, we'll support you. If you're frightened, we'll protect you. If you risk your safety to stop a crime, we'll stand by you. If you risk your life to fight for your country, we will honour you.

Step Five: Conclude
David Cameron often concludes his arguments with a pithy, plain, punchy soundbite to indicate a simple truth:

- 'It's about everyone taking responsibility.'
- 'I get enterprise.'
- 'Time is short.'
- 'Society begins at home.'
- 'You made it happen.'

This is intended to show he is one of the people. And it works! Just like that!

Chapter Nine

The Craft of Media Manipulation

Politicians' speeches are not written for the audience to which they are delivered. Delivering the speech is merely the formality that has to be gone through in order to get the press release into the newspapers.

Yes, Minister (BBC TV)

There are three ways to get a newslead. Announce a new programme, make a prediction, set a goal.

President Eisenhower to his speechwriter, Hardesty[i]

In Ancient Greece, long before radio, television and the web, the only way a speaker could make the message in his speech extend beyond the audience in the room was by making his performances so dramatic and memorable that people felt compelled to tell others about it. That was the age of 'word of mouth' communication. Now it's all about 'word by mouse' communication. Web 2.0, YouTube and iPods have created previously unimaginable opportunities to extend the life, reach and depth of speeches. Instantaneous and infinite reproduction is possible in text, audio or video format for next to no cost.

This is great for people who produce speeches. It's also good news for people who watch speeches. Instead of being served up highlights in the news, we can now watch speeches at a time and place of our choosing, un-spun and unmediated, with footage that puts us right up close to the action. This accessibility is dramatically increasing the audience for speeches. Obama's presidential podcasts regularly pull in 7 million viewers. Dan Hannan MEP attracted 2 million viewers after a fierce speech in the European Parliament in March 2009 attacking Gordon Brown as 'the devalued prime minister of a devalued government'.[ii] The web is now the main auditorium for great speeches. FTSE companies broadcast annual report statements live on the web. Political parties have YouTube channels. But it's not just about disseminating current speeches. The web is also bringing old speeches back to life. Nine million people have watched Martin Luther King's 'I had a dream' speech on YouTube.

It is ironic. The mantra of most commentators is that technological advances have killed the speech but the opposite is true. Voice recognition makes it easier to write speeches than ever before, autocues make them easier to deliver and the web makes them easier to view. The US presidential libraries, historic Hansards and public records are all now available online. These are overwhelmingly positive developments for speechwriters, speechmakers and citizens but, of course, they have a downside. As a good speech can be disseminated wider and faster than ever, so a disastrous speech can shoot around the world in a flash. In fact, the horror videos tend to travel much faster, because this is what interests most YouTube viewers. A typical Gordon Brown speech only attracted a couple of hundred views whereas a million (yes, a million) have tuned in to watch a video of him surreptitiously picking his nose in the House of Commons. The more people watch a video, the higher it climbs up the rankings. New media is not as unmediated as some people claim: it's just it's the masses who do the mediating instead of the media – a much scarier prospect!

This chapter sets out ways to create speeches that meet the

challenging, changing climes of today's modern, multimedia environment. It is based on the view that there will be times when we will want the media to notice what we are doing and times when we won't. So, first, it looks at ways to attract the media spotlight, then it looks at ways to distract the media spotlight.

Ways to Attract the Media Spotlight

Step one: novelty
The first vital ingredient in a news story is novelty. That's why it's called news. There are a number of ways we can create a sense of novelty.

First, our speaker can say that he will do something new. We can publish a Green Paper, a White Paper or a general policy paper. We can say that we are writing a pamphlet, convening a meeting or conducting a review. We can announce an 'eye-catching initiative',[iii] a pilot scheme, or elaborate on previously unrevealed policy details.

We can instigate, publish or comment on research. We can announce new figures which either validate what we do or cast doubt over our opponents' positions. We can set a new target, announce progress on an existing target or declare that we have surpassed an old target. Activity is crucial. When Demosthenes was asked what makes a good orator, he replied, 'Action. Action. Action.'

If our speaker doesn't want to *do* something new, he can say that he *thinks* something new. Speeches are great for 'flying kites'. Because the speech is not quite as formal as a written publication, people are allowed slightly greater licence to drift beyond party lines than usual. In some ways, this is essential, because the speech comes fundamentally from the speaker, not his organization.

Some businesspeople, such as Sir Stephen Green and Sir Alan Sugar, have systematically used speeches to express personal views and establish a reputation that takes them beyond their corporate status, gaining a place on the national stage. Broadcasters such as Michael Grade and Dennis Potter have used speeches to float new and controversial ideas on the future of public-service broadcasting. Bill Gates, George Soros and Sir Alan Greenspan all used speeches to set out their thinking on the future direction of the global economy.

Politicians often use speeches as devices to shift thinking in their parties or departments. In the early years of New Labour, all the leading Blairites made major speeches, attacking the party's sacred cows. Charles Clarke, as Education Secretary, condemned medieval history degrees as 'ornamental'. Stephen Byers, as Industry Secretary, argued that, 'wealth creation is more important than wealth redistribution'. These speeches were well reported at the time because they represented significant shifts. It is through such speeches that attitudes are nudged, opinions revised and parties transformed.

David Cameron deployed a similar strategy with the Conservative Party, making some audacious speeches that repositioned his party on the economy, environment, crime and foreign affairs, cleansing them for a return to office. On the economy, he argued that

'GDP was not as important as GWB (general wellbeing)'. On the environment, he argued that the Conservatives were the party to offer 'sensible green leadership'. On crime, he said that 'hoodies deserve compassion'.[iv] On foreign policy, he declared that Britain needed a new 'solid, not slavish' relationship with America. To the grass roots, it was beyond the pale. But to the voters, i.e. the audience that mattered, it signalled the Tories' re-entry to the human race.

Speeches can also help jockey for personal power. Many of the rows between Blair and Brown were played out through speeches, on issues ranging from the euro to the extension of markets in public services. They used their speeches to send warnings to one another and blow dog whistles to their supporters. When David Miliband was a junior schools minister, he gave a series of low-key but significant speeches setting out a distinct view on the future of public services. The news pages didn't notice but the movers and shakers in the commentariat – who were carefully briefed – did. This meant that, when the time came, he naturally emerged as an obvious ideological opponent to Brown.

If we are not doing or thinking anything new, then we can always have our speaker *talk about something new*. Sometimes the very fact of addressing an issue is enough to create a story, especially when speakers reach beyond their comfort zones. In 2007, Tony Blair gave a lecture entitled, 'Faith and Globalization' in Westminster Cathedral.[v] The speech was instantly noteworthy because UK politicians do not generally talk about religion. This was more significant in Blair's case because Alastair Campbell had explicitly said, 'We don't do God.' Prince Charles also made news in the 1980s by describing the proposed extension to the National Gallery as 'a monstrous carbuncle on the face of a much loved and elegant friend'[vi] in his now-notorious speech to the Royal Institute of British Architects. This went far beyond royal protocols and the press jumped all over it. Bill Gates, Madonna, Angelina Jolie, Bob Geldof, Bono and Geri Halliwell have all also won lots of publicity for speaking outside of their usual areas.[vii] Every year, the World

Economic Forum carefully contrives some interesting combinations of speakers and issues.

We can speak in a new way, using new technologies. Every YouTube or iTunes or iPad first carries potential media interest, as with the Queen's first YouTube Christmas message or Obama's first presidential podcast. Stories about new technologies work particularly well when the speaker's message involves a 'modernization' theme, because the medium supports the message. That is why many cutting-edge companies actively seek out the latest technological wizardry for their presentations. In 2005, Richard Branson launched Virgin Digital by hologram. This kind of thing is great if it works, but if it goes wrong, it is game over. In my career, I've probably seen technology go wrong more times than I've seen it go right. I've seen slides go out of sync, satellite links crash, autocues fail and so on. I once saw a futurologist from BT give a presentation on their next generation product line; he could not get his opening video to play and spent ten minutes cursing his equipment. Ouch!

In my view, there's a lot to be said for going back to basics and making a virtue of traditional speaking, face to face, minus technology. This is what John Major did with his soapbox campaign in the 1992 general election. It's what many American presidential candidates have done with their 'whistle-stop tours'.[viii] And it's what David Cameron did when he cast aside the traditional teleprompter for his 'look-no-notes' speech to the Conservative conference in 2005.

Step two: scale

Scale is another important factor in generating press interest. One universally understood conceptual metaphor is that 'big is good' and 'more is better' so whatever we are doing should be the biggest, best or most on record. In this respect, inflation is a great friend. So too is the steady growth in national incomes. It means, for instance, that every year since 1948 has witnessed record spending on education, health and crime. Most years have also seen record spending in real terms. The 'big is good' metaphor presents a serious presentational dilemma for politicians who believe in a small state; David Cameron leaped this hurdle by talking about the 'big society'.

Even when something is not really the biggest, we can usually make it appear the biggest by carefully repositioning the parameters. We might not be the biggest employer in the world, but we might be the biggest IT employer in the borough. Hyperbole – even when the speaker deflates it – is normally understood and forgiven when it comes to rhetoric. In 2007, the iPhone launch was billed as the 'biggest product launch in the history of electronics'. I once heard a minister say, 'Britain is the best in the world for IT infrastructure – second only to America.' The audience, the company and the media will usually willingly co-conspire in hyperbole because everyone wants the event to appear worthwhile.

Although the usual metaphor is 'big is good', it is sometimes possible to construct an argument that 'less is more' and make it a virtue. We can, for instance, push the argument that crime is down, waiting lists are falling or the number of children being taken into care has tumbled. Likewise, if we are a company, our audience would welcome an announcement that prices are falling or that there are now fewer calories in our chocolate bar than ever before or that our mobile phones are now lighter than ever. Whether our direction is less or more, the essential factor for generating press interest is *scale*.

Step three: conflict

Conflict is another great device for grabbing the press's attention. All of the possible conflicts set out in Chapter Five, the Art of Story-telling (see page 137) represent reliable ways to grab the press's attention.

One of the most notorious ways for a beleaguered politician to grab a cheap headline is to pick a 'fight', usually with a group of people who are unlikely to respond. This technique is now so commonly recognized as the last resort of a desperate politician that it has featured repeatedly in political parodies: in *Yes Minister*, when Jim Hacker uses a speech attacking the European Community for banning the great British sausage to launch himself into Number Ten, even though they had never proposed any such thing; in *Wag the Dog*, when the president launches a war against Albania to distract from a sex scandal back home. Picking fights, particularly against people who are unpopular anyway, rarely does a speaker much harm. The media generally reward the speaker for giving them something entertaining to write about.

Step four: playing to the gallery

One of the easiest ways to get positive press coverage is to *pander to the press's prejudices*. There are several issues – less immigration, lower taxes, anti Europeanism – that a politician can comment on to practically guarantee favourable leader columns, attractive photos and widespread coverage. This is great for those prepared to play the game. Those who aren't or who express contrary views run the risk of serious criticism and personal attacks. It is no coincidence that the few ministers who spoke in favour of Britain joining the euro wound up on the receiving end of some vicious press reporting, including Steve Byers, Peter Mandelson and Keith Vaz.

Another option is to *jump on board a bandwagon*. Throughout his career, Richard Branson has expertly linked Virgin to the big story of the day on a number of occasions. When Concorde was going bust, reports circulated that he was ready to step in as 'white knight'. Similar stories appeared when Northern Rock went bust. Nothing came of it in both cases, but no harm was done: it was a good story and the public had been given hope, albeit fleetingly. Gordon Brown also tried to jump on media bandwagons, but without Branson's landing skills: he issued quotes on all sorts of television programmes from *Big Brother* to *Friday Night with Jonathan Ross* to *Britain's Got Talent*, winning press coverage, but at the expense of his credibility.

The best way to minimize the risk of becoming a 'Billy Bandwagon' is only to intervene in those areas where there is a legitimate link with your own interests, so you don't seem exploitative. This is arguably the difference between Branson's successful interventions and Brown's relative failures. No one could credibly believe that Gordon Brown was watching Big Brother, but the idea of Branson bidding for Concorde was not so far-fetched. There is also a large difference between the levels of media scrutiny to which politicians and businesspeople are subjected.

Ways to Avoid the Media Spotlight

We will not always be looking to attract the media's attention. Just as often, we will look to close a story down. To achieve this, we should deploy the opposite strategies from those used to attract the press's attention. So instead of saying something is new and significant, we say the opposite, namely:

a)   This is nothing new – e.g. 'We've already dealt with this issue thoroughly and there's no point going over old ground.' 'We should draw a line under this.'

b)   This is insignificant – e.g. 'This only affects a very small number of people.' 'This has happened a number of times in the past.'

c)   There is nothing of interest here – e.g. 'No one cares about this issue.' 'What people really care about is jobs, the economy etc. . . .'

We can *be boring*. Harold Wilson once urged his advisers to 'Never underestimate the value of boredom as a political device.' It was said that he went through his speeches deliberately striking out any rhetorical flourishes. Alistair Darling's modest manner also successfully diffused press interest in some red-hot political issues like pensions and transport. Most of the time, he was simply too dull to report.

We can *play for time*. We can say that it is premature, too late or simply untimely to comment. If this doesn't work, announcing an inquiry or review will usually kick most issues into the long grass.

We can *create a deflective source*. As chancellor, Gordon Brown oversaw reviews by Lords Leitch, Turner and Stern into skills, pensions and climate change. By outsourcing responsibility for thinking about these issues, he took heat away from the government both whilst the report was being prepared and subsequently.

We can *shut down the issue*, drawing on timeless excuses such as: 'We're not providing a running commentary'; 'We need to draw a line under this'; 'We can't comment on leaked documents' or 'We can't talk about security issues.'

We can go on *the attack*, aiming fire at our critics ('the person who said this is bitter'), the press ('we've come to expect this sort of questioning from the *Daily Mail*), the line of questioning ('the real issue is …'), the supporting information ('this report is flawed'), the facts ('it's a myth') or the culture that allows such questions to be asked ('it's a shame that the press insist on reducing these issues to personalities').

We can also *be disarmingly open*. When we are being hunted down, sometimes the best strategy is to turn around and face our critics. We can concede errors, acknowledge failings or even apologize, e.g. 'I admit we might have been wrong on Iraq'; 'This has not been the best week ever for the Labour Party'; 'You're right, we haven't done as well as we could have done'; 'There's a lot to this job, and as you saw yesterday, I don't get all of it right'. A *mea culpa* tends to surprise journalists, who are so used to handling ultra-defensive targets they do not quite know how to respond. We shouldn't over-use this strategy though. If we do, there is a danger that we just look incompetent.

Channels and Timing

We should also think about the timing of the story. The best-planned speeches are often briefed on a drip-drip basis, building up a sense of momentum ahead of, during and after the speech. So, instead of pushing all the information out at once, we lead the press through a journey from, 'Next week, X is likely to use his speech to …' to, 'Tomorrow, X is expected to say. . . .' to 'Later today, X will say …' and 'Earlier today, X said …' By releasing the story in chunks, we control the reporting whilst minimizing opportunities for our opponents to steal a march. Handled in the right way, a major speech can get as much as eight days solid coverage, from one Sunday to the next. However, there are risks to pre-briefing, particularly if we are planning to give our audience a hard time. Our speaker will be guaranteed a hostile reception if the audience has already read in the paper that he is to issue them a 'stern rebuke'.

We should also consider how to extend the life of the speech, using additional channels to disseminate our messages to a wider, targeted audience. Many speakers now tweet links to their speeches. We could send extracts to a specialist trade magazine. I recently visited the Department of Business's headquarters in Westminster and saw an electronic display in the foyer transmitting the headline from a speech being given that day by Peter Mandelson in Brazil. This kept staff and visitors bang up to date with the Secretary of State's activities.

More and more speakers are now putting their speeches on YouTube, but this can be overdone. There seems to be a view that, because Generation X watches YouTube, Generation X watches every video that is posted. But this 'pile 'em high, sell 'em cheap' strategy has in some cases led to videos only being seen by a few dozen people, which isn't great value.

We should also think about sending our speech to the commentators: this is unlikely to generate headlines but it can encourage a steady shift of opinion. It's also worth getting to know some journalists, if only because there is a revolving door between journalism and speechwriting: Matthew Parris and Philip Collins of the Times are both ex-speechwriters to prime ministers, whilst Michael Lea, formerly of the *Daily Mail* and the *Sun*, went on to become a chief writer at Number Ten.

Finally, it is not the end of the world if our speech does not get coverage. The truth is that most speeches don't get reported, even truly momentous ones. In May 1803, William Pitt made a speech to the House of Commons about a feared French invasion. This historic speech at this historic moment was not reported anywhere because no journalists were present in the gallery to report.[ix] The truth is that, most of the time, what goes on in Parliament stays in Parliament. As Enoch Powell once remarked, the best way to keep a state secret is to announce it on the floor of the House of Commons.[x]

Summary

- The press demands things that are new.
- The press demands scale.
- The press demands conflict.
- To distract the press, we should show that a story is old and insignificant.
- There are other techniques for distracting the press – being boring, playing for time, creating a deflective source, shutting down the issue, going on the attack or being disarmingly open.

Case study

I have selected Gordon Brown's 2009 speech to the Trades Union Congress to illustrate the techniques in this chapter. This speech was a masterpiece of media manipulation. Brown's position at the time was precarious, his leadership under threat. In his speech, he had to send diametrically opposing messages to the audience inside and outside the room. He had to show the unions that he was committed to public investment, whilst showing the press that he was committed to cuts.

He pulled off the trick with dexterity. The union delegates in the room gave him a standing ovation, convinced they had heard Brown mount a passionate defence of public services. But all the following day's papers ran the opposite line: 'Brown tells TUC – public spending cuts are coming' (*Independent*); ' "We will make cuts," Brown tells TUC' (BBC); 'Gordon Brown faces up to reality on cash cuts' (the *Mirror*); 'A first step towards honesty over cuts' (*Daily Mail*); 'Cuts will be required, admits Brown' (*Daily Express*); 'Gordon Brown finally admits cuts are necessary' (*Daily Telegraph*); 'Gordon Brown says "C" word for first time' (the *Sun*). The *Sun* even captioned Brown's picture with: 'PM . . . set to upset trade unions.'

So how did he convey such conflicting messages from one single speech? He did it by blowing a 'dog whistle', a message that the press heard loud and clear because they were listening out for it, but which the audience in the room missed completely because it had been deliberately smothered with padding.

Here is an edited version of the speech.

Edited extract of Gordon Brown's speech to the TUC in Liverpool, 15 September 2009
Around this time last year, a financial crisis was rolling over the Atlantic towards us.

I knew then that it was going to have to be us, the government, that was going to have to step in directly.

We had to make a big choice: whether to trust the banks or address structural failures.

We had another big choice: to leave the markets to sort it out or to intervene with radical and unprecedented action.

We made the decision to offer financial support to businesses and to help homeowners and the unemployed.

I'll tell you why: because every redundancy is a personal tragedy. Every mortgage repossession is a hope destroyed. Every business collapse is someone's dream in ruins.

We will not walk by on the other side.

Over 200,000 businesses employing hundreds of thousands have been able to keep people in work.

Twenty-two million people have benefited from tax and other changes.

500,000 jobs have been saved.

We have helped 300,000 families with advice with their mortgages.

At no time in our history have we, the British people, done so much to support our homeowners, businesses and the unemployed. This didn't happen by default, but by our decisions.

We still have a choice to make.

Whether we continue to act to help families and businesses or whether we listen to the Tories and withdraw support from families and businesses, cut public services now, and refuse to invest in Britain's future.

If I were to take the advice of our Conservative opponents, I would stop the school leavers guarantee that is giving 55,000 young people a chance of work experience or further education.

I would withdraw the support now available to homeowners, and do nothing to prevent repossessions rising to the rates of the 1990s.

This is not the moment to cut apprenticeships. We will provide 21,000 additional apprenticeships.

This is not the moment to withdraw public support for house-building. We have set aside £1.5 billion to build 20,000 additional affordable homes.

This is not the moment to abandon the help that has kept over 200,000 businesses afloat. This is the time to continue it.

We do this because it's right to help people but also because it's right for the economy.

Because the more jobs and homes we lose now, the higher

unemployment rises, the lower growth is, and the more difficult it will be to secure our recovery, bring our debt down, and keep people in their jobs and homes.

Growth is the best antidote to debt.

Take the National Health Service.

We are now offering personal guarantees to patients about waiting times.

While the Tories want to abandon these guarantees, we are trying to ensure that patients get treatment earlier.

We have given guarantees to everyone worried about cancer. While the Tories want to deny that right, we are making it easier for cancer patients to be treated with speed.

We have given guarantees about GP services that there will be weekend and evening opening. While the Tories want to leave GPs to do exactly as they want, we will ensure that this new right is extended to even more communities.

We will guarantee that every young person will have the right to education not to sixteen but to eighteen.

Previously the only way to get personal tuition was to pay. Now we are extending the right – not through private tuition but free individual tuition.

We will do all these things and more, because we believe that decent education, health and services should be available to not just some, but all of our people.

But we can only make these improvements within a framework of sustainable finances.

That's why we will raise national insurance by 0.5 per cent.

That's why we will remove unfair tax reliefs on higher earners.

That's why we will raise the top rate of tax to 50p for those on the very highest incomes.

We are doing the right thing to make sure that for the future, as we move into a full recovery, we invest and grow within public finances that are sustainable – cutting costs where we can, ensuring efficiency where it's needed, agreeing realistic public sector pay settlements throughout, selling off the unproductive assets we don't need to pay for the services we do need.

Labour will cut costs, cut inefficiencies, cut unnecessary programmes and cut lower priority budgets.

But when our plans are published in the coming months people will see that Labour will not support cuts in the vital front line services on which people depend.

The choice is between Labour who will not put the recovery at risk, protect and improve your front-line services first and make the right choices for low- and middle-income families.

Against a Conservative Party that would reduce public services now and immediately at the very time they are needed most.

Analysis of the speech

The only line the press heard in this speech was, 'Labour will cut costs, cut inefficiencies, cut unnecessary programmes and cut lower priority budgets.' That was the dog whistle. So, how did he make it work?

First, he ensured that they were perfectly primed. The issue of the previous weeks had been, 'Will Brown use the c-word?' With hindsight, this was an issue that Brown had – perhaps deliberately – created. He repeatedly refused to use the c-word, rejecting the opportunity to use it even under direct questioning in interviews and during prime minister's questions. It's also likely that some people in Number Ten had been briefing the press that a row was raging between Ed Balls and Peter Mandelson about the use of the word, thereby leading the agenda.

Second, he ensured that this section of the speech – 'Labour will cut costs, cut inefficiencies, cut unnecessary programmes and cut lower programme budgets' – was dressed in rhetoric (repetition) to ensure it stood out. He also used his delivery to signal to the media that this was the part of the speech that needed to be reported. He paused and looked up to the camera before reading this sentence, and slowed down the pace as he delivered it.

Third, I would be amazed if Brown's press officers had not highlighted that this was the big story of the speech both before and after delivery.

How did he conceal this from the audience? The whole argument of the speech set out a dividing line for the next election between Tory cuts and Labour investment. Three thousand words were devoted to making that argument. Just fourteen words were devoted to the 'we will cut' sentence. What's more, he placed the explosive line between shock absorbers. The preceding paragraph was filled with jargon techno-talk, designed to send anyone into a stupor. The paragraph which followed reinforced the message that the choice at the next election was between Tory cuts to front-line services and Labour investment, therefore allowing anyone – including the assembled trade unionists listening in the Hall – who thought they had heard Brown say something about cuts to conclude they must have been mistaken.

Chapter Ten

The Craft of Performance

Delivery is the dominant factor in oratory; without delivery
the best speaker cannot be of any account at all.

Cicero, *De Oratore*

Your face . . . is a book where men may read strange matters.

William Shakespeare, *Macbeth*

Many have watched its effects. A meeting of grave citizens,
protected by all the cynicism of those pre-prosaic days, is
unable to resist its influence. From unresponsive silence they
advanced a grudging approval and thence to complete
agreement with the speaker: the cheers become louder and
more frequent; the enthusiasm momentarily increases; until
they are confirmed fast by emotions they are unable to control
and shaken by passions of which they have resigned the
direction.

Winston Churchill, *The Scaffolding of Rhetoric*

The '20 hours in America' episode of the *West Wing* opens with
President Bartlett delivering a high gusto campaign speech: chest

puffed out, fist thumping the sky. Then the camera cuts to Toby Ziegler, Bartlett's speechwriter. Toby is pacing up a nearby soybean field, anxious, listening to the president's speech via a distant PA. He is mouthing along with the words, occasionally kicking up a clump of mud from the ground. 'He seems a little tense,' says Cathy, walking alongside him. Josh Lyman explains that he always is when the president is speaking. Cathy asks why he isn't watching in person. Josh explains, 'The president has his blood pressure taken every morning. On higher blood pressure days, Toby isn't allowed to be in the president's line of sight ... You see, he's unable to conceal his displeasure.'

Performance frequently marks the difference between a good speech and a great speech. Yet once the speaker is behind the podium, the speechwriter is powerless. However there are steps we can take to improve our speaker's performance before he reaches the podium. This chapter covers all the essential principles of successful performance, alongside some quick-fire practical tricks.

The Principles of Performance

The first principle is that great orators are not born great, but become great through practice. Demosthenes was said to be a stuttering, stumbling mess in his early speeches. Instead of blundering on blindly, he retreated to a cave to concentrate on improving his art. He shaved off his hair so he would not be tempted to go out. He then subjected himself to a Rocky-esque pre-fight training regime. He put pebbles in his mouth and swilled them around to flex up his jaw muscles. He went to the sea and harangued the roaring waves to improve his projection.[1] When he returned to the stage, he received a thunderous reaction, but only because of the time he had put into practice.

Reagan sharpened his act in Hollywood. Thatcher underwent voice training. Practice matters. So does experience. That's why, traditionally, politicians were recruited from professions which required public speaking, so the Tories recruited barristers and businesspeople whilst Labour recruited trade unionists and teachers. In recent years, this has fallen by the wayside and new 'political class' has emerged, with a number of top politicians being fast-tracked to the Cabinet after brief careers in either journalism or political adviser jobs. Their early performances betrayed all the characteristics of nervousness: talking too fast, blinking furiously, losing their thread. It was barely fair. They hadn't had the chance to learn their trade before being thrust into the spotlight.

The second principle is that the speaker's words and actions must act in concert if our speaker is to be credible. When we are being sincere, our words and actions naturally align. Hitler shook with fury during his speeches because he genuinely believed that Germany had been profoundly wronged. His shrieking voice, shaking hands and jerky actions were seen in Britain as proof of insanity but, to the German people, they proved his authenticity; this is exactly how people behave when they feel aggrieved so it was clear he meant it. Likewise, when Margaret Thatcher told the House of Commons that she had rejected Europe's federalism and she jabbed her head forward, thundering, 'No! No! No!', no one doubted her sincerity. Tony Blair was the true master of the art of melodrama: his shirt drenched with sweat during his 'forces of conservatism' speech; the tear in his eye during the 'People's Princess' speech; his hunted look as he said that Iraq had WMD. Whether he was sincere or not is scarcely relevant – what matters is that most people believed him to be *bona fide*. The man must match the message.

Gordon Brown is a good example of someone whose words and actions were fraught with inconsistencies. He talked about being a 'servant of the people', but thumped the lectern at the same time. He talked about 'fairness and compassion', whilst angrily wrenching at the air. He talked about being 'steadfast in purpose', but his every sign revealed a man tortured by self-doubt: nails bitten to the quick, hunched shoulders, chin buried into chest. Audiences' antennae are instinctively attuned for any signs of inconsistency. When we see this many signs of inconsistency we believe the person we are watching is a being at best oblique, at

worst a liar. Whether they are or not is, again, irrelevant. It doesn't matter. The only thing that matters is what the audience thinks.

Usually though, our antennae are pretty reliable, regardless of how effectively a speaker performs. We cannot prevent our true feelings emerging when we speak. The psychologist Paul Ekman says that we constantly emit what he calls 'micro-expressions' – split-second moments where our face exposes our true feelings, be they anger, reproach or disgust. These signs are not visible to the naked eye but only when watched back in freeze-frame. When Bill Clinton said, 'I did not have sexual relations with that woman – Monica Lewinsky', his brow furrowed, eyebrows rose and jaw tightened just fleetingly: invisible to the naked eye, but a giveaway sign of anxiety for those who noticed.

The third principle is that speakers shouldn't be afraid to consider going over the top. Audiences do not mind because they understand that the drama is primarily for their benefit. Speeches are performances and should be treated as such. However, we should be wary of our speaker getting too carried away, particularly if the speech is being televised: behaviour which seems appropriate in the room can look inappropriate in people's living rooms. He should also keep an eye on levels of decency. I once saw an MP give a speech to Parliament where he intended to say, 'the cuts have gone too far', but he got himself so worked up that he inserted a very unfortunate, stray 'n' into the word 'cuts'.

Step One: Learning the Words

Preparation is vital.[ii] David Davis conceded that the reason his leadership bid bombed was, 'Probably, I didn't prepare [the speech] well enough, and that's the truth of the matter.' The more we familiarize the speaker with the text, the better their performance will be.

There can be no more powerful sign of a speaker's conviction than if he learns the speech by heart. In Ancient Rome, a speech that was not delivered from memory was considered unworthy of attention. Up until the nineteenth century, most orators spoke without notes, including Gladstone's mammoth three-hour long Midlothian Address. Today, the best speeches are still delivered from memory: stump speeches during elections, speeches at rallies and big set-piece product launches.

Memorizing a speech is not as hard as it might seem. There are simple tricks a speaker can employ. The key is to create a pattern of association: you break the speech into manageable chunks, and then create memorable triggers for each of those chunks. Mnemonics is one way to create those triggers (e.g. the word HEAD might cover a speech on Health, Education, Agriculture and Defence). Alternatively, the speaker might assemble a set of visual images, in the form of a storyboard: the bigger and more unusual the pictures and the connections between them, the more likely they will be to stick. For instance, a speaker who wanted to visualize the same sequence (Health, Education, Agriculture, Defence) might use a doctor to symbolize health, a school to symbolize education, fields to symbolize agriculture and tanks to symbolize defence. Put them together into a cartoon narrative and what do you get? How about a wily old doctor putting a comically huge stethoscope on the side of a crumbling old Victorian school, which promptly collapses to reveal a bright yellow field of rapeseed; then tanks come rolling over from the distance. That's pretty hard to forget.

If our speaker is not prepared to memorize the whole speech, he should at least familiarize himself with the crucial sections: the opening lines, the central argument and peroration. This will enhance his credibility. Or maybe he could work from bullets: improvising around a clear structure and set of soundbites.

The worst thing, for speaker and audience, is when it is clear to everyone that the speaker has barely seen the text beforehand. Perhaps the most excruciating example of this was in the 1980s, when Alan Clark delivered a speech to Parliament on equal opportunities: he arrived in the Chamber having just sunk several bottles of wine with Nicholas Soames. He galloped through the text, sometimes passing over two or three pages at a time, because he was so appalled until, eventually, Clare Short intervened. She said that she knew it was un-parliamentary to describe another member as drunk but would the Speaker concede 'there does appear to be some problem'.

The speaker should always read the text out loud at least once before getting to the podium, even if it is on the way to the venue. This will, at the very least, prevent any embarrassing pronunciation gaffes; I once saw a speaker pronounce 'awry' to rhyme with gory.

Step Two: Learning the Actions

Think about which physical and vocal signs might strengthen the speech. A speech is not so much a set of words as a series of signs. Every speaker transmits a huge range of signs when they speak: some conscious, some subconscious. No speaker can control all of these signs – a single minute of speech involves ten to 1,500 neuro-muscular events – but we can at least control some. Research shows that messages about how someone feels are based fifty-five per cent on visual signs, thirty-eight per cent on vocal signs and seven per cent on verbal signs.[iii] Think about it: if you ask how someone's feeling and they say, 'fine', but do so with a pinched face or sharp tone then you'll discount the verbal and trust the visual. Words are often just background noise.

Here are some of the ritualized signs that a speaker can use to underline key messages. We shouldn't go overboard, but a well-timed pause or finger point can make a huge difference.

First, physical signs: an open hand signifies trust, a clenched fist signifies anger, a pointed finger signifies a threat, a thumbs-up signifies good, whilst a raised hand signifies silence/hold back. The face is also very expressive: raised eyebrows mean surprise, widened eyes mean fear or fury, a furrowed brow means worry.

Such signs can give our message extra kick, which is exactly what J.F.K. did when he aggressively jabbed his finger on the italicized words: 'Ask *not* what your country can do for *you*, ask what *you* can *do for your country.*' Bill Clinton also used the jabbing finger in one of his most famous soundbites: 'There is *nothing wrong* with America that can not be cured by what is *right* with America.' By using physical messages to reinforce the verbal, he made it clear that the challenge was heartfelt, supported the rhythm of the rhetoric, whilst also subtly suggesting a 'parent' image (reinforcing the metaphor of the president as 'father of the nation').

George W. Bush was well known as a politician who acted on gut instinct. This impression was literally conveyed in one of his most notorious speeches, when his physical actions pre-empted his words by around a quarter of a second.

> There are some who feel like if they attack us that we may decide to leave prematurely. [Shakes head.] They don't understand what they're talking about if that's the case. [Points and raises eyebrows.] Let me finish. [Stands tall, leans back.] There are some who feel like the conditions are such that they can attack us there. [Arches body forward aggressively, fixes and holds gaze, tosses his hand in the air dismissively, as if chucking away some rubbish.] My answer is bring 'em on.

Our speakers may not want to be so dramatic. But small signs can make a big difference: a nod to show sincerity, a smile to show warmth, an open hand to indicate openness. A speaker's actions set the tone: if he looks at ease, the audience will be; just as an anxious speaker can quickly make an audience feel uncomfortable.

Eyes are very important. If someone's eyes are darting around randomly, his fear will transmit to the audience. I generally advise speakers to pick out three friendly faces in the audience – one on the left, one in the middle and one on the right – and deliberately target their words towards them. If you have ever been to a conference and had the feeling that a speech was being delivered directly to you, it is probably because it was.

Clothes are another physical sign that a speaker can use. Thatcher's blue outfit showed party tribalism, as do Dennis Skinner's red ties. Steve Jobs' turtleneck sweaters and Richard Branson's jumpers show they're non-conformists. Protesters who don a combat jacket or even a balaclava for rallies in Trafalgar Square send an equally powerful signal. Clothes also make us act the part. If someone wears a Versace suit, they are likely to act flashier than if they were wearing Marks and Spencers.[iv] During the 1920s, Gandhi gave hundreds of speeches across India wearing the traditional Indian peasant dress of dhoti and shawl, woven with a yarn that he had hand-spun himself on a charkha. At one of these speeches, a peasant said to him, 'Mr Gandhi. I am listening to all of your speeches. I am hearing the words but I am not understanding what you mean. Tell me, what is your message?' Gandhi replied simply, 'I am the message.'

Our speaker might also use props to reinforce his message. This could be anything, depending on his message and image. A politician of one persuasion might proudly show off a bill that they are piloting through Parliament. An opposing politician might grandly tear up that bill as an example of deregulation. Microphones, glasses, the lectern can all be used as a prop.

Our speaker can also use his voice to reinforce his message. There are three separate elements to voice: pace, pitch and volume.

When it comes to pace, almost every speaker benefits from slowing down a little. Most speakers talk too quickly because they want to get their speech over with as soon as possible. This is perfectly natural, but it is the worst signal to send. Speaking fast signals nerviness; a steadier pace suggests confidence. Most people speak at around 160 to 180 words a minute in normal conversation but practically every great orator clocks in at more like 100 words a minute: Martin Luther King's 'I have a dream' speech was ninety words a minute; Roosevelt's Pearl Harbor 'A day that will live on in infamy' speech was 100 words a minute; Churchill's 'We will fight on the beaches' speech was 116 words a minute (although many were short words). The speeches of Hillary Clinton and Barack Obama were timed during the 2008 Democratic nomination race: Clinton jangled away at 160 words a minute whilst Obama swaggered in at a more statesmanlike ninety.

In terms of pitch, most speakers can afford to speak a bit lower. High pitches indicate anxiety whilst depth suggests gravitas. This creates a dilemma for women. Margaret Thatcher was ridiculed for lowering her voice but it clearly enhanced her power. The pitch of the average woman's voice has dropped by half an octave since the 1940s. Things might, however, now be turning back. Many women speakers now actively exploit their femininity. Likewise, some men are rejecting the old booming style of voice in favour of a more metrosexual tone. David Cameron, Tony Blair and Steve Jobs have had a much higher pitch than great orators of the past.

In terms of volume, there is a careful balance to be struck: too loud seems hectoring; too quiet seems ineffective. The trick is to apply *moderation* to win trust, and *modulation* to grab attention. Hilary Benn adroitly combines both. Like his father before him, he uses volume as a weapon. When I have seen Hilary speak, his sudden shifts in dynamic have almost made me leap out of my seat.

Many speakers benefit a lot from a little work on their voice. A single singing lesson costs around £40 and will provide a speaker with a range of powerful voice techniques, including projection, breathing and posture. He will learn how to warm his voice properly. A professional speaker can make the same preparations as a professional singer: belting out some loud oohs and aahs to get his lungs working, stretching his mouth around different vowel sounds to ensure his diction is full and blowing raspberries to loosen his lips. When the speaker is actually delivering the speech, it might be helpful for him to imagine a piece of string at the top of his head, attached to the ceiling. This keeps his body upright and stretches his rib cage right open.

Step Three: Preparing the Stage

In the final run up to the speech, it's wise to make a few final checks.

Does the speaker have the right script? It's not impossible that the pages have become muddled. Check all the pages are present, correct and tightly bound together. Some spare copies are always useful, for the speaker and for the press, if needed.

The text should be user-friendly. Each speaker has his own personal preferences but the vast majority prefer a large font with one and a half line spacing and no sentences straddling two pages. Each sentence should stand as a separate paragraph, so the final text looks almost like poetry: this helps our speaker anticipate how much breath he needs to get through a sentence. Be careful about writing any instructions or phonetics within the text. I have seen speakers read these out [e.g. 'point towards Derek – he'll be sitting in the front row'].

Check exactly what is required from your speaker. In 1965, John Lennon was Guest of Honour at the Foyles Literary Annual dinner. He did not realize he was expected to give a speech. He was terrified when he was invited to say a few words. Eventually, Lennon shuffled to the podium, said, 'You've got a lucky face,' before scurrying back to his chair as quickly as possible. Cynthia Lennon has said they both found the whole experience excruciatingly embarrassing, understandably.

Practical elements which seem trivial in preparation assume a profound importance if they go wrong. At the 1989 Brit Awards, someone mixed up the microphones of six foot two Mick Fleetwood and five foot one Samantha Fox: so began a whole night of disaster. Someone should check out all the logistical details, including microphone height, lectern height, which side to enter, what will appear on the screen behind the speaker and how he will be announced. It is very important to find out whether or not there is a lectern: this determines whether or not the speaker can read from a full script or just notes. If there is no lectern, most speakers prefer to improvise rather than allow the audience to see their hands shake. In 2009, Prince William delivered a tribute to his mother: there was no lectern available so he held the script in one hand and the microphone in another. The effect was clumsy. He looked unprepared, even though he had clearly thought about his speech very carefully.

If the speech is on autocue, check the autocue guys definitely have the right speech, including last-minute edits. Bill Clinton was once forced to improvise a full fifteen minutes of his State of the Union Address because the wrong speech had been put on the autocue. Incredibly, he remembered it almost word for word. Irish Prime Minister, Brian Cowen, was not so lucky. In April 2009, he inadvertently read President Obama's speech. Cowen began, 'We welcome to the White House a great friend of the United States.'ᵛ

President Obama returned the favour by beginning his speech with, 'First, I'd like to thank President Obama for inviting me here.'

Check that visual aids are lined up and ready to go. Test them before the speaker reaches the stage. There's nothing worse than seeing a speaker play a video to discover the sound isn't plugged in. PowerPoint should generally be avoided. It invites the audience to stare at the screen instead of the speaker. It's also fundamentally an ineffective way of presenting information: its hierarchical structure doesn't reflect the way we think. PowerPoint has been blamed for an increase in bad decision-making in government and business. One respectable report even blamed the Columbia space crash on an endemic use of PowerPoint at NASA, which had fuelled flawed thinking.[vi]

Check that the speaker looks good. Aristotle placed huge emphasis on the appearance of the speaker in *Rhetoric*. He argued that audiences were more likely to trust people who represent physical perfection. The same is true today. We can't do anything about our speaker's height or physique but we can at least ensure they don't have dandruff on their shoulders or anything hanging from their nose.

Check that the speaker feels right. If he is delivering a passionate speech, he should feel passionate. If he is delivering a calm and measured speech then he should feel calm and measured. I knew a press officer who would deliberately wind up her Secretary of State before interviews to ensure he spoke with passion – at least that's what she claimed. In an episode of the *West Wing*, Jed Bartlett's wife cut off her husband's tie thirty seconds before a televised debate to make sure his adrenalin was flowing. Other speakers have different techniques. Enoch Powell would deliberately not go to the toilet in the hours before a speech to give his speech the requisite urgency. David Cameron apparently uses the same technique, although presumably it gets riskier as you get older.

Finally, have a contingency plan in case it all goes wrong. Many speakers have been caught unawares by crowd hostility in recent years: the TV cameras continuing to roll as they endured boos and heckles. If they have a response ready, they can go into autopilot instead of panic mode. As soon as the slow handclaps and jeers start, the speaker is often well advised to simply stop the speech and either tackle the heckler head on or turn to the chair and suggest they move straight to questions as people clearly need to be heard. This restores order and crucially returns the moral high ground to the speaker. If he carries on regardless, pretending the booing is not happening, the risk is he winds up looking arrogant or stupid. The reason people heckle is because they don't feel their opinion is being heard: so let them be heard.

Summary

- Great speakers are not born great but become great through practice.
- A successful speaker's words and actions operate in concert.
- Great speakers are not afraid to go a little over the top.
- Great speakers familiarize themselves with the text.
- Great speakers use physical and vocal signs to underline their key messages.
- Great speechwriters are rigorous in their preparations.

Case study

I have selected Julia Roberts' 2001 Best Actress Oscar acceptance speech for her role in *Erin Brockovich* to illustrate the points in this chapter. I have selected this speech because she looks so at ease with herself. Her words and actions operate in perfect concert, revealing unbridled joy. Oscar speeches involve a balance between going overboard (like Gwyneth Paltrow) and being too terse (like Joe Pesci, who accepted the Best Supporting Actor award for *Goodfellas* by simply saying, 'It was my privilege. Thank you.'). Julia Roberts got the balance just right. Do watch the clip on YouTube.

Julia Roberts' acceptance speech for the Best Actress Oscar at the 2001 Academy Awards Ceremony

Thank you.

Thank you ever so much.

I'm so happy.

Thank you.

I have a television so I'm going to spend some time here to tell you some things.

And sir [points at the conductor of the orchestra] you're doing a great job but you're so quick with that stick so why don't you sit because I may never be here again.

I would like to start with telling you all how amazing the experience of feeling the sisterhood of being included in a group with Joan Allen and Juliet Binoche and Laura Linney and Ellen Burstyn for these last weeks has been. . . .

It just felt like such a triumph for me to be in that list.

My name starts with R so I'm always last but I still love the list.

But . . . I can't believe . . .

This is . . . [looks at the Oscar]

This is . . .

This is quite pretty . . .

I want to acknowledge so many people that made *Erin Brockovich*

But let me make my dress pretty.

Universal. Everybody at Universal. Kevin Micher and Stacey Schneider and Stacey Scheer and . . .

I can't believe I'm remembering everyone's name!

Jersey Films. Danny De Vito.

And everybody over there.

Everyone I've ever met in my life.

This movie was simply fun to make and Albert Finney is my friend and my pleasure to act with.

And Aaron Eckhart and Scotty and Gemmenne and Brittany and Ashley and all the wonderful actors who played my children and Marg Helgenberger.

Turn that clock off it's making me nervous.

Greg Jacobs.

Everyone on our crew who was so great.

Just a few other people . . .

But really the main person . . .

Well Richard LaGravenese and Susannah Grant who wrote such a nice script.

Stephen Soderbergh! Hi! There you are!

You truly just made me want to be the best actor that I suppose I never knew I could be or aspire to.

And I made every attempt.

[Points at conductor again] Stickman! I see you!

So I thank you for really making me feel so . . .

HA HA HA! HA HA HA!!! I love it up here! Yeah!

Anyway, I start working for him again in two days so I can get to you later.

But Benjamin Bratt. My sister Lisa. My brother in law Tony.

Elaine Goldsmith. Thomas who has been my agent since he was a boy.

Jeff Burr. My mum. And just Francis and Marcus and Mike and everybody who's watching at home.

Kelly. Emma. Everybody.

I love the world. I'm so happy. Thank you.

Analysis

She uses her voice to underline the key messages in various ways. She varies her pace dramatically, slowing down for the really important bits. When she says 'I'm so happy' at the beginning her pace is around forty words a minute; when she gets to the laundry list of thank yous at the end, her pace has cranked up to an astonishing 180 words a minute. She also shifts her *pitch* dramatically: when she wants to project gravitas, she speaks within a narrow range of just three semitones. However, at three specific moments of extreme excitement – when she laughs, sighs and cries out 'My mum!' – her voice shoots up by more than an octave. She also shifts her volume dramatically, absolutely yelling 'I love it up here!' at the top of her voice.

She also uses her full range of facial expressions. She flashes the famous Julia Roberts smile time and again. She also makes clear eye contact with individual members of the audience as she name-checks them, comfortably picking out faces from across the theatre, showing she is amongst friends. She also uses her eyebrows – raising them when she is being courteous and screwing them up when she mentions her peers, a touchingly self-deprecating gesture.

She also uses her hands a lot. She grasps the air as if searching for the right word, reinforcing the impression of spontaneity and unpreparedness. She points to those she is addressing, including the conductor, actually motioning for him to sit down. She touches her head several times, as if she can't believe she is really there. And, appropriately, she touches her heart at the two most heartfelt points of her speech: first, when she expresses her amazement at being on a list with her nominees; second, when she talks about the joy of working with Albert Finney.

She does a number of other things which support the impression of spontaneity. She laughs nervously, sighs a lot and says 'um' and 'er' very frequently. She interrupts herself three times: first, to gaze at the Oscar to say how pretty it is, then, to make her dress pretty and finally to scream about how much she loves it on that stage. Most performance coaches would get nervous about the sheer quantity of visual, verbal and vocal signs that are going on in this performance, but together they create the impression of someone who is having the time of her life and who is going to milk every last minute. And good for her, because, as she says, 'I may never be up here again.'

Chapter Eleven

The Craft of Strategy

There are five fundamental factors which determine the results of a war. The first is politics. Politics means the thing which causes the people to be in harmony with their ruler so that they will follow him in disregard of their lives and without fear of any danger. The second is weather. Weather signifies night and day, cold and heat, fine days and rain, and change of seasons. The third is terrain. Terrain means distances, and refers to whether it is open or constricted, and influences your chances of life or death. The fourth is the commander. The commander stands for the general's qualities of wisdom, sincerity, benevolence, courage and strictness. The fifth is doctrine. Doctrine is to be understood as the organization of the army, the gradations or rank among the officers, the regulation of supply routes, and the provision of military materials to the army.

Sun Tzu, The Art of War

Good speeches do not come from nowhere: they take time and patience. Sadly, these are the two commodities in shortest supply for any speechwriter. Instead of lounging around in the luxury of linguistics, speechwriters are most frequently found frantically rushing around, furiously stabbing in the last full stop moments before the deadline. All too often, success means getting the correct title at the top of the page.

The cause of this problem is simple: too many people make too many speeches. If we are churning out six speeches a week, we're not speechwriters, we're sausage machines. Our writing is bound to become perfunctory. So, an integral part of being a successful speechwriter is sorting out the speaker's diary.

This chapter sets out a model for preparing a speech strategy. It ensures the speaker makes high-value interventions and doesn't waste his time with meaningless events about which no one cares.

Speech strategies do not need to be particularly grand affairs. Usually, just setting in place a vague framework represents a dramatic improvement. Nor do they need to be updated particularly frequently: once a year is often enough. The important thing is that you are in control – or, at the very least, are not out of control.

This model is based upon four steps. The first three steps are about preparing the strategy. The final step is about implementation.

Step One: The External Context

We should start by looking at our speaker and organization from an external perspective. An external perspective will ensure that your speaker is addressing real issues of real concern whilst minimizing the risk that they fall victim to what Harold Macmillan called 'events'. It is invariably 'events' that determine the success or failure of any communication strategy. I always begin a speech strategy with an honest, indiscreet and colourful picture of the organization's current position, usually written a tabloid tone.

Step Two: Setting Internal Communication Priorities

There are four essential elements to a communications plan: what are we saying (messages), to whom are we saying it (audiences), when are we saying it (timing) and how (channels).

Messages

A good organization should have a clear messaging architecture, ranging from top-level slogans down to an over-arching narrative. When these are good, they are like gold dust; when they're not, it's in the speechwriter's interests to improve them. The best top-level slogans are usually strikingly short and simple, like Disney's 'Make People Happy' or 3M's 'To solve unsolved problems.' Failure invariably comes from cramming too much or descending into meaningless clichés like 'reaching higher' or 'building bridges'.

Many companies will also have a set of headline messages. Bill Clinton's top three messages in the 1992 election were: a) change versus more of the same; b) it's the economy, stupid; and, c) don't forget healthcare. New Labour's first term in office was also based around: a) no more Tory boom and bust; b) getting people back to work by making work pay; and, c) investing in public services.

The most powerful brands are built on narrative: from Branson's battle with BA to the Google Brothers starting out from their Californian garage. These narratives often have a flavour of strong archetypes, for example, David and Goliath, Dick Whittington or Robin Hood. It might be worth developing a narrative for your organization.

Audiences

There are all sorts of sophisticated models for mapping stakeholders based on power, influence, trust and involvement, but most decisions on stakeholder engagement ultimately come down to a mix of style, history and culture. Some organizations instinctively reach out; others instinctively batten down the hatches. Whichever, we should know our top four or five generic audiences and be able to identify specific events where we can reach them.

Timing

Alastair Campbell famously introduced 'the grid' in Whitehall to co-ordinate news planning. Similar systems have also now been introduced in many private-sector companies. Thinking about this will often present dates, events and opportunities for speeches.

Channels

Today's multimedia environment offers an array of channels. A speech is not always the best channel, even though it is often the first response, e.g. a speech is not the best way to announce a consultation process because speech-making is the antithesis of effective consultation. Maybe a web-based user-generated discussion board would be a more suitable channel?

Where speeches have unique advantages over other channels is in their capacity to:

a)   Present new arguments (because speeches provide a decent uninterrupted period of time to articulate a new way of thinking).

b)   Demonstrate strong leadership (because the iconic act of public speaking invokes images of past leaders).

c)   Set out visions (because speeches can paint powerful pictures and build strong emotional connections).

d)   Trail ideas (because speeches are not as formal as published papers, we can 'fly kites').

e)   Reach limited groups of opinion formers within a relatively informal setting.

Step Three: Developing a Speech Programme

Our speech programme should give anyone who looks at it a clear idea of what's coming up, whether they're the speaker or anyone else in the organization. A grid is a useful format, comprising dates, times, event descriptions and little pen pictures of the individual speeches. A pen picture might comprise a fifty-word summary of the main argument of the speech.

The best way to start is by boiling the various competing demands into two or three really big themes for the term. These should be big themes that get everyone, particularly the speaker, excited. Find some conflict. Latch on to popular topics. Pick something that interests you.

Then, turn these themes into events. Find audiences that match the message. For instance, if a politician is speaking about voter apathy, he shouldn't make a speech to a Westminster think tank but to a group of disillusioned voters. Likewise, if a CEO wants to tell his staff how special they all are, he should take the trouble to tell them in person, not via an awards ceremony on the other side of the world.

We might also pick venues that support our message. Tony Blair launched the 2001 general election manifesto at a school, to demonstrate that education was his top priority. In 2003, George W. Bush declared the Iraq War won with troops standing behind him – a show of strength.

We should weigh up the pros and cons of addressing someone else's conference or hosting our own tailor-made event. Speaking at someone else's conference has the advantage of providing a ready-made, large audience. The downside is that our message will be diluted and the host has prime access to the press.

If we are preparing a speech strategy for an organization with a few different speakers, we should play to their strengths. Rottweilers shouldn't be sent out to deliver touchy feely messages. Many organizations I've worked with seem based around the formula of a cerebral Home Counties born chair and a blunt-speaking Northern chief executive. This formula actually works very well within a speech strategy. The chair does long-range vision speeches whilst the CEO addresses more nuts and bolts issues.

Step Four: Implementation

The speaker and his staff must buy into our strategy if it is to have a chance of success. Whenever I prepare a strategy, I get it to the speaker either in time for the weekend or a holiday, to ensure he gives it a fair crack. The best result is when the strategy returns with loads of scribbles and scrawls: I then have a blueprint for the coming term and a mass of raw material. The worst outcome is when it just comes back with a tick. This usually means he's barely glanced at it.

When the strategy is agreed, we need to avoid the risk of diary creep. When I worked in Whitehall, we established a small group that met every week to consider new invitations. Invitations were subjected to three tests:

a)   Does it take forward policy?
b)   Does it strengthen relations with a stakeholder?
c)   Does it provide an opportunity for press coverage?

If the answer to all three was 'yes', then it was almost certainly a runner. If not, or only one or two seemed likely, then there would be a long argument before it was accepted.

Finally, the strategy must be subjected to some kind of evaluation. Did we take the organization forward? Did we shift attitudes? Did we win press coverage? And, most importantly, did we write speeches that our speaker and audiences enjoyed?

Summary

- A speech strategy will give you the time to write great speeches.
- Start by comparing your internal communications priorities with an external perspective.
- Develop a speech programme based on just two or three key themes. Prepare it in a grid format that clearly shows dates, times, events and pen pictures of the speeches.
- Keep the strategy on track by controlling what engagements go in the diary. Any invitations should be checked to see whether they either a) take forward policy or b) strengthen stakeholder relations or c) provide an opportunity for press coverage.

Case Study

Toyota

Ron Kirkpatrick and Charley Roberts, the staff speechwriters at Toyota, introduced a process for screening invitations. They sold it to the board on the basis that there was a direct correlation between their reputations and the board's share price. They also volunteered to act as 'bad cop' by turning down invitations that didn't pass the test. From then on, all speech invitations were graded by the speechwriting team against four questions:

- Will the speaking forum advance the goals/strategies of the company or lead to more business?
- Will it attract media coverage?
- Is the audience highly influential?
- Can we get extended reach through the host group's website, newsletters, etc.?

The invitation was only accepted if three or more of the answers were yes.

Three years on, they concede that the system's not perfect but it does keep them more strategic. It only took them eight hours to develop but it has saved them bundles more time. It has also shown the board that they are not just good wordsmiths; they are also strategic thinkers who have the company's goals in mind.

Epilogue

Speeches are back in the news again. This is incredibly exciting. When rhetoric flourishes, so does society. Eighty thousand years ago, man was a scattered and wandering species, isolated and alone. We had no way of communicating with one another apart from through grunts and growls, which we used to articulate our most basic needs for food, shelter and warmth. As language developed, so communities grew. The more language evolved, the greater the opportunities for collaboration that arose. The more sophisticated language became, the more civilization advanced. Rarely has progress taken place without oratory's helping hand. That is why I very much hope that the post-Obama revival of interest in rhetoric leads to a full-blown renaissance.

Certainly, it shows every sign of doing so. The number of people Googling speechwriter has quadrupled in the last two years. The BBC has produced an oratorical X-Factor programme 'The Speaker'. There is once again an MA in Rhetoric course in Britain. This great and noble trade, dating back to Antiphon in Ancient Greece, is finally restored to its rightful place in the spotlight. When I first became a speechwriter, a group of Whitehall speechwriters met for lunch at the ICA: there were just five of us. Now, my speechwriters' networking evenings are regularly attended by over fifty people, including the speechwriters to all three of the main party leaders. I predict this interest in rhetoric will only increase: as the differences between political parties narrow and business competition intensifies, a growing premium will fall upon persuasive skill in politics and business. Plus, as issues about the economy and the environment become too complex for most people to reach their own conclusions, judgements will increasingly be determined by credibility. This puts speechwriters centre-stage. There are now more than a thousand full-time speechwriters in the UK and more and more companies are recruiting.

If you want to become a speechwriter, keep an eye on my blog for analysis, (www.bespokespeeches.com/blog), follow my twitter feed (@bespokespeeches), drop me an email (simon@bespokespeeches.com) or come on one of my training courses. I love nothing more than chatting about speeches. I hope that you now feel well equipped in the art of rhetoric. You hold a mighty power in your hands: the power to convince, cajole and carry. Use it with honour, use it with responsibility, use it to make the world a better place. And bear in mind Plato's words: 'The rhetorician ought not to abuse his strength any more than a pugilist or pancratiast or other master of fence; because he has powers which are more than a match either for friend or enemy, he ought not therefore to strike, stab or slay his friends.'[i]

Simon Lancaster
May 2010

Glossary

Active voice When sentences follow a subject – verb – object structure, e.g. 'I went to the park'.

Alliteration A rhetorical device that is based upon repeating the same sound, e.g. 'boom and bust'.

Analogy A technique in argument where something is compared to something else in order to put someone into an appropriate frame of mind, e.g. 'Trying to explain social justice to the Tories is like trying to teach origami to a penguin'.

Anchoring A persuasive technique whereby an appeal for change is anchored within an audience or individual's existing values or beliefs, e.g. 'If you believe in justice then you must support x.'

Asyndeton A rhetorical technique where connective words are removed to produce a clipped, urgent, anxious effect, e.g. '*Veni. Vidi. Vici.*'

Blinding with science A technique of argument in which a speaker deliberately disorientates his opponent by unleashing a bewildering or incomprehensible array of data.

Bracketing A persuasive technique where a proposition is placed within two carefully positioned extremes in order to create the illusion of reasonableness.

Call and response A rhetorical technique where the speaker mimics dialogue by posing and then answering questions, e.g. 'To those that say x, I say y.'

Captatio benevolentae The goodwill of the audience (a term used by Cicero).

Cicero's structure A six step speech structure comprising: a) introduction; b) narrative; c) division between different positions; d) evidence in support of speaker's argument; e) refutation of opponent's argument; f) peroration.

Connotations Associations evoked by a word.

Contrast A rhetorical technique where two ideas are placed in proximity for the purpose of contrast. These may be between opposites, e.g. to be or not to be (antithesis), comparisons, e.g. one small step for man, a giant leap for mankind, corrections of actual positions, e.g. not flash, just Gordon (*correctio*) or phrase reversals, e.g. He would, wouldn't he' (*chiasmus*).

Crisis rhetoric A four-step structure for speeches delivered at points of crisis comprising: a) begin with a statement of facts; b) narrative to date; c) action to be taken; d) appeal to values.

Cum Hoc Ergo Propter Hoc (With this, therefore because of this) A logical fallacy used in argument where a speaker creates the illusion of a causal connection between two unrelated issues by referring to them together, as George W. Bush did by referring to 11 September and Iraq in the same breath.

De Bono's Hats A technique to promote rational thinking by systematically examining an issue from different perspectives.

Dead metaphors Where a metaphor has been over-used to the extent that it has become meaningless, e.g. 'laying down the foundation'.

Denotations The literal meaning of a word.

Depersonalization A technique in argument where a person or group of people are stripped of their human qualities and characterized using a metaphor such as vermin or machines in order to stop people caring about them.

Dialectical reasoning A mode of argument where theories, premises and deductions are tested through an interactive process, such as dialogue.

Deductive reasoning A mode of argument that draws a single conclusion from an arbitrary set of premises. Arguments can be made from authority, from probability, from experience, from opposites, from analogy, from example, from maxim, from assertion, from statistics and from anecdote.

Deflective source A technique in argument where someone will create another issue to take some of the heat, e.g. shifting a debate on standards in public life to a debate on press reporting.

Diabole An argumentative technique that focuses on attacking the credentials of the opponent in argument, e.g. 'He's a liar.'

Enallage A rhetorical style where a speaker deliberately muddles his language to create a sense of disorder, e.g. 'What the f**k?'

Disorientation A persuasive technique where an audience is deliberately disorientated to make them more vulnerable and susceptible to persuasion.

Empathy A persuasive technique used to win the audience's approval, e.g. 'I share your pain.'

Ethos The character of the speaker – one of the essential components of persuasion according to Aristotle. Speakers can demonstrate ethos through association, appearance, analogy, assertion, metaphor, dialect, experience, knowledge, authority, assertion.

False authority A technique in argument where someone falsely creates the impression of authority, e.g. '93.6 per cent of people say this is true.'

False choice A technique in argument where the speaker deliberately creates two false positions in order to make their own position seem more reasonable (also known as bifurcation), e.g. 'The real issue is whether or not we are committed to the National Health Service.'

Flattery A persuasive technique used to win the approval of the audience, e.g. 'You're such a fabulous audience.'

Floating opposites A rhetorical technique where opposites are set against one another, e.g. better food, lower prices.

Framing A technique of argument and persuasion in which the parameters of debate are deliberately controlled to direct opinion.

Generalizations Where general points are used to make a specific assertion, e.g. The Tories have been wrong in the past – therefore their renewable energy strategy must also be wrong.

Hedging A technique in argument where an ambiguity is deliberately created in order to prevent subsequent attacks, 'We will only make spending cuts where they are absolutely necessary.'

Hyperbole A rhetorical style where a speaker deliberately goes over-the-top to demonstrate excessive enthusiasm, e.g. 'This is the most amazing event since the birth of Christ.'

Hypodermic needle model A model of communication prevalent up until the Sixties which assumes a message can be implanted into someone's brain in the same way as a needle plunges a drug into someone's vein.

Ice-breaker A comment used to build a quick connection between a speaker and audience, usually at the beginning of the speech, such as a joke or a story.

Jargon Language which is peculiar to an institution, e.g. 'sustainable', 'benchmark', 'beacon'.

Jumping on a bandwagon A technique used for gaining press exposure where a speaker intervenes on an already running issue.

Knowledge based reasoning A mode of argument that carefully compares and evaluates steps which are taken between premises and deductions.

Labelling A technique of argument in which the speaker will apply a label to something, in order to predispose the audience to thinking about it in a particular light, e.g. 'union barons'.

Legitimizing source A technique of argument in which information is told through the voice of a third party in order to enhance its legitimacy.

Loading language A writing technique where the writer deliberately uses a word which predisposes the audience to a particular line of thought, e.g. 'I am briefing the press, you are leaking, he is spinning.'

Logos The reasoning which underpins the argument – one of the essential components of persuasion according to Aristotle.

Low-balling A technique of argument that starts with an attractive proposition and then slowly escalates.

Maslow's hierarchy of needs A theory about basic human needs used extensively by advertisers to inform persuasive strategies – the needs are wellbeing, safety, love, self-esteem and self-actualization.

Metaphor When one idea is substituted for another for the purpose of illumination or persuasion.

Micro-expressions Physical signs that people subconsciously transmit that reveal their true feelings.

Mimicry A persuasive technique used to win the audience's acceptance.

Mixed metaphors Where two different metaphors are used in close proximity, reducing meaning, e.g. 'gritting our teeth and biting the bullet.'

Moving the goalposts A technique in argument where people shift the argument, e.g. 'I wasn't questioning the substance of your proposal, merely the timing. . . .'

My way or the highway An oppressive technique in argument where a particular route is made to appear more attractive by damning the alternatives.

Oratory The practice of persuasive public speaking.

Over-simplification A technique in argument where a situation is dramatically simplified in order to force people into taking a particular position, e.g. 'You're either with us or you're against us.'

Pandering to prejudices A technique for gaining press attention where a speaker will play to the press's prejudices, e.g. 'Those bonkers Brussels bureaucrats are up to their old tricks again.'

Passive voice A grammatical technique where sentences follow an object – verb – subject structure, e.g. 'The park was visited by me.'

Pathos The emotions of the audience – from Aristotle's holy trinity.

Patronizing A technique in argument where the speaker seeks to make the audience agree by making them feel like children, 'Everyone knows that...' or 'Only a fool could believe that. . . .'

Peroration The climatic ending of a speech.

Personalization A technique where an institution or issue is described using the metaphor of a person in order to enhance people's emotional connections to the institution or issue, e.g. 'The heart and soul of the NHS.'

Physical signs The physical signs a speaker transmits, including facial and hand signals, which can be used to reinforce the words of the speech.

Polemic A technique of argument based on a one-sided assessment that fails to give adequate balance to alternate views.

Playing for time A technique in argument used to distract from the issue, e.g. 'We can't discuss this until the review is complete.'

258

Playing the man, not the ball A technique in argument based on attacking the speaker, rather than the issue, also known as *argumentum ad hominem*, e.g. 'Ask yourself if you can trust the man who was advising Norman Lamont on Black Wednesday.'

Playing to the gallery A logical fallacy, based on the view that if the majority of people think something, then it must be right (*argumentum ad populum*), e.g. 'Let's bomb Russia!'

Playing to fear An emotional appeal to force an audience to act by making them feel afraid – rather like putting a gun to their heads (*argumentum ad baculum*), e.g. 'The whole future of our country is at stake.'

Playing to pity An emotional appeal based on seeking the audience's pity (*argumentum ad misericordiam*), e.g. 'I come on my hands and knees and implore you. . . .'

Playing to shame An emotional appeal in which people are shamed into action (*argumentum ad verecundiam*), e.g. 'Do you want this on your conscience?'

Poisoning the well Discrediting the opponent before they have had a chance to put their own side, e.g. 'You will hear George Galloway making excuses for terrorists later. I'll leave him to make his own case. In the meantime, I want to say. . . .'

Polysyndeton A rhetorical device where a number of unnecessary connecting words are introduced to slow down the pace and create an impression of grandeur, e.g. 'I am extremely grateful for your phenomenally kind invitation to address this illustrious institution today.'

Post Hoc Ergo Propter Hoc (After this, therefore because of this) A logical fallacy whereby the audience is led to believe that, because one sentence follows another, there is a causal connection between the two, e.g. 'In 1997, we gave independence to the Bank of England. We have since experienced the longest uninterrupted period of growth in the country's history.'

Prefix An affix which is adjoined to the beginning of a word, e.g. eco-shopping.

Presumptive assaults A technique in argument where a presumption is made about someone or something, e.g. 'When did you stop beating your wife?'

Priming Putting the audience in the mood where they are more likely to agree with our proposition, e.g. through lighting and music.

Props Physical devices which the speaker can use to reinforce the messages of his speech, e.g. Neville Chamberlain's 'peace for our time' note.

Question – answer A rhetorical technique where a question is asked and then answered, e.g. 'When do we want it? Now.' The question may be implied, e.g. 'You know what happens to people who stay in the middle of the road: they get run over.'

Random connections A brainstorming technique where random ideas are introduced in order to open new trains of thought.

Red herring A technique which can be used in argument to distract the audience: 'As long as the press sees sex and drugs behind the left hand, you can park a battle carrier behind the right hand and no-one's gonna fucking notice.' (From *Charlie Wilson's War*.)

Reducing to absurd A technique of argument in which the speaker defeats his opponent's argument by reducing it to an absurdity.

Repetition A rhetorical technique where a word or clause is repeated for emphasis. Anaphora is when the repetition occurs at beginning of concurrent sentences. Epistrophe is when the repetition occurs at the end of concurrent sentences. Anadiplosis is when the repetition occurs at the end of one sentence and the beginning of the next.

Rhetoric The theory of persuasive public speaking.

Show, not tell A narrative technique that relies on making points through illustration, rather than assertion, e.g. 'Last night, as I sat down for dinner with my family …' instead of 'I am a family man.'

Shutting a story down A common practice in media handling that can be achieved through a number of techniques, e.g. 'No one cares about his story. The real issue is. . . .'

Similes A figure of speech often based around a comparison, often introduced with the word, 'like' or 'as'. Often used as a source of derision, e.g. 'Leaving the Tories in charge of the minimum wage is like putting Dracula in charge of the blood transfusion service.'

Smoothing A persuasive technique where a proposition is framed so that it feels as if it is going with the grain or the past pattern of progress, e.g. 'This is what happened in the 1930s. It's what happened in the 1980s. And it's what will happen now if. . . .'

Soaring and diving A narrative technique based on rapid interchanges between macro-points and minor points, which can be disorientating for an audience, e.g. 'This affects everyone on the planet, including a woman I spoke to last night in Dalston who said. . . .'

Steal and twist Where we take an existing idea or cliché and adapt it, e.g. 'Storm in a TUC cup'.

Straw Man A technique of argument in which a speaker creates a deliberately weak position in order to knock it down.

Suffix An affix that is placed at the end of a word, e.g. 'Bigot-gate' or 'Beatlemania'.

Syllogism A standard three-line argument comprising two premises and a deduction. This can often be used to conceal logical fallacies, e.g. 'A dog has four legs. My cat has four legs. Therefore my cat is a dog.'

System of reward and punishment A tool that can be useful in the act of persuasion in motivating audiences to act, e.g. 'Do we want to continue on the road to recovery, or shall we put all that at risk by taking a turn off now, leading us on the road to ruin.'

Tricolon (the rule of three) When statements are made in three-part lists to create the illusion of completeness and finality, e.g. 'He could not, would not and did not commit the crime.'

Uses and Gratification Theory A model of communication which has been more widely used since the 1970s which is based upon audience focus and understanding what uses and gratifications the audience is seeking.

Vocal signs The signs our voice transmits, generally through pace, pitch and volume.

Bibliography

Chapter One: The Art of Speechwriting

Aristotle and Roberts, W. Rhys (trans.), *Rhetoric* (Digireads, 2005)

Baldwin, Stanley, *On England* (Glasgow University Press, 1926)

Beecher, Henry Ward, *Oratory: A Unique and Masterly Exposition of the Fundamental Principles of True Oratory* (Penn Publishing, 1892)

Booth, Wayne C., *The Rhetoric of Rhetoric: The Quest for Effective Communication* (Blackwell Manifestos, 2004)

Brandt, Carl G. and Shafter, Edward M. (ed.), *Selected American Speeches on Basic Issues, 1850-1950* (University of Michigan, 1960)

Churchill, William, *Secret Session Speeches* (Cassell and Co., 1946)

Cicero, *Orations of Cicero* (Colonial Press, 1900)

Cicero, *Political Speeches* (Oxford University Press, 2006)

Clark, Tom (ed.), *Great Speeches of the Twentieth Century* (Preface, 2008)

Demosthenes, *Orations of Demosthenes* (Colonial Press, 1900)

Dickens, Charles, *Literary and Social Speeches* (John Camden Hotten, 1969)

Habinek, Thomas, *Ancient Rhetoric and Oratory* (Blackwell Publishing 2005)

Heffer, Simon, *Great British Speeches: A Stirring Anthology of Speeches from Every Period of British History* (Marks and Spencer, 2007)

Hoggart, Richard, *Mass Media in a Mass Society: Myth and Reality* (Continuum, 2004)

Jones, Susan, *Speechmaking* (Politicos, 2004)

Kynaston, David, *The Secretary of State* (Lavenham, 1978)

Macaulay, Lord, *Miscellaneous Writings and Speeches* (Longmans, Green and Co., 1891)

MacArthur, Brian (ed.), *The Penguin Book of Historic Speeches* (Penguin, 1995)

Mason, Jeff, *Philosophical Rhetoric: The Function of Indirection in Philosophical Writing* (Routledge, 1989)

Notestein, Walace, *The House of Commons, 1604–1610* (Yale, 1971)

Philip and Ollard, Richard (ed.), *Prince Philip Speaks: Selected Speeches 1956–1959* (Collins, 1960)

Plato, *Plato: Middle Dialogues* (Forgotten Books, 2008)

Safire, William, *Lend Me Your Ears: Great Speeches in History* (W.M. Norton, 1992)

Sebag Montefiore, Simon, *Speeches That Changed the World* (Quercus, 2006)

Vickers, Brian, *Classical Rhetoric in English Poetry* (Macmillan, 1970)

Vickers, Brian, *In Defence of Rhetoric* (Clarendon Paperbacks, 1998)

Warrington, John (ed.), *Aristotle: Poetics; Demetrius: On Style; Longinus: On the Sublime* (Dent, 1963)

Chapter Two: The Craft of Speechwriting

Addison, Joseph, *Maxims, Observations and Reflections: Moral, Political, Divine* (E. Curll, 1719)

Atkinson, Max, *Speechmaking and Presentation Made Easy: Seven Essential Steps to Success* (Vermilion, 2008)

Atkinson, Max, *Our Masters' Voices: The Language and Body Language of Politics* (Routledge, 1984)

Blair, Hugh, *Lectures on Rhetoric* (Exeter, 1822)

Cockroft, Robert and Susan, *Persuading People: An Introduction to Rhetoric* (Palgrave Macmillan, 1992)

Gelderman, Carol, *All the President's Words: The Bully Pulpit and the Creation of the Virtual Presidency* (Walker and Company, 1997)

Graves, Richard L., *Rhetoric and Composition: A Sourcebook for Teachers and Writers* (Boynton/Cook, 1990)

Heller, Richard, *High Impact Speeches: How to Create and Deliver Words that Move Minds* (Pearson Education, 2003)

Hennesy, Peter, *The Prime Minister: The Office and its Holders Since 1945* (Penguin, 2000)

Kaufman, Gerald, *How to be a Minister* (Faber and Faber, 1997)

Noonan, Peggy, *On Speaking Well: How to Give a Speech with Style, Substance and Clarity* (Collins, 1999)

Ritter, Kurt and Medhurst, Martin J. (eds), *Presidential Speechwriting: From the New Deal to the Reagan Revolution and Beyond* (Texas University Press, 2003)

Schlesinger, Robert, *White House Ghosts, Presidents and their Speechwriters, from FDR to George W. Bush* (Simon and Schuster, 2008)

Chapter Three: The Art of Persuasion

Camp, Lindsay, *Can I Change your Mind? The Craft and Art of Persuasive Writing* (A&C Black, 2007)

Charvet, Shelle Rose, *Words That Change Minds: Mastering the Language of Influence* (Kendall Hunt 1995)

Chomsky, Noam, *On Language* (The New Press, 1975)

Davies, Malcolm, *Politics of Pressure* (BBC, 1985)

Gladstone, William, *The Midlothian Campaign 1879–80* (Edinburgh, 1880)

Goldstein, Noaha J., Martin, Steve J. and Cialdini, Robert B., *Yes! Fifty Secrets from the Science of Persuasion* (Profile Books, 2007)

Gulledge, Andrew K., *The Art of Persuasion: A Practical Guide to Improving Your Convincing Power* (iUniverse, 2004)

Jowett, Garth S. and O'Donnell, Victoria, *Propaganda and Persuasion* (Sage, 2006)

Luntz, Dr Frank, *Words That Work: It's Not What You Say, It's What People Hear* (Hyperion, 2007)

Mackay, Charles, *Extraordinary Popular Delusions and the Madness of Crowds* (Three Rivers Press, 1980)

McKenna, Paul, *The Hypnotic World of Paul McKenna* (Faber and Faber, 1993)

Mutz, Diana C. *et al*, *Political Persuasion and Attitude Change* (Michigan, 1996)

Robinson, Bruce, *How to Get Ahead in Advertising* (Bloomsbury, 1989)

Stevenson, Adlai E., *Speeches* (André Deutsch, 1953)

Szántó, András (ed.), *What Orwell Didn't Know: Propaganda and the New Face of American Politics* (Public Affairs New York, 2007)

Thaler, Richard H. and Sunstein, Cass R., *Nudge* (Caravan, 2008)

Yeung, Rob, *Confidence: The Art of Getting Whatever you Want* (Pearson Education, 2008)

Williams, Heathcote, *The Speakers* (Hutchinson of London, 1964)

Windlesham, Lord, *Communication and Political Power* (Ebeneezer Baylis, 1966)

Chapter Four: The Art of Argument

Baggini, Julian, *The Duck that Won the Lottery and 99 Other Bad Arguments* (Granta, 2008)

Berne, Eric, *Games People Play: The Psychology of Human Relationships* (Penguin, 1964)

Bourke, Joanna, *Fear: A Cultural History* (Virago, 2005)

Fisher, Alec, *The Logic of Real Arguments* (Cambridge University Press, 1988)

Kahane, Howard, *Logic and Contemporary Rhetoric: The Use of Reason in Everyday Life* (Wadsworth, 1995)

King, Brian, *The Lying Ape: An Honest Guide to a World of Deception* (Icon Books, 2006)

Lakoff, George, *Don't Think of an Elephant: Know Your Values and Frame the Debate: The Essential Guide for Progressives* (Chelsea Green, 2004)

Mandela, Nelson, *In His Own Words: From Freedom to the Future*

(Jonathan Ball Pubishers, 2003)

Perelman, Chaim and Olbrechts-Tyteca, L., *The New Rhetoric: A Treatise on Argumentation* (Notre Dame, 1969)

Perry, Bruce (ed.), *Malcolm X: The Last Speeches* (Pathfinder, 1989)

Pirie, Madsen, *How to Win Every Argument: The Use and Abuse of Logic* (Continuum, 2006)

Rampton, Sheldon and Stauber, John, *Weapons of Mass Deception: The Uses of Propaganda in Bush's War on Iraq* (Constable and Robinson, 2003)

Tannen, Deborah, *The Argument Culture: Changing the Way We Argue and Debate* (Virago, 1998)

Chapter Five: The Art of Story-telling

Abbot, H. Porter, *The Cambridge Introduction to Narrative* (Cambridge University Press, 2008)

Bal, Mieke, *Narratology: Introduction to the Theory of Narrative* (University of Toronto Press, 1997)

Bettelheim, Bruno, *The Uses of Enchantment: The Meaning and Importance of Fairy Tales* (Penguin, 1976)

Cobley, Paul, *Narrative: The New Critical Idiom* (Routledge, 2001)

Genette, Gerard, *Narrative Discourse: An Essay in Method* (Cornell, 1972)

Herman, David, Jahn, Manfred and Ryan, Marie-Laure (eds), *Routledge Encyclopedia of Narrative Theory* (Routledge, 2005)

Lacey, Nick, *Narrative and Genre: Key Concepts in Media Studies* (Palgrave, 2000)

MacArthur, Brian, *The Penguin Book of Twentieth Century Protest* (Penguin, 1999)

McQuillan, Martin (ed.), *The Narrative Reader* (Routledge, 2000)

Marr, Andrew, *My Trade: A Short History of British Journalism* (Macmillan, 2004)

Morley, Sheridan and Heald, Tim (eds), *The Best of the Raconteurs* (Folio Society, 2000)

Noble, William, *Conflict, Action and Suspense* (Writers Digest Books, 1994)

Reagan, Ronald, *Speaking My Mind: Selected Speeches* (Simon and Schuster, 1989)

Rees, Nigel (ed.), *Dictionary of Anecdotes* (Cassell, 1999)

Taleb, Nassim Nicholas, *The Black Swan: The Impact of the Highly Improbable* (Penguin, 2007)

Toolan, Michael J., *Narrative: A Critical Linguistic Introduction* (Routledge, 1988)

Chapter Six: The Art of Metaphor

Barthes, Roland, *Mythologies* (Vintage, 1970)

Barthes, Roland, *Image, Music, Text* (Fontana Press, 1977)

Berman, Michael and Brown, David, *The Power of Metaphor: Storytelling and Guided Journeys for Teachers, Training and Therapists* (Crown House, 2000)

Burke, Kenneth, *On Symbols and Society* (Chicago, 1989)

Charteris-Black, Jonathan, *Politicians and Rhetoric: the Persuasive Power of Metaphor* (Palgrave Macmilland, 2005)

Cobley, Paul and Jansz, Litza, *Semiotics for Beginners* (Icon, 1997)

Edelman, Murray, *Political Language: Words that Succeed and Policies that Fail* (Academic Press, 1977)

Edelman, Murray, *Constructing the Political Spectacle* (University of Chicago Press, 1988)

Fontana, David, *The Language of Symbols: A Visual Key to Symbols and their Meanings* (DBP, 1993)

Lawley, James and Tompkins, Penny, *Metaphors in Mind: Transformation through Symbolic Modelling* (Developing Company Press, 2000)

Lawrence, Bruce and Howarth, James, *Messages to the World: The Statements of Osama Bin Laden* (Verso, 2005)

Orwell, George, *Why I Write* (Penguin, 1984)

Owen, Nick, *The Magic of Metaphor* (Crown House Publishing, 2001)

Ricoeur, Paul, *The Rule of Metaphor* (Routledge, 1975)

Thody, Philip and Course, Ann, *Barthes for Beginners* (Iron, 1997)

Chapter Seven: The Craft of Editing

Crystal, David, *The English Language: A Guided Tour of the Language* (Penguin, 1988)

Crystal, David, *Words Words Words* (Oxford University Press, 2006)

De Bono, Edward, *Six Thinking Hats* (Penguin, 1985)

Edmonds, Graham, *Bad Language: Words and Phrases to Avoid in Business* (Southbank Publishing, 2008)

Fairfax, John, *Creative Writing: Word Games and Exercises to Help You Get Started* (Elm Tree Books, 1989)

Farb, Peter, *Word Play: What Happens When People Talk* (Alfred A. Knopf, 1974)

Honey, John, *Language is Power: The Story of Standard English and its Enemies* (Faber and Faber, 1997)

Humphrys, John, *Lost for Words: The Mangling and Manipulating of the English Language* (Hodder, 2004)

Lewis, C.S., *Studies in Words* (Cambridge, 1960)

McFedries, Paul, *Word Spy: The Word Lover's Guide to Modern Culture* (Broadway, 2004)

Young, James Webb, *A Technique for Producing Ideas* (McGraw Hill, 2003)

Zinsser, William, *On Writing Well: The Classic Guide to Writing Nonfiction* (Quill, 2001)

Chapter Eight: The Craft of Soundbites

Atkinson, Max, *Lend Me Your Ears* (Vermilion, 2004)

Conc, Steve, *Powerlines: Words That Sell Brands, Grip Fans and Sometimes Change History*, 1st edn (Bloomberg, 2008)

Lanham, Richard, *A Handlist of Rhetorical Terms*, 2nd edn (California, 1991)

Parkinson, Judy, *Catchphrase, Slogan and Cliché: The Origins and Meanings of our Favourite Expressions* (Michael O'Mara, 2003)

Quinn, Arthur, *Figures of Speech: 60 Ways to Turn a Phrase* (Routledge, 2008)

Chapter Nine: The Craft of Media Management

Barker, Dennis, *The Craft of the Media Interview* (Robert Hale, 1998)

Campbell, Alastair, *The Blair Years: Extracts From the Alastair Campbell Diaries* (Hutchinson, 2007)

Cockerell, Michael, Hennessy, Peter and Walker, David, *Sources Close to the Prime Minister: Inside the Hidden World of the News Manipulators* (Macmillan, 1984)

Price, Lance, *The Spin Doctor's Diary: Inside Number 10 With New Labour* (Hodder and Stoughton, 2005)

Sergeant, John, *Give Me Ten Seconds* (Macmillan, 2001)

Chapter Ten: The Craft of Performance

Brown, Derren, *Tricks of the Mind* (Random House, 2006)

Dowis, Richard, *The Lost Art of the Great Speech: How to Write One, How to Deliver It* (Amacom, 2000)

Leanne, Shel, *Say it Like Obama* (McGraw-Hill, 2009)

Lewis, David, *How to Get your Message Across: A Practical Guide to Power Communication* (Souvenir Press, 1996)

Monkhouse, Bob, *Complete Speaker's Handbook* (Virgin Books, 1988)

Prochnow, Herbert V. and Prochnow Jr, Herbert V., *The Public Speaker's Treasure Chest* (A. Thomas and Co., 1965)

Sandford, William Phillips and Yeager, Willard Hayes, *Practical Business Speaking* (McGraw-Hill, 1952)

Smith, David Livingston, *Why We Lie: The Evolutionary Roots of Deception and the Unconscious Mind* (First St Martins Griffin, 2004)

Tufte, Edward R., *The Cognitive Style of PowerPoint: Pitching Out*

Corrupts Within (Graphics Press, 2006)

Walters, Lilly *et al.*, *Secrets of Superstar Speakers: Wisdom From the Greatest Motivators of our Time* (McGraw-Hill, 2000)

Watkins, Dwight E., *Effective Speech: Including Public Speaking, Mental Training and the Development of Personality* (Kessinger Publishing, 2006)

Chapter Eleven: The Craft of Strategy

Bertrand, Ina and Hughes, Peter, *Media Research Methods, Audiences, Institutions and Texts* (Palgrave Macmillan, 2005)

Harvard Business Press (ed.), *Strategy: Create and Implement the Best Strategy for your Business* (Harvard Business Essentials, 2005)

Tzu, Sun, *The Art of War* (Wordsworth Classics, 1988)

Notes and References

Introduction
[i] Burson-Marsteller's 2003 Building CEO Capital Survey

Chapter One: The Art of Speechwriting
[i] Vickers, *Classical Rhetoric in English Poetry*, p.9
[ii] Macaulay, *Miscellaneous Writings and Speeches*, p.72
[iii] Cicero, *De Oratore*
[iv] Luntz, *Words That Work*, p.xii
[v] McKenna, *The Hypnotic World of Paul McKenna*, pp.33–5
[vi] http://www.for68.com/new/2006/5/su664484027162560022 51 52-0.htm
[vii] Ridderstråle and Nordström, *Funky Business Forever*, p.xxii
[viii] Lewis, *How To Get Your Message Across*, p.94
[ix] This is another example of *post hoc ergo propter hoc*
[x] http://www.guardian.co.uk/world/2009/jan/20/barack-obama-inauguration-us-speech

Chapter Two: The Craft of Speechwriting
[i] Schlesinger, *White House Ghosts*, p.116
[ii] Ancient Rhetoric and Oratory, p 36 got in to trouble for getting Seneca the Younger to work as speechwriter for the first major speech of his reign: a funeral oration for his father, Claudius
[iii] p141 *White House Ghosts*
[iv] Carol Gelderman, *All the Presidents' Words*, p128

[v] p17, *White House Ghosts*

[vi] Noonan, *On Speaking Well*, p.124

[vii] According to his advisers, Major 'rejected excessively colourful phrases or personal attacks' when he was editing draft speeches.

[viii] Jones, *Speechmaking*, p.144

[ix] The one exception to this is the big evangelical gatherings in the UK and the US when people can perform 180 degree turns under huge pressure; generally, however, these changes in attitude are not lasting.

[x] Mutz *et al., Political Persuasion and Attitude Change*, p.176

[xi] In 1788, Mozart wrote: 'When I am, as it were, completely by myself, entirely alone, and of good cheer – say, travelling in the carriage, or walking after a good meal, or during the night and I cannot sleep; it is on such occasions that my ideas flow best and most abundantly. Whence and how they come, I know not; nor can I force them.'

[xii] Young, *A Technique For Producing Ideas*, p.15

[xiii] This structure was based on analysis of Presidential statements but it hangs true with British speeches. Tony Blair's speech on 7 July 2007, Kenneth Baker's statement to the House of Commons following the mortar attack on 10 Downing Street and Mrs Thatcher's response to the Brighton bombing all followed this same structure.

[xiv] p172, *The Powers Behind the Prime Minister* by Dennis Kavanagh and Anthony Seldon

[xv] p534, Alastair Campbell diaries

Chapter Three: The Art of Persuasion

[i] Mutz, *et al., Political Persuasion and Attitude Change*, p.134

[ii] This model combines the very best of a number of models taken from the worlds of advertising, hypnosis and propaganda. The model from the world of advertising is known as the AIDA model: a) attention; b) interest; c) desire; d) action. There is a further more generic model of persuasion developed by McGuire (1966), which involves: a) exposure b) comprehension c)

reception d) yielding; e) retention; f) action. There is another model used by advertisers: a) be seen; b) be heard; c) be believed; d) be remembered; e) be acted upon.

[iii] Williams, *The Speakers*, pp.167–8

[iv] Abraham Lincoln, Gettysburg Address, 19 November 1863

[v] Neil Kinnock speech, 15 May 1987, from Safire, *Lend Me Your Ears*, p.1030

[vi] www.alansnyder.com

[vii] http://www.commonwealthclub.org/archive/98/98-07bezos-speech.html

[viii] Aristotle, *Rhetoric*, p.24

[ix] Presenting Sicily with the dubious distinction of having given to the world two enduring, but very different models of conflict resolution: the Mafia and rhetoric.

[x] Habinger, *Ancient Rhetoric and Oratory*, p.9

[xi] Bono, Commencement Address at the University of Pennsylvania, 17 May 2004

[xii] Courtney Love, 'On Piracy and Music' speech to Digital Hollywood Online Entertainment Conference, New York City, 16 May 2000

[xiii] In the 1960s, thirty-eight people peered out of the windows of a New York apartment block watching whilst a woman was stabbed and eventually died. Each of them assumed someone else had rung for an ambulance. In fact, none had.

[xiv] http://www.chrisreevehomepage.com/sp-coliseum-130599.html

[xv] Mutz, et al., *Political Persuasion and Attitude Change*, p.134

[xvi] Gordon Brown, 'On Liberty' speech, 25 October 2007

[xvii] Conceived by the illustrator Norman Rockwell, from Jowett and O'Donnell, *Propaganda and Persuasion*, p.187

[xviii] Robinson, *How to Get Ahead in Advertising*, p.196–7

[xix] Tony Blair, speech on foreign affairs, 15 December 1998

[xx] http://www.guardian.co.uk/politics/2005/jun/23/speeches.eu

[xxi] Chomsky, *On Language*, p.48

[xxii] http://www.nytimes.com/2008/01/20/fashion/20speechwriter.html

[xxiii] Aristotle, *Rhetoric*, p.10

xxiv Episode of the *West Wing*, '100,000 Airplanes'
xxv Gordon Brown, speech to Labour Party Conference, 23 September 2008
xxvi Script can be seen at www.suslik.org/Humour/FilmOrTV/ BlackAdder/ba4-2.html

Chapter Four: The Art of Argument

i http://www.telegraph.co.uk/news/newstopics/politics/ conservative/1908155/David-Cameron-fails-to-end-Punch-and-Judy-politics.html
ii Aristotle, *Rhetoric*, p.6
iii Cockcroft and Cockcroft, *Persuading People*, p.30
iv Aristotle, *Rhetoric*, p.40
v Mandela, *From Freedom to the Future: Tributes and Speeches*, p.27
vi Perelman and Olbrechts-Tyeca, *The New Rhetoric*, p.276
vii Gelderman, *All the Presidents' Words*, p.113
viii Mutz, *et al.*, *Political Persuasion and Attitude Change*, p.130
ix http://www.hitler.org/speeches/05-04-41.html
x Safire, *Lend Me Your Ears*, p.321
xi http://latimesblogs.latimes.com/washington/2008/03/hillary-clinton.html
xii Princess Diana, speech to the Institute for Drug Dependence, New York, 1993
xiii Edmonds, *Bad Language*, p.21
xiv http://bnp.org.uk/2009/06/bnp's-'defining-moment' statement-by-nick-griffin/
xv Barack Obama, speech to crowd in Berlin, 24 July 2008
xvi Longinus, *On the Sublime*, p.169
xvii David Cameron, Prime Minister's Questions, 12 November 2008
xviii Schlesinger, *White House Ghosts*, p.25
xix Rampton and Staubes, *Weapons of Mass Deception*, p.78
xx Anita Roddick, speech to the International Forum on Globalization, 27 November 1999
xxi Quintillian said that we argue from person, causes, place, time,

from resources, from how it is done, from definition, by exposing contradictions or consequents. Hermagoras, a Greek rhetorician, argued that there were seven elements to a hypothesis: who; what; when; where; why; how; from what starting point.

^{xxii} Lewis, *How To Get Your Message Across*, p.95

Chapter Five: The Art of Story-telling

ⁱ http://www.mirror.co.uk/news/tm_objectid=17684874&method= full&siteid=94762&headline=exclusive—how-blair-will-go- name_page.html

ⁱⁱ Edelman, *Words That Succeed and Policies That Fail*, p.25

ⁱⁱⁱ This model is used in the world of movie making.

^{iv} Vladimir Propp said that most great stories had just seven simple characters: the hero, the princess, the villain, the dispatcher, the helper, the donor and the false hero.

^v Orwell, *Nineteen Eighty-Four*, p.390

^{vi} http://www.margaretthatcher.org/speeches/displaydocument.asp? docid=105563

^{vii} http://news.bbc.co.uk/1/hi/magazine/3634126.stm

^{viii} Chadwick and Schroeder, *Applied Ethics in Philosophy*, p.240

^{ix} http://www.guardian.co.uk/politics/2006/jun/20/immigration policy.socialexclusion

^x Edelman, *Words Which Work, Policies That Fail*

^{xi} Campbell, *Diaries*, p.424

^{xii} http://www.guardian.co.uk/politics/2006/may/22/conservatives. davidcameron

^{xiii} http://uk.truveo.com/Clinton-Promises-Pragmatic-Approach/ id/2709901395

^{xiv} http://edition.cnn.com/2001/US/09/20/gen.bush.transcript/

^{xv} http://www.brookings.edu/events/2005/1114poverty.aspx

^{xvi} http://www.labour.org.uk/gordon_brown_conference

^{xvii} http://www.totalpolitics.com/speeches/speech.php?id=344

^{xviii} Anita Roddick, speech to the International Forum on Globalization, 27 November 1999

^{xix} Marr, *My Trade*, p.56

xx   Schlesinger, *White House Ghosts*, p.75
xxi Vickers, *In Defence of Rhetoric*, p.316
xxii http://www.presidentialrhetoric.com/historicspeeches/clinton/memphis.html
xxiii http://www.etan.org/et/1999/february/22-28/24bishop.htm
xxiv Gelderman, *All the Presidents' Words*, p.31
xxv Schlesinger, *White House Ghosts*, p.200
xxvi http://www.nickclegg.com/2008/09/the-only-party-for-a-fairer-britain-autumn-2008-conference-speech/
xxvii http://www.prnewswire.co.uk/cgi/news/release?id=43481
xxviii McQuillan, *Narrative Reader*, p.114

Chapter Six: The Art of Metaphor

i   Bono, Commencement Address, University of Pennsylvania, 19 May 2004
ii   http://www.theatlantic.com/a/green-penn-12-21-06.mhtml
iii Brown, *Tricks of the Mind*, p.242
iv   http://virtualknowledgestudio.nl/staff/sally-wyatt/danger-metaphors.pdf
v   http://blog.ted.com/2009/12/metaphorically.php
vi   Vickers, *In Defence of Rhetoric*, p.299
vii Nietzche, *Rhetoric and Language*
viii http://news.bbc.co.uk/1/hi/events/newsnight/1372220.stm
ix   http://www.uksbd.co.uk/
x   http://www.timesonline.co.uk/tol/news/world/us_and_americas/ article4107327.ece
xi   Edmonds, *Bad Language*, opening chapter 5
xii http://www.theatlantic.com/a/green-penn-12-21-06.mhtml
xiii Charteris-Black, *Politicians and Rhetoric*, pp.41-43
xivv http://www.shunpiking.com/ol0401/0401-MC-ES-infest.htm
xv   http://news.bbc.co.uk/1/hi/education/7451368.stm
xvi Blair was echoing Thatcher's famous 'The lady is not for turning.'
xvii MacArthur, *The Penguin Book of Historic Speeches*, p.304

Chapter Seven: The Craft of Editing

[iv] Orwell, *Politics and the English Language*, p.113

[ii] Churchill, 'The Scaffolding of Rhetoric' (unpublished)

[iii] Lewis, *How To Get Your Message Across*, p.94

[iv] Safire, *Lend Me Your Ears*, p.1036

[v] Credit for many of these ideas goes to McFedries, Word Spy, pp.396-410

[vi] Schlesinger, *White House Ghosts*, p.85

[vii] Kavanagh and Seldon, *The Powers Behind the Prime Minister*, p.99

Chapter Eight: The Craft of Soundbites

[i] Habinek, *Ancient Rhetoric and Oratory*, p.51

[ii] Our bodies work in twos – we have two hands, two arms, two legs, that work imperceptibly together. As we type, we are not consciously thinking which sections are being typed by our left hand and which by the right; they just naturally work in tandem.

[iii] Cixous argues that thought is constructed in terms of binary oppositions. Saussure has shown how language depends on difference.

[iv] We are more attracted to people with symmetrical features, as in the Ancient Greece model of perfection and Michelangelo's David.

Chapter Nine: The Craft of Media Manipulation

[i] Schlesinger, *White House Ghosts*, p.167

[ii] A line that he had in fact stolen: John Smith used exactly the same words against John Major in the dog days of his government.

[iii] A leaked note from Tony Blair to his staff famously demanded he be associated with some 'eye-catching initiatives'.

[iv] He never actually said 'hug a hoody', although that was the line that was spun to the press.

[v] http://tonyblairfaithfoundation.org/2008/04/tony-blair-faith-and-globalisa.html

[vi] http://www.princeofwales.gov.uk/speechesandarticles/a_speech_by_hrh_the_prince_of_wales_at_the_150th_anniversary_187680 1621.html

[vii] http://www.gatesfoundation.org/speeches-commentary/Pages/bill-gates-2000-global-foundation.aspx

[viii] The whistle-stop tour is a wonderfully romantic idea – the reality is rather more gruelling. Clark Clifford, President Harry Truman's speechwriter, described these trips as 'miserable, ceaseless and exhausting'.

[ix] It was this instance that led to the creation of the press gallery.

[x] Marr, *My Trade*, p.137

Chapter Ten: The Craft of Performance

[i] Demosthenes, *Orations*, p.iii

[ii] David Davis interviewed by Andrew Neil on Straight Talk, 24 January 2009

[iii] Borg, *Persuasion*, p.58

[iv] Curiously, the same is true in nature. If you paint a young bird in the colours of a dominant adult, it actually causes it to start acting tougher.

[v] http://www.podiumpundits.com/2009/03/18/the-luck-of-the-irish/

[vi] Tufte, *The Cognitive Style of Powerpoint*, p.8

Epilogue

[i] Plato, *Middle Dialogues*, p.14

Index

acceptance, 83–8
acronyms, 65
active voice, 36
Adonis, Andrew, 16
advertising, 25, 60–1, 75, 92–3, 117
agreement, 88–95
Ahmadinejad, Mahmoud, 81, 112
aims, 57–9
Allen, Lily, 56
alliteration, 194
American Declaration of
    Independence, 122
analogy, 109–10
aponyms, 65
argument, 62–5, 106–7
    attacking opponent, 112–15
    character, 107–8
    defusing emotion, 120–1
    emotional appeals, 115, 116–20
    enhancing logic, 121–4
    establishing speaker, 109–12
    fallacies, 126–9
    framing, 124–6
    Julius Caesar, 131–6
    logical appeals, 121
    priming, 115
    undermining opponent, 129–31

Aristotle, 29, 33, 51, 95, 107, 108,
    115, 121, 167, 237
    The Art of Rhetoric, 22–3, 24, 138
asyndeton, 151–2
attention, 77–83
audience, 55–7, 244–5, 166–7
    audience focus, 23–6, 76–7
    audience's acceptance, 84–8
    audience's agreement, 88–95
    audience's attention, 77–83
Axelrod, David, 15

Ball, John, 18
Ballmer, Steve, 80
Balls, Ed, 16
Barthes, Roland, 138
Beatles, 60, 83
Beckham, David, 120
Bell, Martin, 81
Belo, Bishop, 154
Benchley, Peter, *Jaws*, 138
Benn, Hilary, 235
Bentsen, Lloyd, 113
Bespoke, 11
Best, George, 144
Bevan, Nye, 27, 92, 194
Bezos, Jeff, 81

Biden, Joe, 180
Big Brother, 16
Bin Laden, Osama, 118
Blair, Cherie, 117
Blair, Sir Ian, 128
Blair, Tony, 16, 38, 53, 76, 85–6, 92,
    119, 138, 167, 182, 213, 227, 235
    authority, 110–11
    child poverty, 147, 148
    euro, 108
    forces of conservatism, 145
    Hand of history, 33
    I have no reverse gear, 61, 171
    Iraq, 123–4, 125, 144, 228
    preacher, 166, 168
    Science matters, 97
    Sierra Man, 155–6
    triangulating, 94
    Women's Institute speech, 25
Blake, William, 60
Blears, Hazel, 110
Bono, 86, 213
Booth, Cherie, 27
Bowie, David, 62
brainstorming, 61–2
Brand, Russell, 54
Branson, Richard, 17, 29, 80, 82,
    113, 214, 216, 217, 233, 244
Bright, John, 172
Brit Awards 1989, 236
British National Party, 119
Brown, Gordon, 16, 29, 53, 68, 69,
    70, 71, 76, 87, 98, 113, 126, 140,
    166, 189, 210, 213, 216, 217, 218,
    228–9
    Baby P, 120
    character attacks, 114–15
    civil liberties, 92

social mobility, 147–8
    speech to the TUC 2009, 220–5
    statistics, 110, 122
Bush, George, 36, 126
Bush, George W., 34, 118, 126, 127,
    142, 146, 167–8, 168–9, 170, 189,
    232–3, 246
Byers, Stephen, 212, 216

Cable, Vince, 69, 70
Cameron, David, 16, 38, 68, 69, 70,
    71, 74, 76, 85, 106, 113, 140, 143,
    145, 161, 212–13, 214, 215, 235, 237
    Baby P, 120
    speech to the Conservative
    Party Conference 2009, 198–208
    values, 93
    We can, 117
Campbell, Alistair, 22, 66, 128, 145,
    168, 213, 245
Carroll, Lewis, *Alice in Wonderland*,
    66
Carter, Jimmy, 52, 53
celebratory speeches, 64–5
CEOs, 11, 17, 57, 58, 80, 82, 144,
    246
Chamberlain, Neville, 198
channels, 219–20, 245
character, 107–8
    arguments from character,
    197–8
    character attacks, 114–15
Charles, Prince of Wales, 54, 162,
    213
Charteris-Black, Jonathan, 164
chief executive officers see CEOs
Churchill, Winston, 16, 31, 113,
    169, 194, 195, 234

Iron curtain, 33, 144, 162
speechwriting, 46, 66, 83
Cicero, 18, 83, 107, 115
  Ad Herennium, 63
Clark, Alan, 50, 231
Clarke, Charles, 212
Clegg, Nick, 16, 68, 69, 70, 71, 155, 189
Clinton, Bill, 36, 85, 122, 138, 145, 153, 168, 229–30, 232, 236, 244
Clinton, Hilary, 15, 17, 87, 113, 145–6, 169, 234
Cochran, Jonny, 34, 99–105, 122
common ground, 86–8
communications theory, 25, 93, 169
conclusion (peroratio), 63
conflict, 139, 141–6, 215–16
Conservative Party, 16, 68, 70, 71, 74, 117, 142–3, 171, 212–13
contention, areas of (partitio), 63
contrast, 33–4
Cook, Robin, 108
countdown structure, 65
Cowen, Brian, 236–7
creativity, 49, 82
crisis structure, 64
Cromwell, Oliver, 18
Crosland, Tony, 92

Darling, Alistair, 68, 69, 70, 217
David, Larry, 87
Davis, David, 16–17, 156–9, 230
De Bono, Edward, 61–2
De Gaulle, Charles, 33, 162, 169
Demetrius, 151
Democratic National Convention 2004, 35–6

Demosthenes, 111, 212, 227
dialect, 85–6
Diana, Princess, 33, 59, 117–18
Dickens, Charles, 138
Dyson, James, 146

Ecclestone, Bernie, 111
Economist, 178
Edelman, Murray, 143
editing, 177–8
  bits to cut, 178–80
  bits to improve, 182–4
  bits to replace, 181
  checking argument, 184
  checking style, 184–5
  checking with colleagues, 185–6
  Orwell's six rules, 186–7
  working with speaker, 186–7
Edward VIII, 198
Eisenhower, Dwight D., 144, 151, 185
Ekman, Paul, 229
Elizabeth II, 80
Eminem, 86
emotions, 26–7
  defusing emotion, 120–1
  emotional appeals, 115, 116–20
  emotional arguments, 195–7
empathy, 86
enemies, 88, 142–3
ethos, 22, 31, 51, 167–70, 197–8
  appeals from character, 107–8
  attacking opponent, 112–15
  establishing speaker, 109–12
  President Obama's Inaugural Address, 43
Eurythmics, 82

evidence in support of argument
  (*confirmatio*), 63
exposition (*exordium*), 63

fallacies, 126–9
Favreau, Jon, 39, 45, 95
first drafts, 65–6
first person, 87
flattery, 84–5
Foot, Michael, 113–14
Ford, Gerald, 146
Foster, Jodie, 86
framing, 124–6
fudging, 94–5

Galloway, George, 27
Gandhi, Mohandas, 138, 233–4
Gates, Bill, 98, 122, 212, 213
Geldof, Bob, 213
General Election 2010, 15–16, 171
Gettysburg Address, 31, 33, 122
Ghosn, Carlos, 82
Giddens, Anthony, 94
Gladstone, William, 95, 144, 230
glossary, 252–62
Godfather, The, 26
going with the flow, 89–90
Grade, Michael, 212
Graham, Billy, 144
grammar, 36–7
Green, Sir Stephen, 212
Greenpeace, 119
Greenspan, Sir Alan, 212
Griffin, Nick, 12, 119
Guevara, Che, 140

Hague, William, 16, 68, 69, 70, 71,
  171

Hall, Stuart, 25
Halle, Morris, 94
Halliwell, Geri, 213
Hannan, Dan, 210
Haringey Council, 120
Harman, Harriet, 16
Harper, Stephen, 180
Hawking, Stephen, 122
Hazlitt, William, 90
Heath, Ted, 181, 186
Hemingway, Ernest, 147
Heston, Charlton, 118
Hewitt, Patricia, 10
Hicks, Gill, 144
history (*narratio*), 63
Hitler, Adolf, 12, 113, 118, 142, 169,
  228
  Mein Kampf, 19
  speechwriting, 46–7
How to Get Ahead in Advertising,
  93, 117
Howard, Michael, 95
Howe, Geoffrey, 57, 152–3
Huhne, Chris, 68, 69, 70
humour, 87–8
Humphreys, John, 107
Hurd, Douglas, 181
Hussein, Saddam, 91, 123–4, 126,
  127
Hyman, Peter, 145
hypnotists, 25, 79–80, 161

idea for speech, 59–62
identity, 90–1
imagery, 33, 167–9
inspiration, 59–60

Jagger, Mick, 66

jargon, 54, 181
Jay, Anthony, 138
Jobs, Steve, 17, 57, 80, 98, 116, 185, 233, 235
Johnson, Alan, 9–11, 52, 65, 68, 69, 70, 74
Johnson, Boris, 81
Johnson, Lyndon B., 146, 184
Jolie, Angelina, 213
Jones, Digby, 166
Julius Caesar, 142

Kay, Jason, 171
Keating, John, 180
Kennedy, John F., 26, 34, 39, 43, 49, 50, 52, 59, 147, 189, 232
Kennedy, John F. Junior, 80
Kennedy, Ted, 80
King, Lord, 113
King, Martin Luther, 43, 60, 122, 138, 147, 195, 210, 234
Kinnock, Neil, 16, 59, 80, 112, 116, 180
Kirkpatrick, Ron, 248
Korax, 85

Labour Party, 68, 70, 71, 116, 145, 198
   New Labour, 19, 28, 92, 94, 212, 244
Lakoff, George, 93
Lamont, Norman, 93
Lennon, John, 49, 236
less is more, 29–31
Letwin, Oliver, 16
Levy, Lord, 81–2
Liberal Democrat Party, 68, 70, 71, 74, 126

Lincoln, Abraham, 33, 43, 80
logic, 26, 27–9, 121–4
logos, 22, 31, 51, 171, 190–5
   enhancing logic, 121–4
   fallacies, 126–9
   framing, 124–6
   logical appeals, 121
   President Obama's Inaugural Address, 44
   undermining opponent, 129–31
Love, Actually, 119
Love, Courtney, 89
Lucas, George, 60
Luntz, Frank, 24, 117

Macaulay, Thomas Babington, 22, 27–8, 121
Macchiavelli, Niccolo, The Prince, 95
Macmillan, Harold, 243
   Wind of change, 33, 59, 162, 170
Madonna, 213
Major, John, 53, 214
Malcolm X, 18
Mandela, Nelson, 58–9, 110, 138, 140, 198
   Road to freedom, 33
Mandelson, Peter, 194, 216, 219
Marr, Andrew, My Trade, 151
Marx, Karl, 162
Maslow, Abraham 'Hierarchy of Needs', 96–7
McCain, John, 113
McCartney, Paul, 49, 59–60
McGee, Robert, Story, 139
media manipulation, 209–11
   avoiding the media, 217–18
   channels and timing, 219–20

conflict, 215–16
Gordon Brown's speech to the
TUC 2009, 220–5
novelty, 211–14
playing to the gallery, 216–17
scale, 214–15
metaphor, 33, 71, 110, 160–4
ethos, pathos and logos, 167–71
finding appropriate metaphors,
166–7
perils of metaphor, 171–2
President Obama's victory
speech, 117, 173–6
types of metaphor, 164–5
Microsoft, 80
Miliband, David, 16, 68–9, 70, 71,
74, 113, 213
Miliband, Ed, 16
Millar, Ronald, 57
mimicry, 85–6
Moley, Raymond, 52
Moore, Michael, 57, 76
motivating action, 95–8
Mozart, Wolfgang, 59
Mugabe, Robert, 12

Nazism, 90, 170
Nero, 50, 142
New Yorker, 178
Nietzsche, Friedrich, 163
Nissan, 82
Nixon, Richard, 31, 36, 146, 155
Noonan, Peggy, 39, 54, 121

Oasis, 60
Obama, Barack, 15, 17, 34, 35–6,
38, 58, 60, 76, 87, 113, 119, 138,
210, 234, 236–7

Inaugural Address, 39–42
Iowa speech, 80, 95
victory speech, 117, 173–6
Oldham, Andrew Loog, 66
opinions, 93
opponents, 63, 112–15, 129–31
oratory, 15, 17–19, 21, 83
Orwell, George, 29, 92, 142, 172,
186–7
Osborne, George, 16, 53–4, 68, 69,
70, 74
Oxfam, 119

padding, 152–3
Palin, Sarah, 140
Parris, Matthew, 53, 220
Parry, Chris, 117, 171
passive voice, 36
pathos, 22, 31, 51, 170, 195–7
defusing emotion, 120–1
emotional appeals, 115, 116–20
President Obama's Inaugural
Address, 43–4
priming, 115
Paxman, Jeremy, 107, 168
Peasants Revolt, 18
Penn, Mark J., 169
Pennebaker, James W., 69
performance, 226–7
Julia Roberts' Oscar speech
2001, 238–41
learning the actions, 231–5
learning the words, 230–1
preparing the stage, 235–8
principles, 227–30
peroration, 35–6, 63, 83
personalization, 169–70
persuasion, 75–7

audience's acceptance, 84–8
audience's agreement, 88–95
audience's attention, 77–83
closing speech in O.J. Simpson
  trial, 99–105
motivating action, 95–8
Phillips, Trevor, 141, 179
Pitt, William, 194, 220
plagiarism, 180
Plato, 251
policy statements, 65
Potter, Dennis, 212
Powell, Enoch, 117, 220, 237
Prescott, John, 27, 37, 111, 140, 198
priming, 115
principles of speechwriting, 23–31
  President Obama's Inaugural
  Address, 44
propagandists, 64, 161

Quayle, Dan, 113
Quintilian, 198, 121, 152, 162, 189

random association, 60–1
Ratner, Gerald, 17
Rawnsley, Andrew, 81
Reagan, Ronald, 39, 43, 54, 60,
  111–12, 121, 145, 227
  Evil Empire, 92, 153–4
Reeve, Christopher, 90, 144
refutation of opponent's argument
  (refutatio), 63
research, 54–5
  researching the audience, 55–7
  researching the speaker, 51–4,
  67–8
rhetoric, 18, 19–20, 21, 35, 250–1
  Aristotle, 22–3

post hoc ergo propter hoc, 28, 127
rhetorical devices, 31–4, 189–90
  British politicians, 71–4
  ethos, 197–8
  logos, 190–5
  pathos, 195–7
  President Obama's Inaugural
  Address, 44–5
rhyme, 189, 194–5
Ricardo, David, 162
Richards, Keith, 66
Roberts, Charley, 248
Roberts, Julia, 238–41
Roddick, Anita, 17, 129, 149
Rolling Stones, 66, 79
Ronseal, 25
Roosevelt, Franklin D., 52, 62, 125,
  154–5, 234
Roosevelt, Theodore, 47
Rosenman, Sam, 47
Rotten, Johnny, 60
rule of three, 31–4, 193
Rwanda, 170

Safire, William, 31
Salinger, J.D., The Catcher in the
  Rye, 139
Scargill, Arthur, 27
sentence length, 68–9
  short sentences, 35–6
Shakespeare, William,
  Hamlet, 81, 143–4, 172
  Julius Caesar, 31–2, 33, 131–6
Short, Clare, 231
Shrum, Bob, 52
Silence of the Lambs, 125
Simpson, O.J., 33, 34, 99–105, 122
Smith, Adam, 161–2

Smith, John, 145
soaring and diving, 149
social speeches, 64–5
Socrates, 84
Sopranos, The, 167
Sorensen, Ted, 39, 49, 50, 52
Sorkin, Aaron, 117
Soros, George, 212
soundbites, 19, 31, 53, 188–90
    arguments from character,
    197–8
    David Cameron's speech to the
    Conservative Party Conference
    2009, 198–208
    emotional arguments, 195–7
    logical arguments, 190–5
speaker, 48–9
    researching the speaker, 51–4,
    67–8
speech length, 30–1
speechwriting, 37–8
    three golden principles, 23–31
    three golden rhetorical devices,
    31–4
    top three myths, 35–7
    working as a speechwriter,
    47–50, 67
Spencer, Earl, 33, 59
Stalin, Joseph, 142, 144
statistics, 70, 110, 122
Steinbeck, John, 138
Stewart, Dave, 82
stories, 70, 138–9
    creating something worth
    desiring, 146–7
    David Davis' resignation
    speech 2008, 156–9
    exploration of conflict, 141–6

exposition of protagonist,
    139–41
story-telling techniques, 147–56
storyteller's structure, 64
strategy, 30, 242–3
    audiences, 244–5
    channels, 245
    external context, 243–4
    implementation, 247–8
    messages, 244
    speech programmes, 245–6
    timing, 245
    Toyota, 248–9
Straw, Jack, 143
structure of speech, 63–4
Sugar, Sir Alan, 212

Tacitus, 15
Tebbit, Norman, 93, 114
Thatcher, Margaret, 10, 16, 57, 113,
    138, 142, 145, 167, 168, 227, 233,
    234
    lady's not for turning, 33, 61,
    193
    No! No! No!, 33, 228
    speechwriters, 65–6
timeline structure, 63–4
timing, 219–20, 245
Toyota, 248–9
trade unions, 10, 27, 142
triangulating, 93–4
Truman, Harry, 57
Truth, Sojourner, 37
Twain, Mark, 31

Urban II, Pope, 118

values, 92–3

Van Dyn, Jacobus, 79
Vaz, Keith, 216
viewpoint reinforcement, 25–6, 88
voice-recognition software, 66

Wag the Dog, 216
Waldegrave, William, 186
Wesley, John, 116
West Wing, 34, 97–8, 117, 226–7, 237

White, Hayden, 19
Whitehorn, Will, 29
William, Prince, 236
Wilson, Harold, 97, 217
word length, 68–9
World Economic Forum, 213–14

Yes Men, 89–90
Yes Minister, 9, 138, 172, 216
Young, James Webb, 60